Kennetk Fearing

The Phoenix Poets

KENNETH FEARING
Complete Poems
Edited by Robert M. Ryley, 1994

SAMUEL FRENCH MORSE
Collected Poems
Edited by Guy Rotella, 1994

PARKER TYLER
The Granite Butterfly
a facsimile, with introduction and supplementary material
Edited by Charles Boultenhouse and Michael Fournier, 1994

LOLA RIDGE
Collected Poems
Edited by Elaine Sproat, 1995

Series Editor: Burton Hatlen
Assistant Editor: Sylvester Pollet

Kenneth Fearing
Complete Poems

Edited with Notes and an Introduction
by Robert M. Ryley

THE NATIONAL POETRY FOUNDATION
1994

Published by The National Poetry Foundation
University of Maine, Orono, Maine 04469-5752 USA

Printed by Cushing-Malloy, Inc.
Ann Arbor, Michigan
Printed on acid-free paper

© 1994 by Jubal Fearing and Phoebe Fearing
Introduction, and Notes to the Poems © 1994 by Robert M. Ryley
Cover photograph of Kenneth Fearing, ca. 1940, by Jean Purcell

Library of Congress Number 93-86980
ISBN 0-943373-24-7 (cloth)
0-943376-25-5 (paper)

Designed by Matthew Sweney

This publication is made possible, in part, by a grant from
The Stephen and Tabitha King Foundation

Kenneth Fearing
Complete Poems

Alice Neel. *Kenneth Fearing.* 1935.

Oil on canvas, 30 1/8 x 26" (76.5 x 66 cm). The Museum of Modern Art,
New York. Gift of Hartley S. Neel and Richard Neel. Photograph © 1993,
The Museum of Modern Art, New York.

For Rachel Landon

CONTENTS

Introduction   ix

Bibliography of Major Works by Kenneth Fearing   lxii

A Note on the Text   lxiii

The Poems   1

Notes on the Poems   281

Index of Titles and First Lines   295

Acknowledgments

For permission to cite, quote from, or publish manuscripts, I am grateful to the following libraries: The Poetry/Rare Books Collection, University Libraries, State University of New York at Buffalo; Rare Book and Manuscript Library, Columbia University; Princeton University Library; Harry Ransom Humanities Research Center, The University of Texas at Austin; Special Collections, Margaret Clapp Library, Wellesley College; Department of Special Collections, Memorial Library, University of Wisconsin; Yale Collection of American Literature, Beinecke Rare Book and Manuscript Library, Yale University. I am especially grateful to William L. Allison for permission to publish the manuscript in his collection.

Thanks are due to the following people who provided information in interviews or correspondence: Lionel Abel, William L. Allison, Edith Heal Berrien, Janet Power Bonaparte, Jean Evans, the late Bruce Fearing, Ralph Fearing, Marlys Fixx, James Thomas Flexner, the late Alfred Hayes, Gertrude Hayes, Jeri James, Christine Keller, Ira Koenig, Rachel Landon, the late Nan Lurie, Amy River McCauley, the late Alice Neel, Joseph G. O'Reilly, Carl Rakosi, Louis River, Peggy Ross, Alan Wald.

In a variety of ways, the following people also contributed to the completion of this book: Shareen Brysac, Bill Costley, George Dorris, Katherine R. Dow, Carol Haacke Fearing, Jubal Fearing, Phoebe Fearing, Patrick Gregory, Sam Holmes, David Ignatow, Glenn Lewis, Cynthia Maziarka, Yvonne Schofer, Matthew Sweney.

I owe a special debt of gratitude to York College of the City University of New York for the Fellowship Leave during which much of my research was completed; to the staff of the York

College Library; to my son, Alex Ryley, who prepared the index of first lines; to James A. Perkins, whose meticulous, pioneering bibliography in his "An American Rhapsody: The Poetry of Kenneth Fearing" (diss., U of Tennessee, 1972) laid the groundwork for this edition; to Rachel Landon, for whose help and invaluable friendship the dedication of this book is inadequate thanks; and to the staff of the General Research Division of the New York Public Library, one member in particular—my wife, Alison M. Ryley.

INTRODUCTION

I. The Life

As a senior in high school, Kenneth Fearing was voted wittiest boy and class pessimist. If there had been elections for class cynic and class misanthropist, he would probably have won these as well. After his death, his friends would remember his charm, his eloquence, his almost courtly manners, his prickly independence, his not-quite-hidden vulnerability and innocence—but mostly they would remember his gloomy, sardonic skepticism. In Margery Latimer's roman à clef *This Is My Body*, a character representing Carl Rakosi says to a character representing Fearing (and Rakosi concedes that the sentiments, though not the style, were sometimes his):

> That darkness of yours has changed me. Your damned dead mind is infecting me. . . . Next thing I'll be flippant like you, joking about everything that means a damn. That darkness of yours is like an infection that never heals. . . .

Pessimists are always right in the long run—everybody gets to drive a silk-upholstered six—but Fearing was right in the short run too. His love affairs, his marriages, his politics, his career— all of them went wrong in the end.

At the beginning he must have seemed destined for the best that America had to offer. His father, Harry Lester Fearing, was a successful Chicago attorney who could trace his paternal ancestry back to seventeenth-century Massachusetts and whose great grandmother was a Coolidge, the sister of the thirtieth president's grandfather. Kenneth's mother, Olive Flexner Fearing,

---

N.B.:   Notes documenting the introduction begin on page *xlix*.

was a member of the illustrious Jewish family that, within a generation of emigrating to the United States from Bohemia, produced Olive's cousin Abraham Flexner, the first director of the Institute for Advanced Study at Princeton; and her cousin Simon Flexner, the first director of the Rockefeller Institute. Simon's son and Kenneth's second cousin, James Thomas Flexner, is a distinguished art historian and winner of the National Book Award for his biography of George Washington.

Kenneth was born in Oak Park, Illinois, on July 28, 1902. One day about a year later his mother picked him up and ran away, presumably to Chicago, where his father quickly tracked them down. A divorce followed, the settlement granting each parent six months' custody a year. Soon, however, Kenneth was spending most of his time with the Fearings and being raised by a doting but eccentric aunt, Eva Fearing Scholl, who, it is said, having been abandoned by her mandolin-teacher husband, cut the head out of all of his photographs and later succumbed to malnutrition caused by a diet of spinach and corn flakes. Harry remarried in 1914 and moved out of the Fearing duplex to an apartment some distance away; but even after he returned with his new wife, for some years Kenneth continued to live with Eva in the south side of the house, though happily for his nutrition he ate his meals with his father and step-mother.

Kenneth loved his father and tolerated his mother. Harry was kind, generous, and often playful, and, when his son grew up, surprisingly tolerant of his bohemianism. On the other hand, his mother—or Ollie as she was usually called—was almost wholly without humor, and what little she had was in the vein of the *Beowulf* poet's, a sort of grim irony. Though she sent Kenneth a monthly allowance until his son was born in 1935, it came at a price—her hectoring admonitions about the importance of honest work. "I hope your book is accepted," she once wrote him, "—God knows you need it." When he did publish, she was not impressed. To the woman who cared for her in the last years of her life she never mentioned that her son was a distinguished writer.

A problem that must have raised its head early on was anti-semitism. Ollie claimed she had run away from her husband after hearing one of his sisters say of Kenneth, "Too bad he's a Jew," and later there was an uproar in the family when a younger cousin of his called him an anti-semitic name. He remembered once sitting under a table while Ollie played pinochle and asking, "What are Jews?"—to which Ollie replied, "God's chosen people meld jacks." In spite of marriage to Ollie, or perhaps because of it, Harry seems to have harbored the kind of reflexive anti-semitism typical of middle-class WASPs of the period. On one occasion, conversing amiably with Kenneth's college friend Carl Rakosi, Harry stopped speaking and left the room when Kenneth provocatively asked if he realized that Rakosi was a Jew. Because Kenneth's background was not generally known outside of the family, he encountered no discrimination in Oak Park. But a feeling that he had something to conceal may have contributed to a habit of secrecy reflected in the extreme impersonality of his art. As his first wife once remarked, "Kenneth spent his whole life hiding his inner self from other people."

Kenneth began his generally successful academic career in 1908 at the Whittier School in Oak Park, and at graduation read an essay on the impeachment of Andrew Johnson. At Oak Park-River Forest High School, he followed in the footsteps of fellow Oak Parker Ernest Hemingway by becoming an editor of the student newspaper, the author of a weekly column, and the author of the class prophecy. In the fall of 1920, he entered the University of Illinois and disappeared for two years. All that is known of his time in Urbana are his grades (not bad) and the title of a story of his, "A Tale of Long Ago," listed in an issue of the *Illinois Magazine* but never printed. At the beginning of his junior year he transferred to the University of Wisconsin and within three months was publishing poetry and fiction in the *Wisconsin Literary Magazine*, or the *Lit*, as it was called. By the beginning of his second semester he was on the editorial board, and by the end of the year he had been elected editor-in-chief. This auspicious beginning, however—a pattern is now beginning to establish itself—was followed by an inglorious final semester. He did win the university's William S. Vilas Prize for an essay on the literary criticism of James Gibbon Huneker; but in March 1924 he was forced to resign as editor of the *Lit*, owing partly to financial mismanagement and partly to an editorial policy of which the Committee on Student Life disapproved: too much Modernist obscurity, pessimism, and sexual frankness. Another reason, he reported in a statement to the student newspaper, was that the members of the Committee "could not see that I loved and respected my fellow men." And, he added, "The . . . point is largely true." A final indignity was a "condition" in a mathematics course that kept him from graduating with his class.

In December of 1924 he went to New York to join Margery Latimer, the dazzlingly attractive and exceptionally gifted young writer he had met and fallen in love with at Wisconsin in early 1923. They were almost exact opposites—he slovenly and bedraggled, saturnine, cynical; she immaculate, luminous, mystical, otherworldly. In a letter to a friend, she wittily parodied one of their typical conversations: "'Well, let's get some coffee.' 'O let's do something great, let's get in contact with people, the world, the world—' 'For God's sake let's be plain for a change.'" This improbable relationship—at its best, she shrewdly observed, when they were apart—lasted until the spring of 1928, when she left New York for her hometown of Portage, Wisconsin, hoping he would follow, propose marriage, and offer to give her a child. Instead he began an affair with another woman. He later suggested that they get back together, but after having been almost suicidal over his infidelity, she discovered she no longer needed him. In October 1931 she married the poet and novelist Jean Toomer, and died in childbirth the following August.

Fearing's original plan on coming to New York had been to work as a journalist and do his own writing on the side, but Latimer, who would later blame herself for contributing to his irresponsibility, persuaded him to devote himself to poetry. It could not have taken much persuasion. Until he was well over fifty, he never held a nine-to-five job for more than a few months. In various summaries of his early work-history, he would claim to have been a journalist, a salesman, a millhand, and even—this in an "About Contributors" column, where a man is not on his honor—a lumberjack. Whatever the truth about mills and lumberjacking, he is known to have worked briefly, either during or just after college, at a Chicago newspaper and, for about a month in 1924, at a department store selling pants. In the next thirty years he would take an occasional brief job—with the WPA, with *Time*, with the United Jewish Appeal, with the Federation of Jewish Philanthropies—but for the most part he just wrote. And though he was more serious about his poetry than about anything else, though he made sacrifices in its service, he could never bring himself to regard it as a calling, as something special. "I always begin to get suspicious," he told his son, "when I hear a poet talking about his *work*." He was a professional free-lance writer, and poetry was one of the things he wrote.

Another thing he wrote was pulp fiction, the sale of which, along with a monthly allowance of $15 from his mother, emergency gifts from his father, and loans from Margery Latimer, was probably his main means of support during the early years in New York. To my knowledge no Fearing pulp story has ever been identified, but his half-brother, Ralph, recalls the plot of one from the late 20s, "Garlic and

Dimpled Knees." The story was

> about an artist who painted a portrait of his garlic-eating girlfriend.
> The work was entered in competition at a gallery. On the day of final
> judging, the girlfriend just happened to be standing near one of the
> judges after finishing some garlic-laced lunch. The judge thought
> the painting so elegantly realistic that he actually felt he could smell
> the garlic, so awarded the masterpiece first prize.

Much of Fearing's pulp fiction, however, was soft-core pornography, often published under the pseudonym Kirk Wolff. Writing in 1932 to his wife-to-be Rachel Meltzer, who deplored pulp work as a waste of his talents, he playfully parodied his Wolffian style, envisioning the time when he might "daily draw the seductively curved, palpitating, flame-lipped and dark, laughing-eyed [Rachel] into my masterful embrace and. . . ." He had not, he assured her, written a similar erotic ellipsis in three months.

As for verse, between his arrival in New York in 1924 and the appearance of his first book in 1929, he published 44 poems in 15 periodicals, a quarter of the 44 in the *New Masses*, to which he also contributed essays and reviews. To this journal he was introduced by Latimer. She had received a request for material from James Rorty, one of the editors, and went to his office with samples of Fearing's work. Though the magazine was not yet a Communist organ and was open to literary diversity, Rorty responded angrily, declaring that he wasn't interested in "art for its own sake." Nevertheless, in September 1926 he devoted a page to five of Fearing's poems, and shortly thereafter Edmund Wilson wrote to the magazine praising them and asking for more.

Fearing's first book, *Angel Arms*, containing nineteen of the forty-four poems he had published since coming to New York and five new ones, was issued by Coward McCann in its Songs of Today Series in the spring of 1929. (For bibliographical details concerning this and all other books by Fearing, see the

Bibliography of Major Works on page *lxii*). This collection has been credited with "initiating proletarian poetry as an American literary movement of permanent importance," a claim that lends the book a certain glamour but that reads back into *Angel Arms* attitudes from Fearing's *Poems* of 1935. Edward Dahlberg, comparing *Angel Arms* to *Poems*, speaks of the earlier book's "acid portraits of Woolworth shopgirls." There are no Woolworth shopgirls in *Angel Arms*, but no matter. Dahlberg's inaccuracy expresses a larger truth—that the book is very much a work of the twenties and directs its withering irony everywhere, at the working class and the lumpen proletariat as well as at the bourgeoisie. The term "proletarian literature" has been given a bewildering variety of definitions, but it is hard to imagine one broad enough to include *Angel Arms'* all-encompassing jazz-age iconoclasm.

The book elicited six brief reviews, ranging from the laudatory in the *New Masses* ("brutal frankness, an intellectual hardness and cleanliness rare since Walt Whitman") to the dismissive in, aptly enough, that Eliotic symbol of spiritual emptiness *The Boston Evening Transcript* ("nothing pleasant in the entire volume"). It may have been this paucity of interest, not to mention sales, that led Fearing almost to abandon poetry for fiction over the next six years, during which he would publish only twenty-one poems. On the other hand, the same pattern—a long period of productivity in one genre, followed by a long period of productivity in the other—would repeat itself for the rest of his life.

During this first period of prose, he wrote three unpublished novels: *Jacqueline*, now lost but known to use one of his girlfriends (not Margery Latimer) as a model for Jacqueline; *Robert Ward*, also lost but known to use his friend Harry Ross as a model for Robert Ward; and *Gentleman's Destiny*, surviving in an incomplete manuscript and a plot summary, and known to use his friend Tom Dimitry as a model for the gentleman. This practice of writing novels about his friends suggests a typical 1930s conception of fiction as documentary, but it was also Fearing's way of insuring that he wouldn't write about himself. "The autobiographical first novel is a death knell," he told his first wife, and he later informed his son that "he always wrote himself in as a minor character in order to keep the main character from being Autobiographical." In the case of *Gentleman's Destiny*, the autobiographical temptation may have been especially strong, for the gentleman protagonist is an alcoholic, as Fearing was.

His drinking began at least as early as Wisconsin, where, according to Rakosi, he used to stay up all night writing and slugging whisky. Once in the late twenties he was jailed for drunkenness and had to be bailed out by Horace Gregory. By 1933, when Albert Halper published his novel *Union Square* in which Fearing appears, scarcely disguised, as the "ex-poet" and pulp writer Jason Wheeler, his addiction must have been notorious. Jason is drunk or half-drunk much of the time, and Halper makes his carelessness with cigarettes responsible for the destruction by fire of his apartment building—a prescient invention, for Fearing would later start two or three small fires by falling into a drunken sleep while smoking in bed.

On a blind date in the summer of 1931, Fearing met his wife-to-be Rachel Meltzer. Attractive, intelligent, competent, and affectionate; twenty-seven years old; politically engaged and active in left-wing causes; a trained nurse employed as a medical social worker, Rachel fell in love almost immediately with the filthiest man she had ever seen. His shirts, she recalls, were green with grime, his teeth covered with tartar. For Rachel, however, his very grubbiness may have been part of his attraction. "Kenneth needed someone to take care of him," she has said, and she threw herself into the role of care-giver with a generosity and enthusiasm that belies her claim that she was never cut out to be a nurse. It is not clear whether her love for Fearing was ever requited in full. In a series of thirty-three letters he wrote from Oak Park between January and April 1932, he told her often that he missed her and wanted her, but he also parried all of her arguments in favor of marriage and addressed her in tones of such facetiousness and irony that his true feelings are indecipherable. The letters also foreshadowed what would eventually help to doom the marriage—his reluctance to express affection in person. For while the letters were at least affectionate—in fact, charmingly so—he had to reassure Rachel that he wasn't angry when they parted in New York (he just wasn't very good at leave-taking) and apologize for his aloofness when she telephoned (the family was listening). The time would come when they couldn't Communicate at all, he silent in his toughness and cynicism, she afraid to speak for fear of sounding stupid and sentimental. And yet when they weren't together, he could say on paper what he never said in person. Writing to her in 1937 while they were living apart until they could find an apartment, he declared out of the blue, "Discovered I am horribly in love with you five minutes after I rang the bell at Ruth's and found you'd gone."

Over the objections of Rachel's orthodox Jewish father, who regarded Fearing as a gentile (as did Rachel herself), they were married on April 26, 1933. She then became the family breadwinner, a role that assumed additional importance after the birth of their only son, Bruce, on July 19, 1935, when Fearing's mother decided that Kenneth should assume the responsibilities of fatherhood and stopped his allowance of $15 a month. (When Bruce was older and Rachel wrote pleading for help with his dental expenses, Ollie replied, "Ask your husband.") Except for a few months before Bruce was born and the better part of a year when they were in England on Fearing's Guggenheim, Rachel worked continuously throughout the marriage. During one period, employed by the New York City Welfare Department, she had to travel an hour and a half each way to the Brownsville office in Brooklyn and would get so tired that, much to Fearing's annoyance, she would fall asleep at parties.

As well as the birth of his son, 1935 brought the publication of Fearing's second book. *Poems*, comprising the twenty-one poems he had published since *Angel Arms* and fulsomely introduced by Edward Dahlberg, was issued by Dynamo in an edition of a thousand numbered copies and then, an indication of its success, in paper covers. According to Robert Cantwell, it even made money (though not for the author). Its success was owing not only to its intrinsic merits, which are many, but to its apparent vindication of faith in the power of Marxism to foster poetry of the first rank. Dahlberg's introduction insists on the poems' hostility to capitalism and on their "inexorable, Marxist interpretations," and enthusiastic reviewers hastened to follow his lead, two of them confidently identifying Fearing as a Communist. In fact, however, some of the poems might have been written by the apolitical, iconoclastic Fearing of the 1920s. Nevertheless, the authority of Dahlberg's introduction; the unmistakable Communist implications of many of the poems, especially the last, "Denouement"; and the announcement on the back of the title page that the book was "the first . . . in a projected series which will present proletarian poets"—all of this made it easy to find more Marxism than was probably intended, nor was Fearing at this time averse to having such discoveries made. But was he really serious about Communism? My own answer would be, "It depends."

It depends, for one thing, on what period of his life we're talking about. His first wife reports that at the time he was publishing some of the incendiary poems of *Poems*, he was laughing in private at the pomposity and self-importance of Communist Party members. If this attitude isn't implied, it is at least not contradicted by what he later told the FBI—that "he had become a 'fellow traveler' in 1933 and that prior to that time he had not been very interested in the meetings of the John Reed Club due to the fact that he was not interested in the politics discussed at all the meetings." And the same indifference to politics is evidenced in the thirty-three letters he wrote to Rachel in 1932. These focus on his writing, his money problems, his family, his drinking, his smoking, his reading (murder mysteries), and his boredom. There are only two or three brief references to politics, mainly in response to something said by his correspondent; only two references to the *New Masses*, one having to do with a dance; and only one reference to the Depression—this in connection with his family's citing hard times in an effort to persuade him to stay in Oak Park rather than return to New York.

The answer to the question "How serious was Fearing about Communism?" also depends on what is meant by seriousness. If he was serious enough to become a fellow traveler after 1933, was he serious enough to join the Party? The FBI has a list that says he was, and according to Alfred Hayes, Fearing once turned to Philip Rahv after listening to him hold forth on the evils of Stalinism and said, "And *you* recruited me into the party." Moreover, A. B. Magill told Alan Wald that he recalled Fearing's having been a Party member "for a while." But the FBI list, its provenance unknown even to the Bureau itself, is the merest hearsay; Hayes's anecdote, assuming its accuracy, is open to a variety of interpretations; and Magill's recollection is vague. And against this evidence must be set the contrary testimony of his friends and family, and especially of Fearing himself. In 1950, Anna Marie Rosenberg, President Truman's nominee as Assistant Secretary of Defense, was wrongly identified as a former member of the John Reed Club. It was in connection with the Rosenberg investigation that Fearing was first interviewed by the FBI and then issued a request subpoena by an assistant U.S. attorney in Washington. Testifying under oath and asked if he was a member of the Communist Party, Fearing replied, loudly, "Not yet." This answer, there is every reason to believe, was not only witty but true.

With the critical success of *Poems*, Fearing entered the mainstream of American literary culture. On a Guggenheim fellowship of $2,500, he went with Rachel and Bruce to London for the first eight months of 1937, and returned to a contract offer from Random House for a new book of poems and, somewhat later, another contract for his novel *The Hospital*, which had been drafted in London. In the summer of 1938, he went for his first stay at Yaddo, the writer's colony in Saratoga Springs to which he would often return, and for the first time since 1926, he placed a poem in *The New Yorker*, which became his forum of choice for the next ten years. Much to his amusement, in December of 1938 his degree from the University of Wisconsin was awarded "as of the class of 1924," and in the following year his Guggenheim was renewed. In 1940 he won the Guarantor's Prize of *Poetry* magazine for "Three Poems," and in 1944 an award of $1,000 from the American Academy of Arts and Letters.

This period was also the most productive of his life. Between 1938 and 1943 he published a book a year: *Dead Reckoning* (verse, 1938), *The Hospital* (novel, 1939), *Collected Poems* (1940), *Dagger of the Mind* (novel, 1941), *Clark Gifford's Body* (novel, 1942), and *Afternoon of a Pawnbroker* (verse, 1943). The only critical failure was *Clark Gifford's Body*, whose aggressively avant-garde technique (twenty-three characters narrate a jumbled chronology of sixty years) and pessimistic vision of the future were scarcely calculated to satisfy public taste in the middle of World War II. But even the critically successful works failed to pay, only *The Hospital* and *Collected Poems* earning him more royalties than the advance on each book. Nearly famous and entering his forties, he was still financially dependent on his wife.

But his marriage collapsed in 1942. As early as 1938, in a gentle, affectionate letter from Yaddo, he had broached the subject of divorce, but Rachel, fearful of how the loss of his father would affect Bruce and certain that she couldn't manage without a husband, successfully fought to save the marriage. By 1942, however, Fearing's alcoholism had intensified, a six-month job with *Time* had done nothing to improve his financial prospects, and Rachel had come to believe that she and Bruce would be better off alone. As he was about to depart for another of his stays at Yaddo, she told him she was leaving him and was dumbfounded when he said, inexplicably, "Well, don't pick up any men in bars." Though in later years they would develop a warm friendship, for a long time after the break he nursed feelings of bitterness about what he evidently considered a betrayal.

Consolation, however, came almost immediately at Yaddo, where he met Nan Lurie, a handsome thirty-two-year-old artist. She had grown up speaking Yiddish in New Jersey, gone to Paris on her own after high school, and won a scholarship to study under Yasuo Kunioshi at the Art Students League. She and Fearing met within a week of their arrival at Yaddo and stayed on together during the winter after most of the other residents had left. On Christmas day, with less than a dollar between them, they ate their first meal alone together at a restaurant in the Black district of Saratoga Springs. By the spring, when they were both back in New York, Fearing was wildly, deliriously, giddily in love and writing notes and letters of astonishing sentimentality, even falling into such clichés as "I am not good enough for you." He cherished what he called Nan's "sheer lunacy"—her "vitamins," her "stray cats," her "religious quarter hour," the "confessions" she wrote in the dark, blindfolded. (In his poem "Irene Has a Mind of Her Own," published four years later when his ardor had cooled, he looked on similar flakiness with a less benevolent eye.) In the winter of 1944-45, he moved into Nan's loft on East 10th Street, and, his divorce having become final the year before, they were married in Greenwich, Connecticut, on June 18, 1945.

While still at Yaddo in March 1943, Fearing had been having trouble mapping out a new novel. Inspiration had to wait for two events: the sensational murder in October 1943 of the New York heiress Mrs. Wayne Lonergan, and the publication in 1944 of Samuel Michael Fuller's little-known thriller *The Dark Page*. Transformed and refined, details from the Lonergan case and Fuller's novel would coalesce in Fearing's imagination to produce the plot of his most famous book, which he wrote between August 1944 and October 1945.

Published in the fall of 1946, *The Big Clock* made Fearing temporarily rich. Altogether he took in about $60,000 (roughly $360,000 in 1992 dollars): about $10,000 in royalties and from the sale of republication rights (including a condensation in *The American Magazine*), and $50,000 from the sale of film rights to Paramount. In 1947, Nan won $2,000 in an art competition, a sum they dismissed as negligible but that only two years earlier would have seemed a fortune. But Fearing's successes always contained the germ of disaster. Overestimating his business acumen, he had negotiated his own contract with Paramount, permanently and irrevocably signing away his film rights, and relinquishing his television rights till 1952, by which time, he discovered to his rage and frustration, Paramount was showing late-night reruns and had thus cornered the market. A more immediate problem was alcohol. He told his friend Alice Neel (the model for Louise Patterson, the eccentric painter in *The Big Clock*) that since he could now afford to start drinking in the morning, he was having trouble getting any work done. On one occasion he almost died from a combination of scotch and phenobarbital, and in 1952 he was so shaken by his doctor's warnings about the condition of his liver that he went on the wagon. For Nan, who for years had been trying to get him to stop drinking, this should have been a cause for rejoicing, but she discovered that without alcohol he was no longer "playful" and "romantic" and that she was no longer interested in the marriage.

Stranger at Coney Island and Other Poems appeared in 1948, his "Next to last volume, perhaps," he called it in an inscription to Vincent Starrett. The response of the critics was generally favorable; but beginning as early as the *Collected Poems*, a note of dissatisfaction had begun to sound even in some of the most enthusiastic reviews. Fearing's best work, it was said, had been done before 1938; or the poet was repeating himself; or his methods or his themes or his aesthetic or all three were such as to make major poems impossible. Whatever the justice of these opinions, along with financial considerations they probably contributed to his decision to devote himself thenceforth exclusively to the novel. He abandoned poetry completely until 1955 when, with considerable difficulty and primarily to justify the use of the word "new" in the title, he wrote the "Family Album" section of *New and Selected Poems*.

The last ten years of Fearing's life were embittered by poverty and failing health. Somehow he and Nan had gone through all of his earnings from *The Big Clock*, though their only apparent extravagance, if extravagance it can be called, was to rent a cottage in the country for part of two summers. At any rate, by January 1951 Fearing was beginning to worry about money. His novel *Loneliest Girl in the World* (1951) and the *New and Selected Poems* (1956) provided a little income, but neither of his last two novels, *The Generous Heart* (1954) and *The Crozart Story* (1960), earned enough to pay off his advances. The following fragments of information from his papers at the University of Wisconsin suggest the tenuousness of his solvency throughout the period:

Total annual income, 1954:	$4,878.20
Total annual income, 1955:	$2,975.92
Indebtedness to Harcourt (royalties less advances and books purchased as of 30 June 1955):	($1,353.80)
Indebtedness to Doubleday (royalties less advances as of 31 October 1960):	($1,354.68)

For the first time since the 1930s, he had to write for the pulps again, though now it was crime stories under his own name. And for the first time ever, he held a full-time job for three consecutive years (1955-1958), writing reports and publicity releases for the Muscular Dystrophy Association of America. People who worked with him remember that in the afternoons he would have to put his head on his typewriter and sleep.

These indignities, coming as they did after his affluence of the late forties and in conjunction with the poisonous atmosphere of McCarthyism, led to a radical darkening of his vision. In his last novel, *The Crozart Story*, the only characters not corrupt are those too sketchily portrayed to be morally significant. Steve Crozart, the charlatan and perjurer who has helped to cause, and has vastly profited by, the conviction of Blair Fennister (read Alger Hiss), explains with amoral insouciance the reasoning that underlies his, Crozart's, destruction of the innocent:

> The human sacrifice should be selected with great care. In the classic stories of our age, the protagonist marked for destruction is so well chosen that at first glance it seems unlikely he has really been nominated. He is so favorably situated, he imagines himself so immune to the grotesque indictment, the stereotyped travesty of the accusation, that he believes it is wholly an accident that he, personally, has been designated a leading figure among the category of those about to be condemned. Even when he sees the wholesale abandonment of himself, the universal desertion from his side, his cause and case, even then he doesn't accept that his fate is irrevocably fixed. . . .
>
> And there is a good reason for the choice of such a figure as the

quarry. His complacency adds tone and zest to the whole spectacle. His innocent faith in himself heightens the suspense. His struggles to escape from the fury of the pack become increasingly genuine and desperate because he alone still imagines that it is possible to escape. And the spectators sense this. They know that every move, every turn and twist the dedicated sacrifice makes as he seeks to break out of the gauntlet—all this is genuine.

It's a drama that cannot be counterfeited.

This is satire, of course, but Fearing as satirist is here less a Swift than a Gulliver returned from the land of the Houyhnhnms. In random thoughts set down sometime in the early fifties, ideas that Crozart applies narrowly to security investigations had been generalized by Fearing as his own:

> Cannibalism, the rite of human sacrifice, seems to run through every age and every phase of the human story. In itself both betrayal and atonement, every completed cycle of the process prepares for the next circle of the ritual. Early Spring and late Fall seem to be the favored seasons of the observance.
>
> There is some obscure zest in the act. Religious writers revel in it. It is probably here, even in these observations. In a primitive agricultural society, human sacrifice insured good crops. In complex industrial society, a springtime war means profits.

The Fearing of the fifties differs from Crozart not as Swift differs from Gulliver, but as Gulliver differs from the rest of humanity— in his sickened abhorrence of the Yahooness that everyone else seems to revel in and take for granted. And Yahooness is universal. It governs in the United States, it governs in the Soviet Union. On the same page as his observations on "human sacrifice," Fearing predicts that American security investigations—"the shakedown," "the racket"—will lead inevitably, as their equivalent had done under Stalin, to "mass assassinations." In a brief unpublished essay written at the end of 1952, "Phantoms of the Investigation," he declares that the defense industry, a fiction created by a corrupt establishment to line its own pockets, produces no new military equipment whatsoever, and suggests that there may be an implicit agreement between the U.S. and the Soviet Union to prolong the Korean War. This was the mood that inspired "Reading, Writing, and the Rackets," his furious anti-anti-Communist foreword to *New and Selected Poems*—a foreword in defense of which he almost sacrificed his contract for the book when he thought his editors were trying to censor him. This was the mood that led him to deny to *Mainstream*, the successor to the *New Masses*, permission to reprint "Reading, Writing, and the Rackets." This was the mood that, when he was invited to a meeting to draft a letter of protest against the Soviet Union's refusal to let Pasternak collect his Nobel Prize, led him to snort, "Why don't they give *me* a Nobel Prize. I'll go to a meeting for that."

In the late fall of 1952, Nan had announced that she wanted a separation. When Fearing was about to leave, she went to a movie, telling him to help himself to anything in the loft he thought he could use, but all he took, she discovered when she returned, was a small radio. At the end of the year he wrote a friend that Nan was "sketching churches in Venice" and that, he had finally concluded, "she must be permanently 12 years old." They saw each other only two or three times after the separation, and though he consulted his lawyer about the possibility of a divorce, nothing ever came of it. When he died, she hadn't known he had been ill.

He had begun drinking again in the fall of 1953, and he had never stopped smoking. His half-brother Ralph recalls staying overnight with him sometime in the late fifties and listening as he "coughed his strength away all night long." One day early in 1961, he felt a sharp pain in his back as he started to open a window. By June—at about the time he learned that his mother was arranging to give him a lifetime income of $150 a month— the pain was unremitting. Bruce moved into his 11th Street apartment to take care of him. "That week," Bruce recalled, "he had me covering the village for places to buy codeine cough syrup for a pain killer slugged by the bottle. One week of that & rubbing his back 'there' while he told me how much it hurt, & I figured it was going beyond me. . . ." On the 21st, they went by taxi to Lenox Hill Hospital, where Fearing was admitted with a malignant melanoma of the left chest and pleural cavity.

He died quietly on the 26th.

II. The Poems

Not long after coming to New York from Oak Park, *Newsweek* reported in 1951, Fearing

> was walking along Bank Street near the Ninth Avenue El, polishing in his mind the last two lines of a sonnet about Caesar's centurions, when an El train roared overhead, and this sudden intrusion of contemporary reality on his classical mood led him to determine to give up formal verse from that moment thenceforth, and to work on something closer to the life of the times.

This Pauline conversion sounds too pat to be credible, but the change it mythicizes was real enough, and as transformative in its way as the Christian saint's. Except for a few poems reprinted in *Angel Arms* and one reprinted in *Collected Poems*, Fearing never published formal verse after 1927 and didn't again publish a poem with an ancient setting until 1943. His career thus falls into two unequal periods, the pre-conversion and the post-conversion, and both of these fall into subdivisions of their own.

During the first period, Fearing was a promising but conservative young poet. As late as 1927, he was still publishing works redolent of the Genteel Tradition. Sometimes set in the past and often lacking identifiable settings, these poems treat conventionally "poetic" subjects (death, nature, war, imaginary creatures) in traditional forms (couplets, the villanelle, the elegiac stanza) and in conventionally "poetic," euphonious language ("dim, leaf-strewn retreat," "the perfumed couch of June," "And tell us of / His honey'd eyes"). Some of the poems, however ("Divan and Morris Chair," "Rain," "My Mermaid"), are skillful, charming, and, within the limits of the conventions they observe, wonderfully inventive. Others have a harder edge than the kind of verse they derive from, as if Fearing were trying to break out of the Genteel mode without quite knowing how to do so. In "Man Dead," for example—his first professionally published poem—he cheekily flouts decorum by reducing death and mourning to matters of "nerves," "tendons," and "neurons," but writes in an idiom (no doubt partly imposed by the stanza form) not even remotely close to that really spoken by anybody ("men come dead when stomachs break," "sits a dry-eyed sobbing / beside the muteness.")

At the same time, he was also publishing poems that escape the influence of the Genteel Tradition altogether. (And here it must be emphasized that, since with few exceptions the only dates we have are of publication, his advances and retreats may appear more erratic than they were in fact: Much of the formal verse published after 1925-26 was almost certainly written earlier.) Edwin Arlington Robinson is the model for some of these poems, especially "Scottwell" and "Blair and Blair's Friends," the former a free-verse variation on both "Miniver Cheevy" and "Richard Cory," the latter echoing the intonations, though not the dramatic situation, of "How Annandale Went Out." Fearing's "Ashes" glances both at Robinson and—the only such glance in Fearing's work—at Imagism. "Sonnet to a Prominent Figure on the Campus," a clever satire in which a conformist undergraduate condescends to Abraham Lincoln (whose statue is the "Prominent Figure"), goes directly back to the ironic dramatic monologues of Browning.

Still clinging to formal verse, Fearing made a tentative foray into Modernism in 1925-26 with the publication of "Medusa" and "The Night of a Jew." These poems are in the manner of what David Perkins calls (though not in connection with Fearing, whom he never mentions) "The Poetry of Critical Intelligence": "studied and rigorous in meters and stanzas," "texture of phrasing... dense and active," metaphors "telescoped." Though neither poem is wholly free of old-fashioned poetic diction ("old portals," "From the deep twilight till the morrow"), both violate, flagrantly, Genteel standards of clarity and beauty. The symbolism of both poems is obscure, and some of the imagery is shocking and horrific. However, all experiments of this kind stopped after the conversion, which first manifested itself in print in 1926.

In part, the new Fearing derives from Whitman via Sandburg. He uses the flexible Sandburg line, which can range from lineated prose to a highly rhythmical chant, some of the purposes of meter being served by syntactical parallelism and lexical iteration. He also takes over much of Sandburg's subject matter: cityscapes, working-class and criminal characters, and upper-class fools and scoundrels. But Fearing is no Sandburg clone. He is wittier than Sandburg, with a gift for parody that Sandburg lacks, and more impersonal, more pessimistic, and more cynical. Moreover, he also writes under the influence of the High Modernists, especially Eliot, and is therefore more experimental than Sandburg and more daring in his violation of traditional standards of logic, coherence, and literary decorum. And to this strange amalgam of the Sandburgian and the Eliotic, he makes three contributions of his own: the frequent use, and not always ironically, of a defiantly trite "unpoetic" vocabulary; an occasional fracturing of normal grammar (though never in the manner of Cummings); and a frequently oblique, offbeat approach to otherwise unoriginal subject matter, dramatic situations, or themes. When to all of this is added Fearing's gift for precise but unexpected and quirky turns of phrase, the result is a body of work that escapes easy classification. If Fearing occasionally sounds like another poet, no other poet ever sounds like Fearing.

Though many of the early post-conversion poems are in traditional modes—character portrait, dramatic monologue, narrative—and though some of the portraits may have been influenced by Horace Gregory, the distinctive Fearing manner and voice are already discernible. The portrait "Evening Song," for example, uses throughout what will become a favorite

Fearing device, the imperative mood. McKade is commanded to fall asleep and to have a series of fantasies from which, presumably, the reader is to draw conclusions about his character—that he is sex-starved, that he is afraid of death, that he has social aspirations, and so on. However, the poem makes heavy Modernist demands on the reader's tolerance for uncertainty. Since the imperative mood makes it impossible to determine what information about McKade is literal, there is no way of telling how far his fantasies depart from reality. Where does he actually sleep—under a building, on a bed, or in the street? "Afternoon of Colonel Brady" and "Minnie and Mrs. Hoyne" use the novelistic device of imitating a character's style while maintaining a third-person point of view. Though in the former poem we are in the mind of Colonel Brady, the clipped military accents of his speech are suggested by sentence fragments, and in a kind of modified stream of consciousness we follow his obsessively repetitive recollections of a chambermaid he once seduced and of the sound of guns in the battle of the Argonne. In "Minnie and Mrs. Hoyne," a little masterpiece, it is Minnie's speech we hear, the poet in this instance retaining by means of the third person an ever-so-slight ironic perspective that permits us to see around her character. Minnie's expression "die laughing" or a variant is used five times in the poem until, by the end, the cliché has grown ominous.

The dramatic monologues are also unconventional. "The Drunken Fly," originally titled "Nathan Schaffrin," proceeds by means of what C. K. Stead calls "aggregation": "Pure images . . . added to one another, without the imposition of a structure, without logical or narrative continuity. . . ." In "John Standish, Artist," Standish declares that in order to be an artist and even to survive, he must arbitrarily choose one of the common herd, follow him home, and murder him, the significance of this symbolic act being left entirely to the imagination of the reader. "Andy and Jerry and Joe," reflecting the boredom and unimaginativeness of its three speakers, is flat, rhythmless, and, except for occasional hyperbole, relentlessly literal.

The most daring and original of the early post-conversion poems are the narratives "Green Light" and "St. Agnes' Eve." "Green Light" tells a story, but of what it's impossible to say. The poem's predicates lack subjects and repeatedly force readers to revise their inferences about what is being depicted. Here is the first strophe, with my interlinear comments in brackets:

> Bought at the drug store, very cheap; and later pawned.
>> [The subject is a small object, perhaps a watch.]
> After a while, heard on the street; seen in the park.
>> [The subject is noisy, large, perhaps animate.]
> Familiar, but not quite recognized.
> Followed and taken home and slept with.
>> [The subject is a person.]
> Traded or sold. Or lost.
>> [The subject is an object.]

The effect of moving from fragment to fragment is like that of watching an animated cartoon in which dishes grow legs and run away, a person's flailing arms turn into propellers, and so on. The impression of haste created both by the fragment form itself and the rapidly transmogrifying unexpressed subjects suggests a world of frantic, purposeless bustle, of frenetic changeless change. The narrative of "St. Agnes' Eve" is conventionally coherent but is told in a startling range of tones, from plangent Eliotic solemnity ("Subways mumble and mutter an ominous portent") to comic-strip clowning ("rat-a-tat-tat," "Blam! / Blam-blam!") to journalistic pomposity ("Officer Dolan noticed something suspicious [it is supposed]") to the matter-of-fact ("and Dolan was buried as quickly as possible"). The rhythms are equally varied and unpredictable, sometimes prosy, sometimes almost regularly iambic ("Then Louie sagged and fell and ran"), sometimes child-like ("While rat-a-tat-tat / Rat-a-tat-tat / Said Louie's Gat"). The conventions of narrative realism are violated by the intrusion of drama and film jargon, and by surrealistic, cartoon-like images ("Louie's soul arose through his mouth in the form of a derby hat. . ."). All of these devices make it nearly impossible to feel sympathy for the characters, and this is precisely the point. Not for nothing is the poem called "St. Agnes' Eve," and not for nothing did Fearing place the work at the beginning of every collection he ever published. Both the title and the work are an audacious manifesto, flaunting the contrast between Keats's lush medievalism and Fearing's own brassy, tumultuous modernity. The poem does not fail to achieve, rather it positively refuses to permit, the enjoyment of traditional literary pleasures.

Increasing the range of his subject matter in the post-conversion poems, Fearing also increased the range of his themes but without discarding his earlier preoccupations. "Green Light" implies the nihilism expressed more explicitly in "Moral (OP. 1)," and in "Minnie and Mrs. Hoyne," Minnie—the only developed character in Fearing who explicitly rejects the fantasies of popular culture—is gently satirized, not for sharing this nihilism, as in fact she does, but for failing to recognize its tragic implications, especially for herself. A related theme, adumbrated in the early "Scottwell," is the emptiness of people's lives. Some, like Scottwell, though with more success than he, seek fulfillment in fantasy (Hilda in "Breakfast with Hilda," Feldman in "Angel Arms," McKade in "Evening Song"), some seek reassurance in philosophico-mystical systems (Dr. Barky and his followers in "The Cabinet of Simplicity"), some get drunk ("The Drinkers," William Lowell in "Portrait (1)"), some have too little imagination to be aware of their own dissatisfactions ("Andy and Jerry and Joe," Max and Charlotte in "Saturday Night," the speakers of

"Now"). A new theme, one that will be increasingly important in later works, is the absurdity, the meretriciousness, the sheer chaos of American literary culture, high and low. In the comic "Cultural Notes," which originated as a spoof in prose published in the *New Masses*, the upper-class twits are fatuous middle-brows, the working-class boors are monomaniacal intellectuals. "Aphrodite Metropolis (3)" plays off the traditional eloquence of the *carpe diem* theme against the styles of newspaper headlines, of advertising, of the demotic ("And then they sit down on it, nice"). Jumbling newspaper headlines with passages from a stilted public statement by a condemned killer, "Jack Knuckles Falters" is a funny, slightly scary collage. "St. Agnes' Eve" is a little anthology of American styles, focusing attention not so much on crime and suffering and death as on their transformation into the language of film, newspaper, cartoon, poem, and ordinary speech. It is as if we are meant to see at work in the poem, and at a distance that protects us from its normally irresistible power, the mythmaking machinery of the whole culture.

The crash of 1929, the deepening depression, an atmosphere of crisis affecting the mood and expectations of readers, Fearing's own increasing maturity and closer alliance with the Communist Party—all helped to produce a darkening of tone and an elevation of style in many of the twenty-one poems he published between 1930 and 1935. This change is partly a matter of magnitude, his lines growing longer, sometimes as long as fifty words or more. His sentences are generally longer as well, in three instances a single sentence constituting an entire poem. One of these, "Lullaby," has an inverted word order so complicated that it entangles the poet himself: The "moon" (l. 8) is said to be "filled . . . with the light of a moon" (l. 2). However, this sentence is more than a stylistic flourish, its seamlessness reflecting the seamlessness that must exist, the poem implies, among the

xxxiv

personal, the political, and the economic. In addition to a new grammatical complexity, almost every poem employs, alone or in combination, such devices as insistent parallelism, repeated rhetorical questions, the second person with the future tense, and the imperative mood. The result is a style closer in some of the poems to that of political oratory or religious prophecy than to the slangy colloquialism of much of the earlier verse.

If any doubt remains about Alan Wald's argument that for left-wing poets of the thirties there was no necessary conflict between Marxist thought and the techniques of literary Modernism, the example of Fearing should put it to rest. He now almost wholly abandoned conventional logic and continuity for Modernist methods perhaps even more radical than those in his poems of the late twenties. It is impossible to tell if "Dividends," for example, is a dramatic monologue with interruptions or a series of several different voices. It is equally impossible to know if the "she" of the opening lines of the second strophe is "the woman" of the fourth line, or "Mildred" of the fifth strophe, or both, or neither. The unexpressed grammatical subjects of the earlier "Green Light" metamorphose no more surrealistically than the "you" addressed throughout "1933" ("you" listen to a political speech, forage in an alley, are honored by the king of Italy, and so on), or than the never-defined "it" of "American Rhapsody (2)" ("did you get it," "did you take it, was it safe, did you buy it, . . ."). In "Sunday to Sunday," a summary of a wildly improbable movie plot slides unpredictably back and forth between the fictional world and the real one. In "What If Mr. Jesse James Should Some Day Die?" the tone of the speaker shifts abruptly and inexplicably from fear to oratorical authority ("O, dauntless khaki soldier") to uncertainty to certainty. At the beginning of Part 2 of "Denouement," we see the body of a hanged man, men taking possession of a bed, and cigar coupons in a vase, but whether these make up one scene or three we cannot know. In the same poem, as in many other poems, signals marking a change in speaker are not used, nor is it possible to distinguish a change in speaker from a simple change in tone. Unpredictably, the voice that begins "Denouement" modulates to or abruptly becomes the voice of a judge, the voice of a prosecutor, the voice of a defense attorney (perhaps), the voice of the oppressed, the voice of someone (patient? nurse? doctor? poet?) calling for painkillers, the voice of a naif puzzled by social protest, the voice of a union member, the voice of a political moderate, the voice of a Communist orator.

By such means Fearing manages to be both panoramic and particular, to suggest the chaos of a society thought to be on the brink of ruin, and to control the moral and political implications of his images. But what are these implications? In his introduction to *Poems*, Dahlberg declares that "as the poems in their chronological progression become more incisive and attain Marxian lucidity the ironic comments rise and expand into an affirmative Communist statement." Dahlberg is right about the "affirmative Communist statement," for "Denouement," which concludes the volume, is explicitly Marxist. And though the order of the poems is not precisely chronological, the earliest are grouped at the beginning of the volume. *Pace* Dahlberg, however, Fearing wanders rather than marches to his Communist destination. For one thing, nobody had to consult Marx to be appalled by the inequities of American capitalism in the Great Depression, and unless a poem specifically alludes to Marxism, there is no reason to think its protest motivated by anything other than undoctrinaire American leftism. For another thing, some of the poems imply themes or contain passages apparently inconsistent with or even skeptical of Communism. "Conclusion," for example, the first poem in the volume, glorifies dissent by damning conformity and scorns a yes-man for, among other things, being "found with the many resolved against the few"—

a scorn more consistent with American individualism than with that dictatorship of the proletariat foreseen in "Denouement," in which "millions of voices become one voice, . . . millions of hands . . . move as one." "Winner Take All" is about the psychology of guilt (no wonder Fearing was immediately skeptical of the servile confessions at the Moscow trials) and has more in common thematically with "Jack Knuckles Falters" and "Portrait (1)" than with the later poems. "Resurrection" reflects satirically on a certain kind of Communist ("You will remember the triumph easily defined by the rebel messiah"), as does "American Rhapsody (1)," in which "That proprietor of the revolution, oracle Steve" is implicitly accorded the same moral status as a movie star, a corrupt judge, a thug, and so on. "American Rhapsody (1)" also ends with a god-like longshot view of American life and finds it "strange and significant, and not without peace." "X Minus X" suggests that, for better or for worse, in every individual an irreducible nucleus of feeling remains unaffected by external circumstances of any kind.

And yet these poems may be as effectively anti-capitalist as any in the volume because their images of capitalist degradation have, or pretend to have, an apolitical purpose. The second strophe of "Resurrection," for example, is a tour de force in which a few strategically placed words, most not even pejorative— "friendly," "inhumanly," "triumphant," "glittered," "bought," "clerk," "radiant"—ironically imply a society riddled with violence, guile, hypocrisy, and corruption. The ostensible purpose of the poem, however, is to list the memories that an American might preserve over a lifetime. That some of these memories are favorable ("the cities, the plains, the mountains, and the sea") and that one includes a simple-minded Communist ("the rebel messiah") only enhances the satire by contributing to its aura of objectivity. If "X Minus X" implies that something in human nature is inevitably resistant to its environment, what the poem causes us to remember most vividly is a shoddy American culture—"your friend, the radio," "her dream, the magazine," "his life, the ticker." Fearing is always at his best in the oblique attack of poems like these and of "Obituary," "Dear Beatrice Fairfax," "Dirge," "$2.50," and "Lullaby." In this kind of poem, iniquitous capitalism is made to seem almost incidental, the medium in which Americans of the Great Depression lived, and moved, and had their being.

Only one work had never been published before its appearance in *Poems*, "Twentieth-Century Blues," a poem of considerable obscurity and apparently lacking in political significance. However, that Fearing placed it immediately before "Denouement" in each of its three incarnations suggests that there was, in his mind, an intimate connection between the two works. What that connection might be is a question worth asking for the light it can shed on the meaning of "Denouement" and, by implication, on Fearing's thinking about Communism in 1935.

"Twentieth-Century Blues" is obscure because the questions it asks are unclear in themselves and in their relation to each other. Are they, for example, different questions or the same question asked in a variety of different ways? To spare everybody a long and almost certainly inconclusive explication, let me declare arbitrarily that the poem asks essentially the same question: Is anything that most people want worth having? The answer is no. Nothing satisfies, nothing lasts—riches, personal achievement, sexual fulfillment, none of the tawdry dreams that "fantasy Frank, and dreamworld Dora, and hallucination Harold, and delusion Dick, and nightmare Ned" insist on conjuring up. "Twentieth-Century Blues" is Fearing's "Vanity of Human Wishes."

But "Denouement" provides the solution to the problem that "Twentieth-Century Blues" defines. For "Denouement" suggests that Communism offers the only certainty, the only immortality in a world otherwise given over to death—not the immortality of the Christian afterlife, in which nobody any longer believes (hence those twentieth-century blues) but the immortality of an idea, identification with which insures the believer's symbolic resurrection, both at those moments when, inevitably, the idea overcomes its temporary defeats, and at that final moment when it triumphs once and for all:

> Never again these faces, arms, eyes lips—
>
> Not unless we live, and live again,
> Return, everywhere alive in the issue that returns, clear as light
>   that still descends from a star long cold, again alive and
>   everywhere visible through and through the scene that
>   comes again, as light on moving water breaks and returns,
>   heard only in the words, as millions of voices become one
>   voice, seen only in millions of hands that move as one—

"Denouement" is as close as Fearing ever came to writing a religious poem. Whether he really believed what he wrote is open to question. Typically, however (and prophetically), he ended the poem not on the note of triumph that sounds in the passage I have quoted above but in tones of hopelessness and despair: "no life, no breath, no sound, no touch, no warmth, no light but the lamp that shines on a trooper's drawn and ready bayonet."

Auguring another change in artistic direction, Fearing's first poem after *Poems* was "Pantomime"—apolitical, non-satirical, conventional in technique. Of the twenty-nine additional poems he published over the next three years and collected in *Dead Reckoning*, many return to the shorter line of *Angel Arms*, some are unashamedly light verse, none seems Marxist in its implications, and only eight are indisputably political ("En Route," "Lunch with the Sole Survivor," "Devil's Dream," "Hold the Wire, "C Stands for Civilization," "The Program," and "Ad"). Moreover, these political poems are less concerned with specific evils in American society than with the general atmosphere of crisis produced by the seeming inevitability of war. Perhaps for this reason, there is also a change in Fearing's management of Modernist techniques, a new, unsettling vagueness. Gone, for the most part, are the vivid "close-ups"— the metaphor is his in "American Rhapsody (1)"—of specific scenes from American life, to be replaced by the kind of generalized allusiveness first adumbrated in "Dividends," whose ambiguous pronouns were mentioned above. But whereas in "Dividends" it is clear that, however opaque the meaning of particular passages, a capitalist is feathering his own nest, in "En Route," for example, the nature of the two undercover operatives and their symbolic significance are maddeningly uncertain. M. L. Rosenthal calls them Nazis or proto-Nazis, presumably on the strength of the reference to "our beloved leader," but it is hard to believe that in 1938 Fearing would have expected readers to associate these characters' uncertainty, ineptness, and fear of the police with a political movement backed by the most powerful and dangerous military machine in the world.

The new Modernist poems are also infected by what seems casual whimsy. The conditions required for the next rendezvous in "En Route" (barometer reading "28.28" with "rain and hail and fog and snow"); "an invisible man" for sale in "Hold the Wire"; the "HUMAN GIRAFFE" (a blizzard of uppercase letters is also new) in "Take a Letter"—these lack the pointed clarity of, say, the repeated restorations of virginity in "1933," the huge specter of "Allen Devoe" haunting all of America in "American Rhapsody (1)," and similar satirical fantasticalities throughout the earlier poems.

Some of the new poems, however, eschew Modernist techniques entirely. "Portrait (2)," for example, returns to the kind of character study absent from *Poems* and brilliantly demolishes a complaisant businessman—the speaker, as it were, of "Sonnet to a Prominent Figure on the Campus," now settling into late middle age. "SOS," the only poem Fearing ever published in praise of the beauty of a woman, wittily modernizes Petrarchan hyperbole, upping the stakes of flattery by substituting for the old conceit of the mistress's power to command the lover that of her power to command the imagination of an entire culture, including its engines of publicity. In "Debris," the traditional meditation on a landscape becomes a meditation on an urban apartment the morning after a drunk, and in "How Do I Feel?" the traditional poetic dialogue becomes a comic study in misunderstanding made totally new and totally convincing by Fearing's flawless control of the vernacular.

Many of the poems also return to themes Fearing had subordinated to politics throughout the early thirties. "Q&A" might be said to speak for the emphasis of the whole book when it declares that answers to certain kinds of questions, some of them the most immediately personal and important,

> Will not be found in Matthew, Mark, Luke, or John,
> Nor Blackstone, nor Gray's, nor Dun & Bradstreet, nor Freud,
>   nor Marx,
> Nor the sage of the evening news, nor the corner astrologist,
>   nor in any poet. . . .

To three such questions Fearing returns repeatedly: Is nothing permanent? Is nothing certain? Is nothing meaningful? Sometimes ("Memo," "Requiem") the questions are asked plaintively and negative answers gently implied; sometimes ("A Dollar's Worth of Blood Please," "Longshot Blues," "A Pattern," "Bulletin," "Tomorrow," "Radio Blues") the questions are asked sardonically and negative answers implied or answered in tones of grim satisfaction, as if with contempt for the folly of those who would think otherwise. Other poems ("Happy New Year," "American Rhapsody (3)," "Flophouse," "Take a Letter," "If Money") treat—some with pity, some with scorn—the futility of people's attempts to cope, whatever the means: denial, foolish optimism, hopeless determination, hope.

The twenty poems that Fearing published between 1938 and 1940 were collected under the title "The Agency" in *Collected Poems*. He wrote for the dust jacket of this volume, later authorizing its use on the dust jacket of *New and Selected Poems* as well, a statement that concludes as follows: "I think that poetry must be understandable. Everything in this volume has been written with the intention that its meaning should disclose itself at ordinary reading tempo." Unless he is anticipating C. K. Stead's argument that the High Modernist poem should not have its discontinuities disguised by the laboriously concocted transitions of critics (and should thus presumably be read at normal speed), Fearing is misrepresenting much of his earlier work. His friends, at least, knew he was often obscure. Reviewing *Poems*, Philip Rahv declared that "the transition from detail to detail, from image to image, is one of free association, at times fluid to the point of loss of recognition," and Edward Dahlberg originally wrote in his introduction to the same volume, "Kenneth Fearing's poems are often difficult"; revised this to read, "Kenneth Fearing's poems may at first glance seem difficult"; and then, evidently in despair of reconciling this with his claim that Fearing was "a poet for workers," gave up and omitted the idea of difficulty altogether. Actually, Fearing's statement was a bit of revisionist history, apparently an attempt to make his past practice seem, perhaps even to himself, consonant with the more accessible kind of poem he was now beginning to write. Why he should have wanted to change, however, is a mystery. He may have been reacting against the New Criticism (not yet known by that name) and to the recondite allusions in the kind of poetry that best lent itself to that criticism's methods. In spite of their other difficulties, Fearing's poems had never required more literary and historical knowledge than a high school graduate of his generation might have been expected to command, and his hostility to the New Criticism and to learned obscurity in both poetry and criticism would later be evident in his 1949 parody "A Note on a Note in Poetry." Whatever his motives in 1940, however, the fact remains that from now on he attempted only rarely and hesitantly the kind of discontinuity, fragmentation, and collage-like organization characteristic of so many of the earlier works. The pattern is thus the reverse of what the myth of "proletarian" literature would predict. The use of Modernist techniques in Fearing's poetry waned with the waning of his commitment to the political left and, except for its brief efflorescence in a single poem of the "Family Album" series of 1956, never returned in its most radical form.

One indication of his new commitment to more accessible modes is increasing straightforwardness in the ordering of the poem. The new Fearing is either cautiously imitative of earlier experiments—as in "Public Life," which has some of the discontinuity of "Green Light" without the latter's sentence fragments—or conventionally coherent. For example, though the idea of "Reception Good"—the interference of one radio signal with another—seems to beg for the kind of collage used in "Jack Knuckles Falters," the mingling of messages in the later poem is described rather than enacted. There is also an increase in the number of dramatic monologues, from two in the thirties, to sixteen in the forties. But this is not to say that the dramatic monologues are rigidly traditional. "Engagements for Tomorrow," for example, has to be called a dramatic monologue only because there is no other name for what it is—a series of memoranda jotted to himself by a not quite honest and not very bright businessman. That this melange of cliché and inarticulate vagueness ("and so forth," "stuff, stuff," "and so on, and so on, and so on, and so on") is transmuted into something funny, scathingly satirical, and heartrending is one of the wonders of Fearing's art.

Further evidence of a change in Fearing is his willingness to flirt with the supernatural. In the earlier "Radio Blues," a radio capable of bringing in messages from beyond the grave is, of course, only a metaphor, its function in the poem being in part to evoke and intensify to the level of terror the mood of despair one might feel if, alone and longing for escape, one were to run a radio dial through station after unsatisfying station. But now Fearing sometimes uses the supernatural playfully, without apparent metaphorical or allegorical significance. The literal ghosts of "Thirteen O'Clock" exist only for the droll conceit that the living might haunt the dead, and Gabriel, Satan, and the other mythical figures of "Afternoon of a Pawnbroker" exist only to make possible the troubling experience of the dreamy and bemused pawnbroker. Teasingly, ambiguously, in two other poems Fearing seems to take the supernatural seriously. "Payday in the Morgue" is largely comic until, at the end, one of the cardplaying morgue workers, in language more powerful and more formal than any other in the poem, says of apparently awakening corpses that they are "Either millions of men with feet like lizards and the heads of rats, or gods made of music bathed in blinding light." This extraordinarily vivid image and sudden elevation of tone force an abrupt reconsideration of the easy assumption that one has been reading a joke. "Readings, Forecasts, Personal Guidance," placed at the end of *Collected Poems* as if to impress the reader with its importance, is spoken by a fortune teller, an admitted fraud who nonetheless has come to "feel another hand, not mine, has drawn and turned the card to find some incredible ace. . . ." One possibility among the many a reader must consider in interpreting this poem is that the breach in the speaker's skepticism reflects a breach in the poet's own. Whether playful or seriously mystical, however, such poems are almost unthinkable in the work of the stern political moralist of the early thirties.

And the political moralist had almost stopped writing about politics. Between 1939 and 1948 he published only five political poems—"Pact," an indirect comment on the Hitler-Stalin pact; "A Tribute and a Nightmare," a satire on Martin Dies; "A la Carte" and "Five A.M.," oblique allusions to the contemporary international crisis; and "Decision," a Kafkaesque evocation of a menacing bureaucracy. Gone is anything comparable to the flood of specific names in the great political poems of the Depression—"Mr. Hoover," "Will Hays," "Al Capone," "Father Coughlin," "Aimee Semple McPherson," "Adolph Hitler," "Laval," "Pius XI," "D.A.R.," "Ku Klux Klan," "Wall Street," "Moabit," "the Tombs." This decline in specificity is evident in other ways. As an admirer unknown to Fearing told him sadly in a fan letter of 1943, *Afternoon of a Pawnbroker* contained no sense at all of wartime New York. In fact, only a month earlier, *The New Yorker* had published his "Monograph on International Peace," a witty slice of homefront life and full of wartime vocabulary and allusions. But, almost as if he had determined to sit out the war, he never reprinted the poem, and never published another like it. Except for quotations from typical but presumably fictional radio war-news in "Reception Good" and a sardonic untitled poem on war bonds (here titled "Somebody's War Bonds") printed only on the dust cover of *Afternoon of a Pawnbroker*, World War II has no place in Fearing's verse. The Holocaust is never mentioned, and nuclear weapons appear only in "Family Album (3)" of 1956.

But if Fearing's poetry is now less experimental, less political, less topical than in the past, it is not less accomplished. The wonderful comic sense is still there in "Art Review," in "Beware," in "The Joys of Being a Businessman," in "Sherlock Spends a Day in the Country," in "Irene Has a Mind of Her Own." And the gift for evoking despair is still exceeded only by Eliot's. I am thinking here not of the poems explicitly about death, such as

"Finale [1]" and "Elegy," admirable as they are, but of poems in which the images suggest, with a power out of all proportion to their constituent parts, a heartbreaking desolation—the "familiar rooftops wrapped first in summer sunlight and then in falling snow" in "Piano Tuner"; "the bartender, and the elk's head, and the picture of some forgotten champion" in the Hopperesque "4 A.M."; the "rainy corner where the busline does not run at all" in "Certified Life." Reviewing *Stranger at Coney Island*, Selden Rodman asked with some exasperation if Fearing was "never simply happy to be alive, or in love, or just enjoying something." The same question might be asked with equal justice of Eliot. As for "enjoying something," in the satirical poems, including those in the somber *Stranger at Coney Island*, fascination and even delight with the victims are never far below the surface of the mockery and the ridicule. And to dwell on evanescence is to insist on the value of what is lost.

It is fitting that after sixteen years of near-total political silence, Fearing should have re-emerged in "Family Album" as the scourge of McCarthyism. Each of the first three poems in the series continues, effectively, the relatively conventional discursive mode of the later verse and, what is rare in Fearing's satirical poems, maintains the same ironic perspective throughout. "Family Album (1)," spoken as if by a future historian, and "Family Album (2)," spoken as if by somebody browsing through an album of ancient photographs, use the satirical device of undeserved praise to ridicule "the investigators" of the fifties, ironic sparks flying every which way in the scrape and rasp of conflicting connotations: "the diaries they commissioned"; "the first crude registry of licensed Truth"; "Armed and equipped to perfection with the weapon she gave the sorcery of her special art, / The recorder snuggled in its holster. . . ." "Family Album (3)" is spoken as if by a future popularizer of archaeological scholarship who summarizes two theories about the origins of a boat uncovered in a desert. Only in the last line is it revealed that the desert is in Idaho and that the boat is part of a nuclear weapons test. And only then does the mistaken theory of the earlier strophes, that the boat is a pagan "funeral vessel," reveal its own delicious irony.

"Family Album (4)" returns to the discontinuities of Fearing's earlier work in the Modernist mode, but it is not a successful poem. Most effective are the jumbled questions that grow increasingly incantatory as they repeatedly interrupt the collective voice of the primary speakers, presumably "investigators" of a time contemporaneous with, or later than, that of the archaeological discovery in "Family Album (3)." But the details of the laboratory they stumble on are (unlike those of the bizarre appliance in "Suburban Sunset, Pre-War, or What Are We Missing?") surrealistic without being either interesting or evocative. Presumably the "investigators" are about to blow themselves up: "Open the valve, who's got a match?—" However, this no doubt satisfying denouement seems less significant than the implied prophecy—happily, it now seems, mistaken—that the cycle of investigation and destruction will persist into an unimaginably distant future. One could wish that the "Family Album" series, and Fearing's poetic career, had ended one poem earlier. But, as he never tired of telling us, it is always unwise to expect a happy ending.

Let us hope, therefore, that this edition of all of his poems is not an end but a beginning. Let us hope that it will stimulate a reconsideration of the map of American poetry, from which—on the road that leads from Mt. Whitman across Sandburg Ridge through the *terra incognita* of the Depression to the Foothills of the Beats—a certain strange but fascinating geological formation has for too long been omitted. Let us hope that it will stimulate a reconsideration of the ranking of the poems in the Fearing canon, without regard for the opinions of anthologists, of the editor of this book, or even of the poet himself, who by his selections may have undervalued some of his own best work. Let us hope that it will stimulate the application to Fearing of Eliot's test for recognizing a major poet, one whose individual works give the greater pleasure as knowledge of the total oeuvre increases. Whether he will pass this test, as I think he should, and all the other tests that canon-makers will devise, may not be known for generations. Meanwhile, as Hayden Carruth has observed (and Carruth, to his credit, called for a revival of Fearing as early as 1963), there can be no shame attached to survival as a minor poet. "What else is there—" he rightly asks, "except oblivion on one hand and the fluke of greatness on the other?"

Notes to the Introduction

The following abbreviations and short titles are used in the notes:

Annotations   Autograph annotations by Carl Rakosi of various pages photocopied from Margery Latimer's novel *This Is My Body*. The original annotations are in the collection of the editor; photocopies of the annotations are in the Carl Rakosi Collection, Memorial Library, University of Wisconsin-Madison.

BF   Bruce Fearing, Kenneth Fearing's son.

BMW   The Blanche Matthias Collection of the Letters of Margery Latimer, Memorial Library, University of Wisconsin-Madison.

KF   Kenneth Fearing.

KFW   Kenneth Fearing Collection, Memorial Library, University of Wisconsin-Madison. Except for those to Rachel Landon, letters by Fearing in this collection are carbon copies.

NL   Nan Lurie, Kenneth Fearing's second wife.

RL   Rachel Meltzer Fearing, now Landon, Kenneth Fearing's first wife.

RHC   Random House Collection, Rare Book and Manuscript Library, Columbia University.

RMR   Robert M. Ryley.

RNL   Forty-three numbered reminiscences of Kenneth Fearing by Nan Lurie, in the collection of the editor.

Texas   Harry Ransom Humanities Research Center, University of Texas at Austin.

Yale   James Weldon Johnson Collection, The Beinecke Rare Book and Manuscript Library, Yale University.

Unless otherwise identified, all communications are personal letters. Source material is cited by means of selected catch phrases in the order of their occurrence on a particular page.

ix   wittiest boy, class pessimist: Oak Park-River Forest High School *Senior Tabula* 26 (9 Jun 1920): 55. The school newspaper once identified KF as a "noted cynic" ("Curiosity Killed the Reporter," *Trapeze* 21 May 1920: 3).

ix   Latimer, Rakosi: Margery Latimer, *This Is My Body* (New York: Smith and Cape, 1930), 207; Annotations, 207.

ix paternal ancestry: Twila Shoemaker Fearing, "The Fearing Family in America," mimeographed paper, 1967, rev. ed. 1981, excerpt provided by Jeri James, ltr. to RMR 8 Aug 1984; Jeri James, *The Fearing Tree*, newsletter of the Fearing Family Organization, no. 18 (Jul 1984): 2-3. Harry Fearing was born in Davenport, Iowa, in 1868; graduated from the University of Iowa around 1889; taught for a few years in Iowa grammar schools; graduated from Chicago Kent Law School around 1895 and was admitted to the bar and began to practice in that year (Elizabeth Dipple Delay, et al., "The Family Ancestors of Donald Stewart Dipple I," mimeographed paper, 1981, 9-10; Ralph Fearing to RMR, 16 Dec 1985).

x illustrious Jewish family: James Thomas Flexner, *An American Saga: The Story of Helen Thomas and Simon Flexner* (Boston: Little, 1984), 4-6. Olive Flexner was born in St. Louis, Missouri, on 7 Feb 1880, the daughter of Estelle Bondy and Leopold Flexner (birth certificate of Olive Estelle Fearing, collection of RMR). Leopold was the youngest brother of Moritz (or Maurice) Flexner, father of Abraham and Simon (James Thomas Flexner to RMR, 4 Mar 1984). By the early 1890s, Leopold had moved the family to Davenport, Iowa (*Stone's Davenport, Iowa, City Directory*, 1892-93), where Olive met Harry Fearing, probably around 1898 (KF, "My Ancestors," KFW). Altogether she married four times (not seven as has been inaccurately reported), but Kenneth was her only child (RL, personal interview, 16 Apr 1984).

x quickly tracked them down: Patricia B. Santora, "The Life of Kenneth Flexner Fearing (1902-1961)," *College Language Association Journal* 32 (1989): 310. This article is often inaccurate, especially in its account of KF's paternal ancestry and in its dating of certain events in his life.

x eccentric aunt: RL, personal interview, 16 Apr 1984.

x Harry remarried: Ralph Fearing to RMR, 2 Apr 1984.

x loved his father, tolerated his mother: RL, personal interview, 6 Jun 1983; NL to RMR, 23 Jul 1984.

x monthly allowance: RL, personal interview, 16 Apr 1984.

x "I hope your book": Olive Flexner Power to KF, 30 Jan 1937, KFW.

xi woman who cared for her: Janet Power Bonaparte to RMR, 9 Aug 1984.

xi Ollie claimed, uproar: RL, personal interview, 6 Jun 1983.

xi "What are Jews": BF to RMR, 8 Dec 1982.

xi   conversing amiably: Carl Rakosi, *The Collected Prose of Carl Rakosi* (Orono, ME: National Poetry Foundation, 1983), 91-92.

xi   no discrimination: Neither Edith Heal Barrien, who used to go dancing with KF in high school, nor Amy River McCauley, the sister of his closest Oak Park friend, was aware that KF was half Jewish until so informed by RMR (Edith Heal Barrien, personal interview, 26 Jun 1986; Amy River McCauley to RMR, 16 Jul 1986).

xi   wife once remarked: RL in conversation, date unrecorded.

xi   at graduation, editor and weekly column: Frederick Ebersold, "Who's Who in O.P.H.S.," *Trapeze* 19 Mar 1920: 4. Fearing occasionally wrote his column, "What's What in O.P.H.S.," using the pseudonym Oso Verdant.

xi   class prophecy: *Senior Tabula* 26 (9 Jun 1920): 47-53.

xi   his grades: U. of Illinois transcript of Kenneth Flexner Fearing.

xi   story of his: "A Tale of Long Ago," *Illinois Magazine* Oct 1921 (Santora 311).

xii   forced to resign: the financial and other troubles of the *Lit* and its editor can be followed in the *Wisconsin Daily Cardinal* throughout the first three months of 1924.

xii   Committee "could not see": "Weimer Elected Editor of *Lit* to Replace Fearing," *Wisconsin Daily Cardinal* 21 Mar 1924: 1.

xii   "condition" in a mathematics course: R. L. Johnson, Supervisor, Degree Summaries and Verification, U. of Wisconsin-Madison, to RMR, 10 Dec 1986.

xii   letter to a friend: Latimer to Meridel LeSueur, [summer 1930], Yale.

xii   at its best: Latimer to Blanche Matthias, [winter 1925], BMW.

xii   she left New York: For a somewhat different version of the breakup, see Nancy Loughridge, "Afterword: The Life," *Guardian Angel and Other Stories* by Margery Latimer (Old Westbury, NY: Feminist, 1984), 222. My version is based on two letters from Latimer to Blanche Matthias, [both summer 1928], BMW; her letter to Perry Goldman, 31 Jan 1930, Yale; and her letter to Carl Rakosi, [Mar 1931], Texas.

xiii   blame herself: Latimer to Perry Goldman, 6 Apr 1930, Yale.

xiii   his work history: For KF's own accounts of his work history, see "About Contributors," *The Reviewer* 5 (1925):56; the blurb on the dust jacket of *Poems*; KF to Amy Bonner, undated letter [1942], Texas; KF to Dr. Joseph Gennis of William Douglas McAdams,

Inc., letter with résumé, 11 Feb 1957, KFW. In the résumé, Fearing says that he was employed as a reporter by the *Chicago-Herald Examiner*, the *City News Service*, and the *Pioneer Press*, but according to Carl Rakosi, KF worked only "as a police reporter in Chicago, on a night shift. He stood it for 2 weeks and then gave the job to me. . . . Neither of us had had a day's experience on a paper. He had lied about our experience. . ." (Annotations, pp. 299-300). KF had, however, been the high school correspondent for *Oak Leaves*, his home town newspaper ("Poet Fearing Is Author of Novel," *Oak Leaves* 7 Sep 1939: 6). On his job at a department store (the Fair Store), see KF to Carl Rakosi, [Nov 1924], Texas. In the late thirties, Fearing taught poetry writing for the League of American Writers (*Writers Teach Writing* [New York: League of American Writers, n.d.], 5); for a week in the summer of 1948, he taught fiction writing at Indiana University (*1948 Writers' Conference Program* [Bloomington: Indiana U, 1948]).

xiii he told his son: BF to RMR, 30 Jan 1982.

xiii recalls the plot: Ralph Fearing to RMR, 30 May 1983.

xiv Writing in 1932: KF to RL, 31 Mar 1932, KFW.

xiv received a request: Latimer to Carl Rakosi, [Mar 1926], Texas.

xiv Rorty responded: Latimer to Carl Rakosi, [summer 1926], Texas.

xiv Edmund Wilson wrote: Latimer to Carl Rakosi, [early fall 1926?], Yale. The conjectural Yale date, summer 1926, seems erroneous, since KF's first contribution to the *New Masses* didn't appear until September.

xv collection has been credited: Allen Guttmann, "The Brief Embattled Course of Proletarian Poetry," *Proletarian Writers of the Thirties*, ed. David Madden (Carbondale, IL: Southern Illinois UP, 1968), 252.

xv "Woolworth shopgirls": Edward Dahlberg, Introduction, *Poems* by Kenneth Fearing (New York: Dynamo, 1935), 11.

xv "brutal frankness": Nicholas Moskowitz, "Four Poets," *New Masses* Sep 1929: 19.

xv "nothing pleasant": F. M., "Some Songs of the Hour," *Boston Evening Transcript*, 1 Jun 1929, Book Section: 4.

xv *Jacqueline*: In a letter to RL (9 Feb 1932, KFW), KF mentions that this novel took him two years to write. On the model for the title character: RL, personal interview, 9 Jul 1984.

xv *Robert Ward*: This title is announced in KF to RL, 21 Mar 1932, KFW. Harry Ross is identified as the model for the title character in KF to RL, 9 Mar 1932, KFW, and in other letters in this series.

xv incomplete manuscript: KFW.

xv plot summary: Elaine Gilbert, 4 Sep 1942, Editorial Correspondence, RHC.

xvi Tom Dimitry: RL, personal interview, 9 Jul 1984.

xvi "death knell": RL, personal interview, 10 Jun 1987.

xvi "wrote himself in": BF to RMR, 24 Jan 1983.

xvi Rakosi: *The Collected Prose of Carl Rakosi* (Orono, ME: National Poetry Foundation, 1983), 91.

xvi jailed: RL, personal interview, 6 Jun 1983.

xvi Jason Wheeler: Albert Halper, *Union Square* (New York: Literary Guild, 1933), 10-15, 24-31, 55-57, 65-66, 111-114, 167-172, 202-206, 252-253, 258-265, 272-279, 280-296, 302-304, 339-342, 367-369, 375-376.

xvi small fires: Peggy Ross, personal interview, 6 Oct 1983.

xvi blind date: RL to RMR, 22 Dec 1982.

xvi filthiest man: RL, personal interview, 10 Jun 1987.

xvi "needed someone": RL, personal interview, 16 Apr 1984.

xvii series of letters: 2 Jan-13 Apr 1932, KFW.

xvii arguments in favor of marriage: 4 Feb, 2 Mar 1932, KFW.

xvii wasn't angry: 6 Jan 1932, KFW.

xvii his aloofness: 23 Feb 1932, KFW.

xvii couldn't Communicate: RL, personal interview, 16 Apr 1984.

xvii out of the blue: 7 Sep 1937, KFW.

xvii as a gentile: RL, personal interviews, 16 Apr 1984, 24 Jul 1985.

xvii stopped his allowance: RL, personal interview, 16 Apr 1984.

xvii "ask your husband": RL, personal interview, 6 Jun 1987.

xviii would fall asleep: RL, personal interview, 24 Jul 1985.

xviii made money: Robert Cantwell, "A New York Letter," *Pacific Weekly* 21 Jun 1935: 296.

xviii "Marxist interpretations": *Poems*, 11.

xviii two of them: Peter Monro Jack, "New Books of Poetry," *New York Times Book Review* 3 Nov 1935: 15; William Rose Benét, "The Phoenix Nest," *Saturday Review of Literature* 15 Jun 1935: 18. Benét uses a lower-case 'c'.

xviii laughing in private: RL, personal interview, 14 Aug 1989.

xviii told the FBI: "Re: KENNETH FEARING," FBI report of interview with KF on 15 Dec 1950, FBI no. NY 62-10641.

xix 'fellow traveler': In 1935 KF signed the call for the American

Writers' Congress, and in 1939 the call for the Third Congress of the League of American Writers and the open letter of 14 August that branded as fascist the charge that Germany and the Soviet Union were equally totalitarian. According to Alfred Hayes, KF's disillusionment with the Party began at the time of the Moscow trials in 1937-38 (to RMR, 2 Jan 1984); according to Alice Neel, the last straw was the Soviet invasion of Finland in November 1939 (personal interview, 11 Oct 1983). KF's last contribution to the *New Masses* had appeared a year earlier ("Ad," *New Masses* 8 Nov 1938: 10); and in the summer of 1938, when Joshua Kunitz of the *New Masses*, citing the Popular Front, had insisted that he remove a disparaging reference to Pius XI from his poem "The Program," he had replied, "No pope, no poem," and published it elsewhere (KF to RL, 7 Jul 1938, KFW; RL personal interview, 6 Jun 1983; on the publication history of "The Program," see Notes on the Poems, page 289).

xix thirty-three letters: KF to RL, passim., but see especially 6, 11, 25, 29 Jan; 15, 19 Feb; 17 Mar; 13 Apr 1932, KFW.

xix FBI list: "Communist Party Members," 28 Aug 1942, FBI document number not readable. KF's name is followed by the notation "DW, 12/24/31, p. 3." In answer to questions about the authenticity and significance of the list, Charles E. Mandigo, Supervisory Special Agent (FBI New York) replied that "due to the drastic procedural changes that have obviously taken place during the last 40 years regarding this type of material, the significance of a 1942 document is quite obscure, as well as the meaning of the 'DW, 12/24/31, p. 3' notation . . ." (to RMR, 11 Sep 1986). A check of p. 3 of the *Daily Worker* for 24 Dec 1931—conceivably the referent of "DW, 12/24/31"—reveals nothing by, about, or relevant to KF.

xix Alfred Hayes: letter to RMR, 2 Jan 1984.

xix A. B. Magill: Wald interviewed Magill on 22 Oct 1989 (Alan Wald to RMR, 17 Oct 1993).

xix testimony of his friends: RL, who was certainly in a position to know, has not only repeatedly denied that KF was a Party member but regards the very idea as absurd. She dismisses KF's remark in the Hayes anecdote as "a ploy" (to RMR 20 Feb 1984). Carl Rakosi writes, "Kenneth was not, and from what I know of him, couldn't have been, a CP member. It would have been out of character." As for the Hayes anecdote, Rakosi says, "Rachel [Landon] is exactly right. It was 'a typical example of [Fearing's] irony'" (to RMR 19 Jul 1984). Lionel Abel regarded KF as not really interested in politics, though sympathetic to Stalin and the Soviet Union (personal interview, 20 May 1987).

xix   request subpoena: Ira Koenig (KF's attorney), telephone interview, 21 Feb 1984. In a panic, KF had appeared near midnight at the door of Koenig's apartment. Koenig pointed out that KF was not obliged to answer a request subpoena but advised him to do so because he might otherwise be served with a subpoena requiring his testimony before a grand jury. KF told Koenig that he had never joined the Party.

xx   Fearing replied: NL accompanied KF to Washington and waited outside in an anteroom while he testified. Immediately afterwards, KF told NL that he had said "Not yet," and "in a loud voice" (RNL #1).

xx   London: At the end of Dec 1936, the Fearings sailed for Europe on the *Normandie* with the first contingent of American volunteers on their way to fight in the Spanish Civil War. In England, they lived at 8 Russell Gardens, Golders Green, NW11. KF, who liked to relax by taking long walks, said that walking in London was like "finding your way around a plate of spaghetti" (RL, personal interview, 6 Jun 1983).

xx   contract offer: Bennet Cerf to KF, 11 Oct 1937 and 11 Jul 1938, RHC.

xx   Yaddo: KF to RL, 7 Jul 1938, KFW.

xx   to his amusement: RL quoted, Santora 312. RL assumes that owing to KF's new eminence, Wisconsin made him a gift of a passing grade. However, BF believed (to RMR 9 Oct 1986) that his father had completed the course during the summer of 1924, and Margery Latimer, writing home from New York the following November, told her mother that he had "got his degree" (to Laurie B. Latimer, 7 Nov 1924, Yale). The registrar's records show only that he "was given permission to take a special examination in Mathematics on or after Jun 28, 1924" and that "this work was not completed until December 14, 1938" (R. L. Johnson to RMR, 10 Dec 1986). If BF and Latimer are correct, the 1938 Wisconsin registrar was quietly correcting a fourteen-year oversight.

xx   failed to pay: Emanuel E. Harper, memo to KF [Aug 1942], RHC. In 1943, KF still owed $430.50 on the advance for *Clark Gifford's*

Body, and as late as 1946, $26.13 on the advance for *Dead Reckoning* (Random House royalty statements, KFW).

xxi letter from Yaddo: KF to RL, 25 Aug 1938, KFW.

xxi fearful: RL, personal interview, 6 Jun 1983.

xxi job with *Time*: KF to Joseph Gennis, 11 Feb 1957, KFW.

xxi "Well," he said: RL, personal interview, 10 Jun 1987.

xxi bitterness: Alice Neel, personal interview, 11 Oct 1983.

xxi She had grown up: NL, telephone interview, 19 Jul 1984.

xxi She and Fearing met: RNL #15.

xxi On Christmas day: RNL #38.

xxi writing notes and letters: There are eight extant letters postmarked between 4 Mar 1943 and 10 Oct 1944, one of them (29 Jul 1943) evidently written after a quarrel and cool to the point of hostility (collection of RMR).

xxi "I am not good enough": KF to NL, 29 Aug 1943, collection of RMR.

xxi "sheer lunacy," "confessions": KF to NL, 10 Oct 1944, collection of RMR.

xxi "vitamins," "cats," "religious quarter hour": KF to NL, 4 Jan 1944, collection of RMR.

xxii a new novel: KF to NL, 4 Mar 1943, collection of RMR.

xxii murder: Fearing acknowledges his adaptation of the Lonergan case in a letter to Henry Volkening, 20 Nov 1946, KFW. Mrs. Lonergan had been found bludgeoned and strangled in the bedroom of her apartment in the east fifties. The initial suspect, her escort the night before the murder, was cleared when a cab driver corroborated his alibi—to wit, that he had taken Mrs. Lonergan home in a taxi and left her alive in the vestibule of her apartment. Ultimately tried and convicted was the victim's estranged husband, but no one could place him in the vicinity of the Lonergan apartment at the time of the murder. See Hamilton Darby Perry, *A Chair for Wayne Lonergan* (New York: Macmillan, 1972), esp. 31, 44, 63, 86, 89, 171, 231, 277, 281. The Lonergan case also accounts for the novel's seemingly gratuitous references to homosexuality, "a principal theme" of newspaper accounts of the murder, according to Walcott Gibbs, "The Wayward Press," *New Yorker* 6 Nov 1943: 89.

xxii little-known thriller: Samuel Michael Fuller, *The Dark Page* (New York: Duell, 1944). In this novel a newspaper editor murders a woman, takes charge of the investigation himself, insures that all evidence is given to him rather than to the police, and is confronted in his office by a witness who can identify him as the wanted man but does not do so. Motion Pictures Investors Corporation, owners of the screen rights to Fuller's book, threatened to sue Paramount for infringement of copyright when the latter announced its plans for filming *The Big Clock*. Fearing acknowledged having read *The Dark Page* but rightly insisted that the "plot, characters, background and philosophical implications of The Big Clock are entirely my own creation; there is no similar combination to be found elsewhere in literature" (KF to Henry Volkening, 20 Nov 1946, KFW).

xxii   between August 1944 and October 1945: Harcourt, Brace contract, 1 Aug 1944, KFW; John Woodburn to KF, 16 Oct 1945, photocopy kindly supplied by Patricia B. Santora.

xxii   he took in: I rely here on RNL #42 but have never seen confirming evidence. Since by the early fifties KF was again nearly penniless without, apparently, ever having changed his style of life, it is possible that NL's memory inflated KF's 1946 income. KF was also paid $1000 in three installments for revising the manuscript of the novel *John Barry* (1947), written by Donald Friede and H. Bedford Jones, and published under the pseudonym Donald F. Bedford (contract with Creative Age Press, Inc., 15 Dec 1945, KFW).

xxii   condensation: "The Judas Picture," *American Magazine* Oct 1946: 157-180.

xxii   Nan won: RNL #42. The painting, *Blue Table Still Life*, is reproduced in *The Art Digest* 1 Oct 1948: 9.

xxii   told his friend: Alice Neel, personal interview, 11 Oct 1983. According to Neel, KF said to her concerning his portrait of Louise Patterson, "I didn't do you justice."

xxii   almost died: RL, personal interview, 6 Jun 1983.

xxii   so shaken: NL, telephone interview, 19 Jul 1984.

xxiii   she discovered: NL, telephone interview, 19 Jul 1984.

xxiii   "Next to last": Quoted from KF's inscription by Christine Keller of Norfolk-Hall, Ltd., booksellers, St. Louis, MO, letter to RMR, nd (1983).

xxiii   note of dissatisfaction: On *Collected Poems*, see the reviews by Ruth Lechlitner, *New York Herald Tribune* Books 17 Nov 1940: 27, and by F. W. Dupee, *New Republic* 103 (1940): 597; on *Afternoon of a Pawnbroker*, see those by Oscar Williams, *Tomorrow* 3 (Mar 1944): 54, and by Delmore Schwartz, *New York Times Book Review* 7 Nov

1943: 34; on *Stranger at Coney Island*, see those by William Abrahams, *Poetry* 74 (May 1949): 118-120, and by Selden Rodman, *New York Times Book Review* 24 Oct 1948: 18.

xxiii with considerable difficulty: James Ashbrook Perkins, "An American Rhapsody: The Poetry of Kenneth Fearing," diss., U. of Tennessee, 1972, 144, 147.

xxiii rent a cottage: NL to RMR, 23 Jul 1984; RL, personal interview, 22 Mar 1992. NL mentions only one cottage, in Woodstock, New York, to which KF's mother came as a visitor. RL reported that KF rented another cottage during the same period, presumably 1947-50.

xxiii worry about money: KF to Diarmuid Russell, 8 Jan 1951, KFW.

xxiii fragments of information: KF to Ira Koenig, 2 Mar 1954, 3 Apr 1955; Harcourt, Brace royalty statement, 25 Oct 1955; Doubleday royalty statement, 31 October 1960, KFW.

xxiv write for the pulps: "Murder Wears Four Overcoats," (true crime) *American Weekly* (Hearst Sunday Supplement), 14 Jun 1953: 22-23; "The Jury," *Manhunt*, Mar 1955: 102-111; "Shake-up," *Manhunt* May 1955: 38-49; "Three Wives Too Many," *Michael Shayne Mystery Magazine* Sep 1956: 91-108; "Champagne and Bitters" (true crime), *Ed McBain's Mystery Book* No. 2 (1960): 71-81. "Three Wives Too Many" was anthologized three times within five years of its first publication.

xxiv full-time job: KF résumé, 23 Oct 1959, KFW.

xxiv people who worked with him: Jean Evans, telephone interview, 19 Jul 1984; Joseph G. O'Reilly, personal interview, 12 Feb 1986.

xxiv "The human sacrifice": *The Crozart Story* (Garden City: Doubleday, 1961), 41.

xxv generalized by Fearing: Untitled observations, KFW.

xxv "Phantoms of the Investigation": 2-3, KFW.

xxvi almost sacrificed his contract: Perkins, 146.

xxvi deny to *Mainstream*: Perkins, 101.

xxvi invited to a meeting: Lionel Abel, personal interview, 20 May 1987.

xxvi separation: RNL #43.

xxvi wrote a friend: KF to Marlys Fixx, 30 Dec 1952, collection of RMR.

xxvi saw each other: RNL #41.

xxvi consulted his lawyer: Ira Koenig to KF, 29 Jan 1953; KF to NL, 22 Nov, 8 Dec 1953, KFW.

xxvi had begun drinking: BF to RMR, 2 Apr 1982.

xxvi   "coughed his strength away": Ralph Fearing to RMR, 30 May 1983.

xxvi   pain in his back: BF to RMR, 31 Jan 1984.

xxvi $150 a month: Olive Power to KF, 2 Jun 1961, KFW.

xxvi   Bruce recalled: BF to RMR, 10 Jan 1982.

xxvii   malignant melanoma: Santora, 321.

xxviii   *Newsweek* reported: "Microphone Girl," review of *Loneliest Girl in the World*, 6 Aug 1951: 86-87. At this time KF was reviewing books for *Newsweek* under Robert Cantwell.

xxix   David Perkins: *A History of Modern Poetry: Modernism and After* (Cambridge, MA: Belknap-Harvard UP, 1987), 75.

xxx   more impersonal: KF's impersonality is temperamental and existed well before he came under the influence of Eliot. In all of KF's poems, only one personal pronoun clearly refers to himself: the startling "mine" in the third line of "Manhattan." "Any Man's Advice to His Son" sounds autobiographical, especially the final strophe, but implies a child considerably older than five year-old Bruce.

xxx   especially Eliot: Notice that KF's disparaging allusion to Eliot in "American Rhapsody (1)" says nothing about his poetry, whose images, diction, and rhythms KF often echoes. Earlier he had written that in Eliot "rhythm assumes a meaning more exact than any word" ("Beyond Estheticism," *Menorah Journal* 15 Sep 1928: 286). F. W. Dupee complained in 1940 that KF's imitations of other poets were becoming mechanical and cited Eliot's "Difficulties of a Statesman" as typical of a poem that would "show its face again and again in [Fearing's] pages like a family ghost" ("Sinister Banalities," *New Republic* 28 Oct 1940: 597). According to Alfred Hayes (to RMR, 2 Jan 1984), KF cherished a letter from Eliot praising his poetry. Since no one else seems to have heard of this letter, I suspect that Hayes's memory betrayed him, but the error itself is probably significant of Eliot's importance to KF.

xxx   trite "unpoetic" vocabulary: For example, adjectives and adverbs often overused in conversation—"wonderful," "incredible," "marvelously," "very," "terrible," "fantastic." And perhaps no other poet has ever made more use of numbers and numerals—not only the word "million" (or "millions"), which, combining euphony with grandeur of connotation, appears about twenty times in KF's poems of the late twenties and early thirties, but more pedestrian numbers as well, of which there are at least seventy, not counting repetitions.

xxx   fracturing of normal grammar: Not only the practice of writing poems entirely or almost entirely in sentence fragments ("Green Light," "Lunch with the Sole Survivor," "Engagements for Tomorrow"), but the use of pronouns without antecedents and of such locutions as "Whether the truth was then or later" ("No Credit") and "What do you call it . . . When it's just like a fever shooting up. . ." ("Twentieth-Century Blues").

xxx   Horace Gregory: Margery Latimer had believed that KF had influenced Gregory but was told by KF that the influence went the other way (Margery Latimer to Horace Gregory, [1930?], photocopy kindly supplied by Patrick Gregory).

xxxi   C. K. Stead: *Pound, Yeats, Eliot and the Modernist Movement* (New Brunswick, NJ: Rutgers UP, 1986), 39.

xxxi   symbolic act: M. L. Rosenthal suggests that "Standish expresses the need to revolt against the formless mass-civilization in some drastic manner" ("Chief Poets of the American Depression," diss. New York U, 1949, 1: 268). The cogency of this interpretation is confirmed by another, different response to mass culture in "George Martin," originally published as a companion piece to "John Standish, Artist" but omitted from all of KF's collections.

xxxiv   spoof: "The Village is a Sham," *New Masses*, 3 May 1927: 18.

xxxiv   His sentences: The long one-sentence poem is anticipated by "John Standish, Artist," though in *Angel Arms* conservatively punctuated with semi-colons. "Invitation" is not a single sentence, though so punctuated.

xxxv   Alan Wald's argument: "Erasing the Thirties," *New Boston Review* 6 Feb 1981: 20-22; *The Revolutionary Imagination: The Poetry and Politics of John Wheelwright and Sherry Mangan* (Chapel Hill: U of North Carolina P, 1983; *The New York Intellectuals: The Rise and Decline of the Anti-Stalinist Left from the 1930s to the 1980s* (Chapel Hill: U of North Carolina P), Ch. 3.

xxxvi   Dahlberg declares: *Poems* 12.

xl   M. L. Rosenthal: II: 323-324.

xlii   C. K. Stead: *The New Poetic: Yeats to Eliot*, rev. ed. Philadelphia: U of Pennsylvania P, 1987), 148-151, 162-168.

xlii   Philip Rahv: "In the American Jungle," *Kosmos* Jul 1935: 32.

xlii   Edward Dahlberg: Printer's copy of the typescript of *Poems*, collection of RMR, p. 3 (actually 4, an unnumbered page having been inserted between 2 and 3). The phrase "a poet for workers" appears in the published version on p. 13.

xliii   his 1949 parody: "A Note on a Note in Poetry," *Tiger's Eye* 8 (Jun 1949): 10-13.

xliii   not very bright businessman: KF's œuvre is an exception to the following accurate observation by Dana Gioia: "The business world, including the huge corporate enterprises which for better and for worse have changed the structure of American life over the last fifty years, is generally absent from the enormous body of poetry written in this century" ("Business and Poetry," *Poetry After Modernism*, ed. Robert McDowell [Brownsville, OR: Story Line, 1991], p. 102). In addition to "Engagements for Tomorrow," see "Dividends," "Portrait of a Cog," "The Joys of Being a Businessman," "Yes, the Agency Can Handle That," "Five A.M.," "Bryce & Tomlins," and "Museum."

xlv   fan letter: Gloria Beckerman to KF, 13 Dec 1943, collection of RMR.

xlvi   Selden Rodman: "New Verses by Fearing," *New York Times Book Review* 24 Oct 1948: 18.

xlviii   Eliot's test: T. S. Eliot, "What Is Minor Poetry," *On Poetry and Poets* (New York: Noonday-Farrar, 1961), 44-45.

xlviii   Hayden Carruth: *Working Papers: Selected Essays and Reviews*, ed Judith Weissman (Athens, GA: U of Georgia P, 1982), 56, 189.

Bibliography of Major Works by Kenneth Fearing

Angel Arms. New York: Coward McCann, 1929.

Poems. New York: Dynamo, 1935.

Dead Reckoning. New York: Random House, 1938.

The Hospital. (novel) New York: Random House, 1939.

Collected Poems of Kenneth Fearing. New York: Random House, 1940.

Dagger of the Mind. (novel) New York: Random House, 1941.

Clark Gifford's Body. (novel) New York: Random House, 1942.

Afternoon of a Pawnbroker. New York, Harcourt Brace, 1943.

The Big Clock. (novel) New York: Harcourt Brace, 1946.

John Barry. (novel) [as "Donald F. Bedford," *pseud.*] New York: Creative Age, 1947. (Written by Donald Friede and H. Bedford Jones, revised by Kenneth Fearing.)

Stranger at Coney Island. New York: Harcourt Brace, 1948.

Loneliest Girl in the World. (novel) New York: Harcourt Brace, 1951.

The Generous Heart. (novel) New York: Harcourt Brace, 1954.

New and Selected Poems. Bloomington, IN: Indiana UP, 1956.

The Crozart Story. (novel) Garden City, NY: Doubleday, 1960.

A Note on the Text

In general, the poems in this edition are printed in the order of their first serial publication. Any poem whose date of composition is known, however, is placed according to that date, and any poem published only in a Fearing collection and otherwise undatable is placed more or less according to its placement in that collection. Dates of publication and, if known, of composition, are provided in the Notes on the Poems.

Except for poems not previously published, the texts are those of the last published versions. To spare the reader the distractions of an intrusive scholarly apparatus, textual variants, of which there are many having both aesthetic and political significance, are not recorded. The publication histories in the Notes on the Poems will facilitate the research of scholars who may want to study these variants on their own. A few obvious typographical errors have been silently corrected.

Nan Lurie. *Kenneth at work.* circa 1945.

Ink on paper, 8 1/2 x 11". #9 in a series of 15 sketches.
Collection of RMR. Reproduced by permission.

Complete Poems

TESTAMENT

Unto the panoramic skies,
To worship them, my dead wide eyes—

Unto some dim, leaf-strewn retreat,
The dust of my adoring feet—

Unto the earth, to seal them fast,
My all belying lips at last—

Unto mankind, to be his part,
The ashes of my wastrel heart.—

VILLANELLE OF MARVELOUS WINDS

Patient are the winds that blow
Around the crannies of the town,
And gather and spend the drifting snow.

Quaint patterns in a ceaseless show
Go up and up, and down and down:
Patient are the winds that blow.

None watch them all; none really know,
Save only the winds that muse and frown
And gather and spend the drifting snow.

Winds, do you seek in flux and flow
Some ultimate, some fitting crown?
Patient are the winds that blow!

What are you thinking as you go,
With hushed white spume to breathe renown,
And gather and spend the drifting snow?

And is there time—you are so slow—
For cloud and flame and sage and clown?
Patient are the winds that blow,
And gather and spend the drifting snow!

VIOLENCE

I

Tip-toeing softly through the sky,
The curved white dagger of a moon
Hiding in straggled clouds, goes by
To seek the perfumed couch of June.

II

Ho, Guard!
　　There's murder . . .
　　　　God; too late . . .
The moon, with stealthy slink and crouch,
A scarlet dagger dripping hate,
Glides home to its October couch.

ASHES

A cigarette burning—
The paper curls back, and disappears,
Revealing delicate, finely-wrought flakes and
        strands
Of grey ashes.

Hampton's face was like that—
Life had stripped it stark
And left intact the old lines of himself—
Grey ashes.

SCOTTWELL

Scottwell could project his soul
Into incredible grandeur
In five minutes dreaming.

Unfortunately, he could also
Watch the sublime trajectory of himself
From the ground.

That is why Scottwell shot himself—
With a superb, ironic frown,
And an apologetic giggle.

DIVAN AND MORRIS CHAIR

Like a window blind that shakes all night;
Like rain that spatters through the night;
Something in me you could not know;
Something in you I could not know,
Kept flickering behind the light,
And could not come, and would not go.

SECRET

Silent . . something white . . went "flick" . .
And waiting for the baton's click
Is tidal music. Soul, be quick . .

Heart, heart, be red tonight!
Down there . . passed a something white
Suddenly against the light.

Something in the deepest black
Came stealing to a soft attack . .
Felt at the door . . and then turned back.

Who goes there? . . Soul! brain-bolt the gate
And after him like sullen fate . .
I think it was . . it was . . too late . .

BLAIR AND BLAIR'S FRIENDS

Poem? You call that a poem—that little line
 Etched between his eyes and down his cheeks?
 Or perhaps a chronicler that mutely speaks
The drama of a life. Oh, something fine,
Beyond a doubt. Blair himself would assign
 A mystic soul-or-something, but Blair seeks
 Oil for the engine of his life, that creaks
Damned flatly, like a half-heroic whine.

I'll try my hand. The thing's a monument
 To everything Blair didn't know. Grotesque
 As love, as quaint as hope that men will scrawl
On the odd wan face of Grief—from reverent
 Waiting for nothing to happen, at a desk,
 With ignorance clamped down upon it all.

MAN DEAD

Next door there's happened something strange.
    It's death has happened,
And crêpe. (I wonder if he's marveling
    At the change.)

His eyelids, they are cold and tight;
    But underneath,
The pupils of his eyes are up,
    His eyes are white.

For men come dead when stomachs break—
    (His did, it seems)—
Their nerves and tendons cease to jerk,
    Their hearts to shake.

However, sits a dry-eyed sobbing
    Beside the muteness.
She grieves for him all night, with neurons
    Mightily throbbing.

BAL MASQUE

Cold street beneath the winter moon;
    Three leaves, a pop-corn bag, two straws
Whirl an ecstatic rigadoon
    To a fiddle wind that whines and saws.

They dance, with nods and pirouettes,
    Now in the gutter, now in the street,
Battered Pierrots, antique Pierrettes—
    From what far corners crept to meet?

Each by each these ancient elves,
    Gay tatters of a weary day,
Cackle and nod among themselves—
    My God, it's cold to make such play!

Cold street, cold wind, the moon's cold light—
    Six nondescripts hold revelry—
Come on, dance up! What's doing tonight?
    Ho, comrades, comrades, wait for me!

MORAL (OP. 1)

It does no good
To call life a bad coin
And thump it loudly on the table.

Slip it to some one quietly
With pious fingers
Covering the hole.

MORAL (OP. 2)

Read, as the dreamer reads,
Only between the lines.

Everything else is indubitably
A misprint, a devilish misprint.

SONNET TO A PROMINENT FIGURE ON THE CAMPUS

Poor old codger! you seem to realize
    There's something wrong about your being there;
Head bowed, abashed, half-slumping in the chair,
    You seem afraid to meet our fine young eyes
As though you knew the way we criticize
    Your baggy, unpressed trousers, shaggy hair
    And rough hands; you pretend that you don't care,
And stiffly try to look aloof and wise.

Diable man! Just how did you get in?
    And did you check that Springfield tongue outside,
That made all heaven snicker with its sin?
    You always were a little—odd; look here—
To be quite frank—would you have tried and tried
    For Skimmed Milk night? Would you have made Big Beer?

CANNIBAL LOVE

These small, cool kisses, love, what good are they?
I famished for your flesh not always thus!
Remember you, my sweet, that Afric day
My naked tribe stole forth, adventurous,
And when we'd laid your village waste, by fire,
I found you, weeping, with averted head,
And took you home with me, for my desire,
And bit your ebon breasts until they bled;
Then with my thirsting teeth, in one mad flood
Of love, I gored your body, foot to crown,
And tenderly I drank your coy, hot blood,
And in a final rapture, ate you down?

Oh now in kisses you seem hardly real,
My little cannibal cookie, my leg of veal . . .

BUTTERFLY ARRAS

A butterfly whose wings
    Are sparks of the white foam,
Is a vessel that brings
    Poetry to Rome.

While sails of the pure gold
    In a winking dance,
Will have casks in the hold,
    Bearing wines to France.

It would take nine years to log
    The scarlet boats that go
Away with wisps of fog,
    Returning a flake of snow.

But there are stranger ships
    Than all of these together,
Riding in the slips
    Of drowsy autumn weather.

Best not to think long
    Of those that clip the night
With hulls of utter song,
    And sails all of light.

FINALE

The furious giant who rifled him
In all the fissures of brain and breath,
Towered up at last like an ocean's brim
And smoothly pitched him into death.

A maze of gears that fitted like notes,
Damp archives where kindled eyes would crawl,
Moons, and firmaments of motes,
Stopped, like a bullet on a wall.

HELL

Somewhere beyond the wall of blue
In a tavern quieter than air,
Danton, Marat, Robespierre
Sit like statues in a dream
Listening to the Emperor
Grow devious on Waterloo.
Napoleon, his eyeballs gleam!

Outside, the devil makes red tea,
But here, frost sparkles on the mould,
And icicles are turning cold.
Marat is bathed, white as cream,
His colleagues swallow labouredly;
They listen, and speak no word, these three,
But God their popping eyeballs gleam!

TO A DYING MAN

Flourish your cigarette,
    Guzzle your beer;
Human, you will appear
    Royal yet.

God, you are a crowned thing,
    Filled with holy death,
Sharing your least breath
    With a king.

Tell us in what calm guise
    He came, and where he is,
And tell us of his
    Honey'd eyes.

Clown that was all alone,
    You are all royal now,
With your soft, living brow
    Pressed on stone.

CARMICHAEL

"You are sure you love me?
Why do you love me?"
These were the words of Carmichael,
As slim and beautiful as Carmichael,
The tawny pennon of manhood
Snapping and curling in a gale.

"But your eyes are strange.
Hoofbeats on the nightroad past my bedchamber
        are not so strange.
I love you."
And Thyra was the youngest of the court dancers.

Then he would show her of love
As keen as it was in him.
And from the palace's highest battlement
Carmichael listened to the falling scream.

Few women find them the lover Carmichael,
Carmichael the sheer.

MEDUSA

A man is a maze of ants in dark endeavor.
  What did the ants do with Medusa's head?
  They stood on her brow, sweating beads of lead,
And pried up her nose, with their need for a lever.
The way an ant is valorous and clever
  Is in his deep bowels; they never get fed.
  And a maze of ants in the dark fields of dread
Are eating their Medusas down forever.

There may be one exception to that rule.
In vines of crooked lightning a hushed fool
  May see lost roads that skirt his memory.
  He hears old portals vibrate windily,
And listens back to them, locked as a vow.
This is the time he hears them shut . . now, now.

OLD STORY

The drummer lad who marched away,
His uniform was bright with braid.
They may have wondered what he meant,
Or he himself wished he could say.
Doubtless he took his drum and played,
But what does it matter where he went,
And who cares whether he was gay,
Or whether he came back, or stayed?
His uniform was bright with braid,
His uniform was bright with braid.

JACK KNUCKLES FALTERS
(But Reads Own Statement at His Execution While Wardens Watch)

HAS LITTLE TO SAY
Gentlemen, I
Feel there is little I
Care to say at this moment, but the reporters have urged that I
Express a few appropriate remarks.

THANKS WARDEN FOR KINDNESS
I am grateful to Warden E.J. Springer for the many
        kindnesses he has shown me in the last six months,
And I also wish to thank my friends who stuck by me to the last.
As one who entered his nation's defense

STAGGERS WHEN HE SEES ELECTRIC CHAIR
Five days after war was declared, I was hoping for a pardon
        from the governor,
But evidently the government has forgotten its veterans in
        their moment of need.
What brought me to the chair

WILL RUMANIAN PRINCE WED AGAIN?
Was keeping bad companions against the advice of my
        mother and companions.
How I

WISHES HE COULD HAVE ANOTHER CHANCE
Wish I could live my life over again. If I
Could only be given another chance I would show the world
        how to be a man, but I
"I AM AN INNOCENT MAN," DECLARES KNUCKLES
Declare before God gentlemen that I am an innocent man,

22

As innocent as any of you now standing before me, and the
    final sworn word I

POSITIVE IDENTIFICATION CLINCHED KNUCKLES
    VERDICT
Publish to the world is that I was framed. I
Never saw the dead man in all my life, did not know about
    the killing until

BODY PLUNGES AS CURRENT KILLS
My arrest, and I
Swear to you with my last breath that I
Was not on the corner of Lexington and Fifty-ninth Streets at
    eight o'clock.

SEE U.S. INVOLVED IN FISHERY DISPUTE
EARTHQUAKE REPORTED IN PERU

APHRODITE METROPOLIS

I

When the stars speak out above
The city in a tree of sparks
The exiled casuals of love
Come out with the wild shrinking of
Marvelously wounded larks
That never can be still enough.

Hydras from the matchless thigh
Of the smiling Aphrodite,
Walk at the foot of the straight sky,
Fabulous with misery,
Searching love in steppes of night,
Or among their Lorelei.

APHRODITE METROPOLIS

II

"Myrtle loves Harry"—It is sometimes hard to remember a
    thing like that,
Hard to think about it, and no one knows what to do with it
    when he has it,
So write it out on a billboard that stands under the yellow
    light of an "L" platform among popcorn wrappers and
    crushed cigars,
A poster that says "Mama I Love Crispy Wafers So."
Leave it on a placard where somebody else gave the blonde
    lady a pencil moustache, and another perplexed citizen
    deposited:
"Jesus Saves. Jesus Saves."
One can lay this bundle down there with the others,
And never lose it, or forget it, or want it.
"Myrtle loves Harry."
They live somewhere.

APHRODITE METROPOLIS

III

Harry loves Myrtle—He has strong arms, from the
     warehouse,
And on Sunday when they take the bus to emerald meadows
     he doesn't say:
"What will your chastity amount to when your flesh withers
     in a little while?"
No,
On Sunday, when they picnic in emerald meadows they look
     at the Sunday paper:
GIRL SLAYS BANKER-BETRAYER
They spread it around on the grass
BATH-TUB STIRS JERSEY ROW
And then they sit down on it, nice.
Harry doesn't say "Ziggin's Ointment for withered flesh,
Cures thousands of men and women of moles, warts, red
     veins, flabby throat, scalp and hair diseases,
Not expensive, and fully guaranteed."
No,
Harry says nothing at all,
He smiles,
And they kiss in the emerald meadows on the Sunday paper.

APHRODITE METROPOLIS

IV

Broadway was a rash of fire,
the bay as dark and quiet as the bell buoys
laughing among themselves at the pit of it
the night Harry got it from Myrtle
in a room.
Harry was nobody's fool.

THE NIGHT OF A JEW

Illimitable grief, at night,
Screams in the desert of the sky.
Within the skulls of stars, bleached white,
Jehovah's hungry spiders creep
And clamorously lust, and die . . .
The Lord Jehovah cannot weep,
Yet how his hand goes out and closes
About the crumbled flesh of Moses!

We also are Jehovah's blest—
White spiders in his web of grief.
But we are shrewd; we feign unrest
From the deep twilight till the morrow
While blind Jehovah's stark motif
Is sweet with lusting and rich sorrow . . .
High above him, and far behind,
Derisive tides of darkness wind.

BUSINESS AS USUAL

This is the poet
Who wrote the sonnet
And was paid three dollars
And sixty-five cents.

This is the artist,
The man who has drawn it
(For twenty-five bucks)
A margin of nymphs—
The nymphs in the sonnet
That earned three dollars
And sixty-five cents.

Here is the printer
Who published the page
(Clearing upon it
A hundred or so)
Of nymphs, and the sonnet
That earned three dollars
And sixty-five cents.

This is the empty
Bottle of gin
That cost three dollars
And sixty-five cents
That enabled the poet
To write the sonnet
That earned three dollars
And sixty-five cents.

BALLAD OF THE SALVATION ARMY

On Fourteenth street the bugles blow,
    Bugles blow, bugles blow.
The red, red, red, red banner floats
Where sweating angels split their throats,
Marching in burlap petticoats,
    Blow, bugles, blow.

God is a ten car Bronx express,
    Red eyes round, red eyes round.
"Oh where is my lustful lamb tonight,
His hair slicked down and his trousers tight?
I'll grind him back to my glory light!"
    Roll, subway, roll.

Heaven is a free amusement park,
    Big gold dome, big gold dome.
Movies at night: "The life she led."
Everyone sleeps in one big bed.
The stars go around inside your head.
    Home, sweet home.

On Fourteenth street the bugles blow,
    Bugles blow, bugles blow,
The torpid stones and pavements wake,
A million men and street-cars quake
In time with angel breasts that shake,
    Blow, bugles, blow !

ST. AGNES' EVE

The settings include a fly-specked Monday evening,
A cigar store with stagnant windows,
Two crooked streets;
The characters: six policemen and Louie Glatz.

Subways rumble and mutter a remote portent
As Louie Glatz holds up the cigar store and backs out with

$14.92.

Officer Dolan noticed something suspicious, it is supposed,
And ordered him to halt,
But dangerous, handsome, cross-eyed Louie the rat

Spoke with his gat
Rat-a-tat-tat
Rat-a-tat-tat
And Dolan was buried as quickly as possible.

But Louie didn't give a good God damn,
He ran like a crazy shadow on a shadowy street,
With five policemen called to that beat
Hot on his trail, going Blam! Blam! Blam!

While rat-a-tat-tat
Rat-a-tat-tat
Said Louie's gat,

So loud that Peter Wendotti rolled away from his wife,
Got out of bed to scratch his stomach and shiver on the cold floor
Listening to the stammering syllables of instant death met on
    secret floors in the big vacant galleries of night.

Then Louie sagged and fell and ran.
With seven bullets through his caved-in skull and those feeble
    brains spilling out like soup,
He crawled behind a water hydrant and stood them off for
    another half minute.

"I'm not shot," he yelled. "I'm not shot," he screamed. "It
    isn't me they've shot in the head," he laughed. "Oh,
I don't give a damn!"

And rat-a-tat-tat
Rat-a-tat-tat
Stuttered the gat
Of Louie the rat,
While the officers of the law went Blam! Blam! Blam!

Soft music, as the wind moans at curtained windows and
    shuttered doors.
The vibrant throats of steamships hoot a sad defiance at
    distance and nothing.
Space lays its arm across the flat roofs and dreary streets.
Bricks bulge and sag.

32

Louie's soul arose through his mouth in the form of a derby
        hat that danced with cigarette butts and burned
        matches and specks of dust where Louie sprawled.
Close-up of Dolan's widow. Of Louie's mother.
Picture of the fly-specked Monday evening, and fade out slow.

DEATH AND TRANSFIGURATION OF
FOURTEENTH STREET

Fourteenth street, with a bad cold in its head,
Lay in a back bedroom on Fourteenth Street,
Not counting the rheumy flies that nailed the years
Speck upon speck to the walls overhead,
Not listening, dully, to the sleet, sleet, sleet
Of noise it had somehow sired by hoofs and gears
Drumming the xylophones of its deep stones,
Not knowing that Fourteenth Street would abruptly stop
When Murray opened his radio shop.

Tenderly over the corpse of Union Square
Murray's loud-speaker blats professional woe.
The malign, anemic whoop of Fourteenth Street
Chokes sickly on the opera-tainted air,
Laocoon to the hugely brooding flow
Of stuffed serpents, too glistening, and sweet.
The toil of many flies is snow-capped, and done.
The angels weep while Murray, in the mist,
Paddles the pants of Fourteenth Street with Liszt.

JAKE

Too bad for her with the kids and all
(Certainly is) and the room's too small
For all those undertaker chairs.
(The choir had to sit on the stairs.)
Jake's played his last ace, finished the race,
Lilies for Jake and a harp to play.
We all must come to it some day. (Hey?)
Last Saturday Jake was roaring tight.
Good-bye (forever), old poker-face,
See you at Joe's next Saturday night.

REVEILLE

They tremble in the morning eye
Like people walking on a blade.
They bounce in barrels or lean from windows
And bay out at the cavalcade.

None of their faces are cooked enough,
Save their eyes, charred by a single scorch.
They shrink from the sun's adroit rapier,
And the smoking street, a shattered torch.

THE DRUNKEN FLY

Sounds at night
Are only bats that fly
Among the lofts of darkness
Through broken rooms
Where stars are chips of fallen lime,
Bleached and dry.
But sounds are nothing:
Old drowned boats
Crawl around the harbor bed
And go up the sky,
Barking, with throats
Choked by fog and dread.

Only silence lives at night,
Silence and fear,
With something warm as melody
Ringing through distant streets
I cannot go near.
Cannot, for the winds that play
Around and through and over me
As though I were a shred of straw
Blown down an alley-way.

Then there is nothing, any more
But rags and bits of glass in corners,
And the sound of dust
Softly raining on an iron door.
Then there is nothing, and no one,
The people are gone
Like an army that has rolled on
Over deep canyons choked with men.

LOUIS MENDELE

Blood in my veins that seems not mine
Rises to stain the quiet sky,
Nights that are strong as poisoned wine,
When stars drop from the stiff, black vine,
And lightning moods blaze up and die.

Pythons in deep, warm swamps, whose eyes
Are scarlet suns, would relish this
Old blood where clouded furies rise,
With violent gestures and sharp cries,
And sink back in a dark abyss.

ALAN STRACHE

The falcon is a star that broods of plunder
Or he wakes, and pivots to the spire of height.
Space gathers and spins under his cold rise,
The spread of his wing is a cry of wonder.
How should he hear the marsh gnats hiss their spite,
Or know he drops a feather as he flies
That quells their whimpers like a pillar of thunder?
The falcon, who is the javelin's edge of flight,
A vertigo unleashed by silent skies.

ANTON RUBIN—ARTIST

In me slumber the strong secrets
That play behind all men and dreams.
The royal desires and bleak regrets
Men walk among bewilderedly—
Slumber in me in broad streams,
Immaculate, and warm, and free.
Prison'd in sleep, they slip away,
Yet I will waken them, some day.

What will the people think of me?—
My forms, to mirror and transcend
The pathos and stark futility
Bred in the hollow of all bone?
Calm rivers I must knot and bend
To strange, bright shapes that are my own . . .
Horizons I shall re-create . . .
Will they applaud me? . . . Call me great?

MY MERMAID

My darling spurns the tea cup's waves,
Terrac'd on tiptoe to watch her swim.
Valiantly she dives to the dark naves
That shadows build on floors of sea.
There around the oval moon
Of a monstrous silver spoon
Wander the lonely whales of tea.
My mermaid! These lagoons are rife
With both mirage and disenchantment . . .
She goes down to find the dim
Scorpion at the heart of life,
Glowing from a coral dungeon.
But, in the cosmos of the cup,
The moon stirs round! and she darts up,
Fearfully gains the tea cup's brim,
Dances in sunlight on the rim.

TRIUMPH

One time across the hills of Rome,
Twenty-one miles of war came home.

Twenty-one miles of Triumph came
With plumes and eyes like tufts of flame.

Jewels and slaves five hours and more,
With Titus homing from the war.

Twenty-one miles the roadway rang,
A crawling, golden boomerang.

Twenty-one miles of rumbling wheels,
And the hungry march of iron heels.

Then "They have lived!" was heralded;
Now, by the crash of triumph, dead!

Titus, in his high-decked car,
The veil, the prisoner god, the scar

Swept from the hearth of earth, at last,
Emptily, like a trumpet blast.

Their lances, that were loud with war,
Muter than weed on an ocean floor.

But that serpent made of light
Can never be content with night.

Nor can the tides of silence after
Take back the sword's bright, perfect laughter.

Mars! how the heart still runs to meet
Twenty-one miles of marching feet,

And will not believe they are thrice-dead men
Who thread the standing arch again!

ANGEL ARMS

She is the little pink mouse, his far away star,
    The pure angel in his sleep,
    With skirts blowing back over stark, bright thighs,
    And knees that are ivory, or white, or pink,
Pink as the little pink mouse, his far away star,
    The pure angel in a deep dream, his lonely girl.
She is going to be Feldman's girl some day.
    No damn immoral scum will ever kiss her lips,
    No crazy black fiend will ever stain her thighs
    With a touch, or a glance,
    Or dare to think of them,
    Not even Feldman,
    Not anyone, she is so clean,
    She is so pure,
She is so strange, she is so clean,
She is a little pink mouse
    Squeaking among the rubbish and dried tobacco juice of
        black alleys,
    A blazing star among dirty electric lights in warehouse lofts,
    A Bible angel smiling up at him from a starched bed,
    Telling him to be a good, pure Feldman . . That's what he
        is . . That's what he is. .
Do they think he is a woman-faced roach,
    A walking sewer, with his girl a bottle-fly buzzing on the
        rim,
    Do they think he is a hunch-backed yellow poodle
    Screaming under the wheels of red engines that squawk
        through streets?
Some day he is going to kill all the morons,
    Be applauded by crowds,
    Praised in the churches,

Cheered by the gang,
Be smiled upon by the little pink mouse, his faraway star,
   His pure angel with her skirts torn away over blinding
      thighs,
   She is going to be Feldman's girl some day.
Hand in hand, heart joined to heart,
   A new day dawned,
   Happy and sweet and sunny and pure.
Some hot summer night
   When the city trembles like a forest after battle
   And Feldman's brain is an iron claw
   She will drop from an "L" train sliding through the sky
      like a burning snake
   And give him the wink, and he will come along . .
He will come along . .
She is the little pink mouse that whispers "Coo-coo, Feldman!"
   A touch-me-not star,
   His smiling angel with her soft angel arms
   Jerking the barbed wire caught in his bones.

BRACELET

Return to me now,
For I am a thousand arms
Spread out to you like an open fan;
A thousand gargoyles whose stone mouths
Will twist into shadowy smiles
When you return.
Walk in my night,
Far among the taut strings
Of my veins, that will tremble with sound.
And in my brain, panel'd with broad mirrors,
Be blood-red sparks by thousands
That walk and walk.

EVENING SONG

Go to sleep, McKade;
Fold up the day, it was a bright scarf;
Put it away;
Take yourself apart like a house of cards.

It is time to be a gray mouse under a tall building;
Go there; go there now.
Look at the huge nails; run behind the pipes;
Scamper in the walls;
Crawl toward the beckoning girl, her breasts are warm.
But here is a dead man. A lunatic?
Kill him with your pistol. Creep past him to the girl.

Sleep, McKade;
Throw one arm across the bed; wind your watch;
You are a gentleman, and important;
Yawn; go to sleep.

The continent, turning from the sun, is dark and quiet;
Your ticker waits for tomorrow morning,
And you are alive now;
It will be a long time before they put McKade under the sod.
Sometime, but not now.
Sometime, though. Sometime, for certain.

Take apart your brain,
Close the mouths in it that have been hungry, they are fed for
    a while,
Go to sleep, you are a gentleman, McKade, alive and sane, a
    gentleman of position.

Tip your hat to the lady;
Speak to the mayor;
You are a friend of the mayor's, are you not?
True, a friend of the mayor's.
And you met the Queen of Rumania? True.

Then go to sleep;
Be a dog sleeping in the old sun;
Be an animal dreaming in the old sun, beside a Roman road;
Be a dog lying in the meadow, watching soldiers pass;
Follow the girl who beckons to you;
Run from the man with the dagger; it can split your bones;
Be terrified of strangers, and the sea, and of great height;
Forget it, then; curl up and dream in the old sun that warms
        Manhattan.
Sleep, McKade.
Yawn. Go to sleep.

AFTERNOON OF COLONEL BRADY

He, forty-five years old,
> One time religious,
> Colonel of marines in the Argonne,
> One time in Chicago salesman of motor cars,
> Seducer of a Swiss chambermaid in Detroit, years ago.
Pouring whiskey now, drinking it,
> Warm, gay,
> Feeling simple, alone, thinking of nothing,
> Considering the night's amusement,
> Staring at slow, white clouds beyond the window,
> Thinking of the air that snapped with invisible fingers in
>> the Argonne,
Pouring whiskey, drinking it.
Heard: "Ha! Ha! You wicked man!"
> When? Detroit. Where? Detroit. A chambermaid.
> "Ha! Ha! You wicked man!" Detroit.
> Who? What wicked man?
He, forty-five, ex-Colonel of marines,
> Red-haired boy playing with a kite,
> Boy in the tall trees by the still river,
> Sun on the trees,
> Boy sailing a kite in the blue sky,
Religious one time, afraid to die,
> Young, curious, in love,
> Young man with an idea for a new kind of fountain pen,
> Young man who knocked out two men in a bar-room
>> brawl,
> Afraid to die.
He, forty-five years old,
> "Ha! Ha! You wicked man!"
> Once in Chicago, a salesman of motor cars,

Too good for that,
Snap. Commanded the battalion advance. Snap. Snap-
   snap.
Died there?
Drank whiskey now.
   Considered the night's amusement.
   Thought he would go for a short walk.
   Choose a revue to see that night.
   Looked out of the window.
   Looked at the slow, white clouds.
   Felt gay. Warm.
   Wise. Strong. Secure.
   Felt small. Strange. Forgetful.
   Restless. Thin. Confused.

CULTURAL NOTES

Professor Burke's symphony, "Colorado Vistas,"
In four movements,
I Mountains, II Canyons, III Dusk, IV Dawn,
Was played recently by the Philharmonic.
Snapshots of the localities described in music were passed
      around and the audience checked for accuracy.
All O.K.
After the performance Maurice Epstein, 29, tuberculosis,
      stoker on the *S.S. Tarboy*, rose to his feet and shouted,
"He's crazy, them artists are all crazy,
I can prove it by Max Nordau. They poison the minds of
      young girls."
Otto Svoboda, 500 Avenue A, butcher, Pole, husband,
      philosopher, argued in rebuttal,
"Shut your trap, you.
The question is, does the symphony fit in with Karl Marx?"

At the Friday evening meeting of the Browning Writing
      League, Mrs. Whittamore Ralston-Beckett,
Traveler, lecturer, novelist, critic, poet, playwright, editor,
      mother, idealist,
Fascinated her audience with a brief talk, whimsical and caustic,
Appealing to the younger generation to take a brighter,
      happier, more sunny and less morbid view of life's
      eternal fundamentals.
Mrs. Ralston-Beckett quoted Sir Henry Parke-Bennett: "O
      Beauty," she said,
"Take your fingers off my throat, take your elbow out of my eye,
Take your sorrow off my sorrow,
Take your hat, take your gloves, take your feet down off the table,
Take your beauty off my beauty, and go."

In the open discussion that followed, Maurice Epstein, 29,
        tuberculosis, stoker on the *S.S. Tarboy*, arose and
        queried the speaker,
"Is it true, as certain scientists assert, that them artists are all
        of them crazy?"
A Mr. Otto Svoboda present spoke in reply,
"Shut your trap, you. The question is, what about Karl Marx?"

THE CITY TAKES A WOMAN

"Twilights that are deathless
I walk in my garden,
Knowing that I die.
The great iron idols
Are dark and breathless,
And stand a little higher
When I walk straight by.
Flowers of cold light
Come out in their crowns,
Nodding to me, smiling,
Far across the sky—
Broad fields of poppies,
Purple, red, white,
Blazing on steel vines
Where marble birds cry
Terribly at night.
Twilights that are deathless,
With a body that dies,
I walk in my garden
Higher than the sun.
Beautiful flowers there:
I pick none."

CARICATURE OF FELICE RICARRO

"Etch me in black and white.
Describe me as a jet mark
Fixed on a straight horizon.
Pierce me with a wide arc,
One curving line, to show
Wind swept down from a cold sky,
Back into withering height.
Make it a winter scene,
The ground a vacant space,
White, for an ice plateau.
Have nothing else, no trace
Of color and no breath
Of angry, secret life.
Omit the diamond spark
Veiled in the human eye.
Nor will you hint of death.
Do not suggest the stiff dark
Compact men who lie
In ichor-bleeding cliffs,
Silent and sweet, that stretch
Beneath this vacant snow.
Caricature me so.
Scratch your personal mark
In the corner. But the sketch
I want simple, and stark."

RAIN

Dragons love the world in rain.
They crawl among the watery feet
Of its sheeted cliffs in coats of chain,
Catching glimpses of blazing scales
Through shifting pockets in the discreet
Grey rain. They love to stand and look
On Saracens locked in holy wars,
Waving crimson scimitars.
More do they love to twist their tails
And stare in through a window-pane
At a man bent over a printed book,
Drinking from a crystal flagon.
But nothing is like the dragon's joy
At seeing a portrait of a dragon
Crawling in rain, catching sight,
Through mist, of blazing scales that stain
The watery cliffs, watching the fray
Of Saracens with scimitars bleeding,
Staring, in ecstasies that pain,
Through blurred windows on a man reading,
On portraits of dragons who crawl away
Helpless with wonder in the rain.

OLD MEN

They are the raw, monotonous skies,
The faded placards and iron rails
Passed by in narrow streets of rain.
Theirs are the indistinct thin cries
Heard in a long sleep that fails
In strange confusion and numb pain.

But old men have their deep dreams
They follow on quiet afternoons
At intervals, through distant streets.
Their lives come near them in warm streams
Of tonic hope. And orange moons
Shine magically on stark defeats.

BREAKFAST WITH HILDA

Coffee for Hilda,
Hilda being gay,
(Hilda walking in sunlight forever
On streets bright as diamonds;
Hilda dancing,
Hilda dressed in a new green gown.)

Coffee for Hilda, while she makes toast.
(She is always looking at the sky
As her lover bends down to bruise her mouth
And smooth her hand.)
Now, however, in the hushed cathedral,
A multitude gathered before the draped bier of Hilda, the
       martyr, kneels in reverent prayer.
Hilda in white.
Hilda sad.
Hilda forgiving the lover who has martyr'd her,
And smoothed her hand.
Hilda always kissing him.
Hilda always dancing in an ivory palace, while poets and
       princes are shooting at each other, and stabbing
       themselves.

She is neither awake,
Nor asleep, nor dreaming, quite,
Merely singing, forever and ever and ever,
While Hilda makes toast, and Hilda makes coffee,
For Hilda, the gay.

LITHOGRAPHING

These are the live,
    Not silhouettes or dead men.
    That dull murmur is their tread on the street.
    Those brass quavers are their shouts.
Here is the wind blowing through the crowded square.
    Here is the violence and secret change.
    And these are figures of life beneath the sea.
These are the lovely women
    And the exhilarations that die.
    Here is a stone lying on the side-walk
    In the shadow of the wall.
Hey? What saith the noble poet now,
    Drawing his hand across his brow?
    Claude, is the divine afflatus upon you?
    Hey? Hey Claude?
Here are a million taxi drivers, social prophets,
    The costume for an attitude,
    A back-stage shriek,
    The heat and speed of the earth.
Here is a statue of Burns.
    There is the modern moon.
    That song is the latest dance.
Hey? Of what doth the noble poet brood
    In a tragic mood?

THE DRINKERS

Except for their clothing and the room,
Gonzetti's basement on MacDougal,
The men are a painting by Franz Hals,
Flemish Drinkers or *Burghers of Antwerp.*
We have a speakeasy here, however,
Four men drinking gin, three of them drunk.
Outside is the street that sleeps and screams,
Beyond it are other sleeping streets,
And above us, above the paper'd ceiling,
Above Gonzetti's private roof,
Is a black, tremendous sky that crawls.

We have a Village speakeasy here,
One curtained room with ochre lights,
Four men drinking gin, three of them drunk.

Four new men are born in their brains
That would not show in a painting by Hals.
They do not hear each other now—
They listen to voices in themselves,
Mad with perfect sanity.
Hals could not show Gonzetti's room
Reeling and stretching out in space.
Hals could not show their brilliant eyes
Watching a thing beyond the walls
Step from air and beckon them
To follow through streets, and nights, and days . . .

We have a speakeasy here, tonight.
Gonzetti, for three dollars cash,
Is giving the drinkers ten thousand things
Not Hals or any man could show.

ANDY AND JERRY AND JOE

We were staring at the bottles in the restaurant window,
We could hear the autos go by,
We were looking at the women on the boulevard,
It was cold,
No one else knew about the things we knew.

We watched the crowd, there was a murder in the papers, the
     wind blew hard, it was dark,
We didn't know what to do,
There was no place to go and we had nothing to say,
We listened to the bells, and voices, and whistles, and cars,
We moved on,
We weren't dull, or wise, or afraid,
We didn't feel tired, or restless, or happy, or sad.

There were a million stars, a million miles, a million people, a
     million words,
A million places and a million years,
We knew a lot of things we could hardly understand.
There were liners at sea, and rows of houses here, and clouds
     that floated past us away up in the sky.
We waited on the corner,
The lights were in the stores, there were women on the
     streets, Jerry's father was dead,
We didn't know what we wanted and there was nothing to
     say,
Andy had an auto and Joe had a girl.

GEORGE MARTIN

Bankers and priests and clerks and thieves,
    Fear and death and money and rage,
    They are always there,
    In electric-lights, in bill-boards,
    In churches, theatres, bar-rooms, cabarets,
    In the moon—
Always there, seen and dreamed about and known,
    More known than the smile of the moving-picture
        sweetheart,
    Familiar as the honest eyes of beggars, patriots, nuns,
    More known than public love and joy,
    Salesmen and judges and whores and marines,
    Terror and pain and rage and death,
    Known more than I ever know myself,
    And what am I?
What am I, listening to speeches baited for millions?
    Stunned by fearless, honest, automatic, terrible
        applause—
    Trapped by cunning innocence—
    Linked with the virtue of the moving-picture queen—
    Chained to the patented souls of lady geniuses, gentlemen
        heroes—
Bankers, plumbers, clerks, thieves,
    Ten of them die when one speaks,
    Read the papers, write the novels, sing the melodies,
    Their courteous fingers reach for my throat in dreams . .
    Ten are born when one of them dies . .
    Nod, and speak, and smile, and pass . .
    Speak to the lost, smile at the beaten, nod to the mad,
    Walk with the doomed—

Honor to triumph, honor to the mob,
    Honor to the heroine,
        Twist her skirts higher, I will be rich . .

JOHN STANDISH, ARTIST

If I am to live, or be in the studios,
If I am to be in the quiet halls and clubs,
Quiet at tea,
If I am to talk calmly at dinner, when evening falls,
If I am to breathe—

When it is night, and millions are awake, moving like a sea,
    not human, not known,
When millions are aroused to stare, to laugh, to kill,
When I feel them,
When they have no voices, but they have mouths and eyes,
When their wants are confused, but implacable,
When a theory about them becomes nothing, and a portrait
    of them would look well on no studio wall,
When they cringe, when they scowl, when they are counted
    by millions,
When they have no meaning to me, to themselves, to the
    earth, but they are alive—

If I am to live, if I am to breathe,
I must walk with them a while, laugh with them, stare and
    point,
Pick one and follow him to the rotted wharves,
Write my name, under his, in gray latrines, "John Standish,
    artist,"
I must follow him, stumbling as he does, through the docks,
    basements, tenements, wharves,
Follow him till he sleeps, and kill him with a stone.

NOW

Now that we know life:
Breakfast in the morning; office and theater and sleep; no
      memory;
Only desire and profit are real;
Now that we know life in our own way,

There is no war, no death,
There are no doubts, no terrors, and we make no mistakes;
There is a forest of bones in the earth but above it, now there
      is peace;
The fury is gone;
The purposes are gone;
For a little while, the agony is gone;
We have our own thoughts, we know life in our own way,
The world is quiet and green—

As it is where bubbles rise in the waters of swamps;
Where bubbles of gas rise and break among the reeds;
And the reeds are green;
And the frogs are loud, the water is warm where the bubbles rise;
The reeds are still;
The reeds are green, the water is warm, the sky is blue.

SATURDAY NIGHT

That is not blood on the shiny street
Where heroes and heroine appear, in taxis bound for bright
　　　cabarets.
That is not blood along the pavement, though it could be;
It is dirty water,
Not the blood you think might be there after crowds have
　　　scraped and cursed and hammered upon it all day.

9:29 Saturday night;
Elite Max;
Charlotte, the beautiful magazine girl;
They want to hear music;
They only want to hear some music play.

A packed house in Madison Square Garden finds delirium in
　　　a prize fight,
And elsewhere, others are entertained by Senator Horgan's
　　　speech,
But suave Max and lovely Charlotte seek their pleasure at the
　　　Blue Swan.

10:38 P.M.;
Battling Bolinska sleeps on the canvas mat;
Senator Horgan is a true statesman of the old school;
Shall we go to the Parakeet instead of this place?
It is kind of dull here.
Yes. Give the waiter ten dollars.

That sum represents one day's mental travail on the part of
　　　nonchalant Max,
Elite haberdasher whose cut-priced hosiery shines in a

modest window;
But there is no blood on the street,
Though crowds have struggled and lied and hurried upon it
    all day long;
There is no blood along the pavement from Max, Charlotte,
    or anyone,
To pay for the hosiery, the *Blue Swan*, and the fatigue.

11:45 Saturday night,
On penny arcade and gin palace and senator alike.
11:45, the great leveller.

That is rain-water on the shiny street,
Not eyes, not blood, not fingers, nerves, rags, glass, bones,
Where now in a taxi suave Max and exquisite Charlotte roll
    onward in each other's arms,
Roll on into the big silhouette of gaiety,
Roll on through Saturday night.

MINNIE AND MRS. HOYNE

She could die laughing,
On Sunday noon, back of the pawnshop, under the smoke-
    stack, with Mrs. Hoyne.
She could hide her face in rags and die laughing on the street.
She could snicker in the broom closet. In the dark of the
    movies. In bed.

Die, at the way some people talk.
The things they talk about and believe and do.
She and Mrs. Hoyne could sit together and laugh.
Minnie could snicker in the dark alone.

Jesus, what do they mean?
Girls trying to be in love.
People worried about other people. About the world. Do they
    own it?
People that don't believe a street is what it looks like. They
    think there's more.
There isn't any more, the cuckoos.
She could die laughing.
Free milk for babies, Mrs. Hoyne.

Crazy liars, all of them, and what next?
Minnie will be a millionaire.
Mrs. Hoyne will fly a balloon.
Give my regards to the Queen of France when you get there.
Ask her if she remembers me. "Say, Queen, have you got any
    old bloomers you don't want, for Minnie Spohr?"
She could die, grinning among the buckets at midnight,
Snicker, staring down the elevator shaft,
Minnie doesn't care. Get the money, that's all.

She could die laughing, some time,
Alone in the broom closet among the mops and brushes on
the forty-third floor.

NOCTURNE

The floor of the blue night,
Steeped in ether,
Is fixed beneath the muffled floor of time.

In the blue, ether night,
Buildings rise in marble streams that do not end.
Night does not end.
Motionless vapor on the vacant street thins the barren cries
     that strike through distance,
And drains the heatless lamps that stretch away forever within
     a scene that does not change.
Night does not change.
Yesterday has shrunk to a news bulletin
Read under a gray light in an all-night restaurant on the floor
     of the blue night that will not end because there is no
     end to the cold night that seeps through marble walls.

From the blue, icy walls
Rise giant pillars, filled with spiral stairs, upholding towers of
     sculptured night
Where pure ether tides unroll in corridors that have no end
     and rise in mist
Through windows on the blue night.

On the floor of night there is no time.
Men cough and walk away.

PORTRAIT (1)

William Lowell is drunk again.
He has escaped the skull-faced men that whisper and wait.
    Forgotten the filed documents.
Now there is a reason for his smooth desk, for the rustling
    papers and white corridors.
Now there is a reason for his thousand defeats.
There is a reason for having gone with the whores, lain awake
    in black rooms, walked through vacant streets, talked to
    cats in deserted halls.
If the world knew, there are reasons for having lied and
    betrayed and cringed.

If the world knew his life,
Knew the hundred forces seeking to destroy him;
If there were an eye of God to see him as he is, know his
    motives in spite of evasion and compromise,
See him alone in desolate rooms, broken by remorse—

William Lowell, born under blue skies,
Child dreaming under broad pillars of sunlight rising beyond
    the clouds,
No fever then, no profane dreams, no skulls following him in
    roaring subway tunnels to stare through his eyes into a
    soul on fire,
Peace, and no crazy venom in those lost days—

If the world knew,
There is a reason for his thousand failures, vows, treacheries,
    lies, escapes,
And if the world would hear him,
William Lowell would be at peace with all mankind for one

hour before the white corridors and echoing streets and
staring skulls knew him no more,
William Lowell, the child of blue skies.

THEY LIKED IT

They watched the lights go on when night fell.
Away below them streets glowed up like topaz necklaces on
     black silk.
They liked the red eye in the Metropolitan.
And they liked Broadway.

Blake had nothing to do for a while. He talked.
No one in the office paid attention.

"Listen," he said, "I want advice.
You remember that Swede I was telling about?
I saw her again last night.
I'm going crazy."

They liked the muffled hammer and rasp of the city's life.
They liked its size.
They liked to hear liners in the harbor howl at the sky.

"We went to a flat on Sixty-second.
There were a lot of her friends along, and she took on six of
     them right under my eyes.
But when I barely touched her she laughed in my face.
'I'll take any man in the world,' she says, 'but never you.'
I've followed her around for two years.
She's driving me crazy.
What should I do?"

Blake wore checkered socks, carried a cane, had a wife in the
     Bronx.
No one knew where he lived.

"You lying half-wit," said one of them, "the last time you told
        that story the girl was a wop.
Before that she was Irish, and it happened in Brooklyn.
You don't have to tell us, we know you're crazy."
Blake laughed.

They liked to feel the city, away below them, stretch out and
        breathe.
They liked the Metropolitan's red eye, and Broadway.
They liked to hear liners on the river baying at the sky.
They liked it all.

GREEN LIGHT

Bought at the drug store, very cheap; and later pawned.
After a while, heard on the street; seen in the park.
Familiar, but not quite recognized.
Followed and taken home and slept with.
Traded or sold. Or lost.

Bought again at the corner drug store,
At the green light, at the patient's demand, at nine o'clock.
Re-read and memorized and re-wound.
Found unsuitable.
Smashed, put together, and pawned.

Heard on the street, seen in a dream, heard in the park, seen
        by the light of day;
Carefully observed one night by a secret agent of the Greek
        Hydraulic Mining Commission, in plain clothes, off
        duty.
The agent, in broken English, took copious notes. Which he
        lost.
Strange, and yet not extraordinary.
Sad, but true.

True, or exaggerated, or true;
As it is true that the people laugh and the sparrows fly;
As it is exaggerated that the people change, and the sea stays;
As it is that the people go;
As the lights go on and it is night and it is serious, and just
        the same;
As some one dies and it is serious, and the same;
As a girl knows and it is small, and true;
As the corner hardware clerk might know and it is true, and

pointless;
As an old man knows and it is grotesque, but true;
As the people laugh, as the people think, as the people
        change,
It is serious and the same, exaggerated or true.

Bought at the drug store down the street
Where the wind blows and the motors go by and it is always
        night, or day;
Bought to use as a last resort,
Bought to impress the statuary in the park.
Bought at a cut rate, at the green light, at nine o'clock.
Borrowed or bought. To look well. To ennoble. To prevent
        disease. To entertain. To have.
Broken or sold. Or given away. Or used and forgotten. Or
        lost.

INVITATION

We will make love, when the hospitals are quiet and the blue
    police car stops to unload prisoners,
We will sleep, while the searchlights go across the sky,
We will dine, while the destitute actor shakes hands cordially
    in an uptown bar,
We will be alone, we will go to the theater, we will be drunk,
    perhaps we shall die, and there will be a thousand lovers
    on the bus-tops, they will find the suicide lying on the
    floor of a furnished room.

It will be morning when the old men are dreaming again in
    sunlit parks,
It will be night when the movie heroine smiles once more
    through perfect tears,
Night when the bank cashier is blackmailed and crowds are
    muttering in the square, night when a girl walks with
    head turned back to watch the shadows following
    through dim streets,
It will be night when the judge drinks with the salesman and
    the lady novelist bares her soul,
Night when we laugh,
It will be night when pleasure turns to agony, agony to terror,
    terror to rage, rage to delight,
It will be morning when we forget,
It will be morning when the air grows warm, and we read the
    news.

Here we will be invited by thundering feet, desolate faces,
    laughter, cunning eyes, eyes bright with love, lips
    tightened in pain,
Here we will be urged by reality confused with dream,

We will be urged by the hunger of the live, trapped by the
     relentless purposes of millions,
With the millions we will know this, and we will forget,
We will be aroused, we will make love, we will dream, we will
     travel through endless spaces, and we will smile across
     the room.

THE CABINET OF SIMPLICITY

It will be known as Doctor Barky's cabinet, a new magic,
    Something for which there can be no substitute.
    May be used as an ornament or worn like a hat.
    Neat. Genteel.
    Doctor Barky's patented magic cabinet of strict, strict
        simplicity.
    Doctor Barky is the type of man who, were he to see a
        photograph of the Himalayas,
    Or of a Zulu headhunter, or of an octopus,
    Would believe that what he saw was, somewhere, real.
    Naïve, credulous as a child, easily excited,
    The doctor's imagination indeed knows no bounds.
    He has looked at an Egyptian mummy and expressed
        faith that it once laughed.
    That problem, however, remains unsolved.
    But the cabinet, the magic box
    In which Doctor Barky has projected the universe
    And reduced life to its simplest terms—
    That is no dream.
    Upside down in a darkened room
    Among an excitable audience, credulous and naïve,
    The creaking of the cabinet's hinges could be mistaken
    For a wordless whispering through space,
    For discords struck from violent streets,
    For the giant harmonies of death itself.
But a word here about its creator, and what gave life to the
        invention.
    Doctor Barky has traveled far.
    One time in a dream he cut off his head and gave it to a
        girl with stone lips.
    When she drank the acid of his skull,

And later he found her twisted body stretched by the sea,
    burned from within,
The doctor felt sick regret.
But dining on her lips that calm twilight by the frozen waves,
Watching the motionless gulls, listening to far-off
    laughter, and musing on the depth of land and sky,
He grew content.
When the heat swelled in his bones, he shrieked and died.
    Centuries later, this time no dream
    The doctor as a young boy playing on the beach
    Uncovered his smooth skull buried in the sand.
    What a meeting!
    What undercurrent of pathos was in that gay reunion!
These and other severe but pointless experiences
    Have whetted in Doctor Barky a need to arrange the
        world so that he can understand it,
    And still more, to create a fixed world.
See then the cabinet as it will appear before all eyes,
    Swung into space above the stars.
    Magnificent! Magnificent! Magnificent!
    Imagine now the doctor as he doffs his hat,
    Steps forward, bows.
"This is my weapon, the mechanical heart that tames chaos.
    In its lower left-hand drawer I have caused to be placed
    Spices, gems, perfumes, fruit-rinds, nails,
    Mottos for all family occasions,
    A government investor's guide for the year 1857,
    And half a deck of playing cards said to have been used by
        John Brown
    On the night before he was hanged.
"In the lower right-hand drawer I have placed a set of
        Tennyson,
    And a copy of 'Will the Stars Grow Dim?'—that

immortal novel by the world-renowned author,
My friend, Mr. B. Phillipston Gibbs.
I do this thing that the spiritual needs of man be not
    neglected.
"The large upper-chest I have left empty, for the public's
    convenience,
Save for a small bottle containing my right kidney,
The result of a most painful operation.
I thought the public might be interested," said Doctor
    Barky shyly.
"The kidney is preserved in alcohol." He chuckled
    whimsically,
There was a twinkle in his eye. "Lucky kidney!"
The doctor has finished.
He steps back into the shadows forever.
Tall candles burn before the magic box.
Inscrutable and still, the mechanical heart draws into itself
The veins and arteries of chaos.
Earth, time, and space, with a gesture
Are wound and set again in motion.
Comrade, this is no poem,
Who touches this
Touches Doctor Barky's patented magic cabinet of
    certified, strictly guaranteed simplicity and truth.

WINNER TAKE ALL

Innocent of the mean or stupid, and innocent of crime,
Still, justice denied you, from this extremity there is no
　　　escape.

Say to the accusing eyes, say to the doctor standing at your
　　　deathbed, say to the memory of your mistakes, say you
　　　are innocent,
Say to the telegram announcing death you are innocent of
　　　death,
Say to the ticker that wipes you out this failure was not to be
　　　foreseen,

Tell the black headlines, shouting your infamy to millions,
　　　that even a judge has to have what he has to have
(And they say you've been bought, fixed, call it a bribe when
　　　you borrow money from a friend).

Yes, tell the neighbors,
After he's gone, calling you a lowdown doublecrossing tramp,
Tell them you are innocent
(A woman's got to have what she's got to have, and you had
　　　to have that man).

Say to the world you are a man to be valued, beyond the
　　　reach of brisk refusal and command,
Say you are a gentleman, untouched by the pettiness forced
　　　upon you,
Say you, also, are a motion-picture queen, innocent of vacant
　　　nights, useless desires, bargain heroes,

Go on, tell the jury you are innocent of murder

(Shooting at an arm reaching for a gun to drop you dead),
Robbery, yes, but you never meant to kill that crazy fool, yes,
    robbery,
But who knows how you needed money?—
You've got to have what you've got to have, you're going to
    do what you've got to do,
And you are innocent of what has to happen,
Innocent, when they put you out on the street, when they
    look at you and laugh, when you grow old and fade
    away, when they strap you in the electric chair,
Tell them all you are innocent, innocent of this.

What if they don't listen, and there is no escape?
Still you are innocent, and brave, and wise, and strong.

OBITUARY

Take him away, he's as dead as they die,
Hear that ambulance bell, his eyes are staring straight at
    death;
Look at the fingers growing stiff, touch the face already cold,
    see the stars in the sky, look at the stains on the street,

Look at the ten-ton truck that came rolling along fast and
    stretched him out cold,

Then turn out his pockets and make the crowd move on.
Sergeant, what was his name? What's the driver's name?
    What's your name, sergeant?
Go through his clothes,
Take out the cigars, the money, the papers, the keys, take
    everything there is,

And give a dollar and a half to the Standard Oil. It was his
    true-blue friend.
Give the key of his flat to the D.A.R. They were friends of
    his, the best a man ever had.
Take out the pawnticket, wrap it, seal it, send it along to the
    People's Gas. They were life-long pals. It was more than
    his brother. They were just like twins.

Give away the shoes,
Give his derby away. Donate his socks to the Guggenheim
    fund,
Let the Morgans hold the priceless bills, and leaflets, and
    racing tips under lock and key,
And give Mr. Hoover the pint of gin,
Because they're all good men. And they were friends of his.

Don't forget Gene Tunney. Don't forget Will Hays. Don't
    forget Al Capone. Don't forget the I.R.T.
Give them his matches to remember him by.
They lived with him, in the same old world. And they're good
    men, too.

That's all, sergeant. There's nothing else, lieutenant. There's
    no more, captain.
Pick up the body, feed it, shave it, find it another job.

Have a cigar, driver?
Take two cigars—
You were his true-blue pal.

CONCLUSION

You will give praise to all things, praise without end;
Idly in the morning, bluntly at noon, cunningly with the
      evening cigar, you will meditate further praise;
So will the days pass, each profitable and serene; so will your
      sleep be undisturbed; so you will live;
No faith will be difficult, rising from doubt; no love will be
      false, born of dread;

In the flaring parks, in the taverns, in the hushed academies,
      your murmur will applaud the wisdom of a thousand
      quacks. For theirs is the kingdom.
By your sedate nod in the quiet office you will grieve with the
      magnate as he speaks of sacrifice. For his is the power.
Your knowing glance will affirm the shrewd virtue of clown
      and drudge; directors' room or street-corner, the
      routine killer will know your candid smile; your
      handclasp, after the speeches at the club, will endorse
      the valor of loud suburban heroes. For theirs is the
      glory, forever and ever.

Always, more than wise, you will be found with the many
      resolved against the few;
But you will be a brother, on second thought, to all men.

The metropolitan dive, jammed with your colleagues, the
      derelicts; the skyscraper, owned by your twin, the pimp
      of gumdrops and philanthropy; the auditoriums,
      packed with weeping creditors, your peers; the morgues,
      tenanted by your friends, the free dead; the asylums,
      cathedrals, prisons, treasuries, brothels, shrines—upon
      all, all of them you will find reason to bestow praise;

And as you know, at last, that all of this will be,
As you walk among millions, indifferent to them,
Or stop and read the journals filled with studied alarm,
Or pause and hear, with no concern, the statesman vending
    manufactured bliss,

You will be grateful for an easy death,
Your silence will praise them for killing you.

AMERICAN RHAPSODY (1)

Let us present,
This night of love, and murder, and reckoning, and sleep,
Evening of illusion, night filled with thousands intent upon
    ordained ends,
Let us introduce, among a few leading citizens in unrehearsed
    acts,

That popular ghost, Allen Devoe, serial hero of the current
    magazines,
The exact, composite dream of those who read.
An artist in innocence,
Tonight the ectoplasm of Mr. Devoe hovers inescapably
    everywhere about us,
That profitable smile invisible above the skyscrapers, those
    serene eyes piercing night-courts, clinics, tenements,
    that exclusive nicety available in remote villages and
    farms,

That breadline,
Salvation before coffee and rolls.
"Last night a number of you gentlemen hurried through the
    banquet and dashed around to the mission next door
    for another slice of bread.
Is that gratitude? Is that decency? Certified scabies? Starvation
    common, or TB preferred?"

That genius, that littérateur, Theodore True,
St. Louis boy who made good as an Englishman in theory, a
    deacon in vaudeville, a cipher in politics,
Undesirable, in large numbers, to any community.
Closing prices: Is This Really a Commercial Age?—100. That

Anguished Soul of Marcel Proust—150. Liberty or
Dangerous Freedom, Which?—210. That Unknown,
Patriotic, Law-abiding Corpse—305.

We present that motion-picture star, and the superfilm:
"Will the daughter of the humble call-house magnate wed the
    patrician wardheeler, O America?"
And the Blumberg twins (magistrate Ike, gorilla Mike) in
    conference with that blonde, blonde evangelist.
The senator at that microphone again. Those spinster sibyls,
    again in the rotogravure. That proprietor of the
    revolution, oracle Steve.

"I killed her because she had an evil eye." "We are not
    thinking now of our own profits, of course." "Nothing
    can take back from us this night." "Let me alone, you
    God damn rat." "Two rickeys." "Cash."

These, however, are merely close-ups.
At a distance these eyes and faces and arms,
Maimed in the expiation of living, scarred in payment exacted
    through knife, hunger, silence, hope, exhaustion, regret,
Melt into an ordered design, strange and significant, and not
    without peace.

[IT HAPPENED IN FAR OFF FROZEN NOME]

It happened in far off frozen Nome,
One blistering Fourth of July:
John Brown and his body were pardners
Against Jesse James and I!

Brown cut the cards and Jesse dealt;
While the silence that fell on the room
Was loud as the noise of the Saxophone Boys
Rehearsing in Grant's grey tomb.

"No trump," called John beginning the game,
I passed in answer staid;
"Double," Brown's body, his pardner, spoke,
And Jesse remarked, "One spade."

"One diamond," up spoke the bold John Brown.
"One club," I ventured to say;
Said the pardner of Brown with a terrible frown,
"Do you think it will rain today?"

"Two spades!" "Two hearts!" "Two diamonds!" "Two clubs!"
And the terrible pardner of Brown
Called out with a smile of tigerish guile,
"Three spades, though I do go down."

Three hearts, three diamonds, then followed three clubs.
The clock on the wall struck eleven;
Then four and five, then six, and Jesse
Yawned as he whispered, "Seven."

Seven hearts, seven diamonds, seven clubs;
They followed like bullets from a Thompson gun;
The bidding might have lasted forever—
Indeed, I had just begun—

But the pardner of Brown, that courteous ghost,
Asked the time in a moment's lull.
"It's a dreadful shame to spoil the game,"
He sighed, "though it has been dull."

"But I've got to be going at midnight
Back where the grave diggers delve.
D'you think it'll rain?"—and just then
The clock laughed and whispered "Twelve."

RESURRECTION

You will remember the kisses, real or imagined;
You will remember the faces that were before you, and the
      words exchanged;
You will remember the minute crowded with meaning, the
      moment of pain, the aimless hour;
You will remember the cities, and the plains, and the
      mountains, and the sea,

And recall the friendly voice of the killer, or the voice of the
      priest, inhumanly sweet;
Recall the triumphant smile of the duped;
You will not forget compassion that glittered in the eyes of
      the money-lender, refusing you, not forget the purpose
      that lay beneath the merchant's warmth;
You will not forget the voice of the bought magistrate
      quivering in horror through the courtroom above
      prostitute and pimp,
The majesty of the statesman at the microphone, the sober
      majesty of the listening clerk,
The face of the fool, radiant on newspaper and screen;

You will remember hope that crawled up the bar-room tap
      and spoke through the confident speech of the lost,
Happiness clearly displayed on the glaring billboards,
Love casually revealed in the magazines and novels, or stated
      in the trembling limbs of ancient millionaires;
You will remember the triumph easily defined by the rebel
      messiah, by the breadloaf in the hand of the ghetto
      wife, by the inscription on the patriot tomb;
You will remember your laughter that rose with the steam
      from the carcass on the street
In hatred and pity exactly matched.

These are the things that will return to you,
To mingle with the days and nights, with the sound of
 motors and the sun's warmth,
With fatigue and desire,
As you work, and sleep, and talk, and laugh, and die.

1933

You heard the gentleman, with automatic precision, speak the
    truth.
Cheers. Triumph.
And then mechanically it followed the gentleman lied.
Deafening applause. Flashlights, cameras, microphones. Floral
    tribute. Cheers.

Down Mrs. Hogan's alley, your hand with others reaching
    among the ashes, cinders, scrapiron, garbage, you found
    the rib of sirloin wrapped in papal documents. Snatched
    it. Yours by right, the title clear.
Looked up. Saw lips move in the head thrust from the
    museum window: "Unconstitutional."

And ran. Escaped. You returned the million dollars. You
    restored the lady's virginity.
You were decorated 46 times in rapid succession by the King
    of Italy. Took a Nobel prize. Evicted again, you went
    downtown, slept at the movies, stood in the breadline,
    voted yourself a limousine.
Rage seized the Jewish Veterans of Foreign Wars. In
    footnotes, capitals, Latin, italics, the poet of the Sunday
    supplements voiced steamheated grief. The RFC
    expressed surprise.
And the news, at the Lucky Strike Hour, leaked out.
Shouts, Cheers. Stamping of feet. Blizzard of confetti.
    Thunderous applause.

But the stocks were stolen. The pearls of the actress, stolen
    again. The bonds embezzled.
Inexorably, the thief was pursued. Captured inexorably.

Tried. Inexorably acquitted.
And again you heard the gentleman, with automatic
    precision, speak the truth.
Saw, once more, the lady's virginity restored.

In the sewers of Berlin, with the directors prepared, the room
    dark for the seance, she a simple Baroness, you a lowly
    millionaire, came face to face with John D. Christ.
Shook hands, his knife at your back, your knife at his. Sat
    down.
Saw issue from his throat the ectoplasm of Pius VIII, and
    heard "A test of the people's faith." You said amen,
    voted to endorse but warned against default, you
    observed the astral form of Nicholas II, and heard
    "Sacred union of all." Saw little "Safe for democracy"
    Nell. Listened to Adolphe "Safety of France and
    society" Thiers.
And beheld the faith, the union of rags, blackened hands,
    stacked carrion, breached barricades in flame,
No default, credit restored, Union Carbide 94 3/8, call
    money 10%, disarm, steel five points up, rails rise,
    du Pont up, disarm, disarm, and heard again,
Ghost out of ghost out of ghost out of ghost,
The voice of the senator reverberate through all the morgues
    of all the world, echo again for liberty in the catacombs
    of Rome, again sound through the sweatshops,
    ghettoes, factories, mines, hunger again repealed, circle
    the London cenotaph once more annulling death, saw
    ten million dead returned to life, shot down again,
    again restored,

Heard once more the gentleman speak, with automatic
    precision, the final truth,

Once more beheld the lady's virginity, the lady's decency, the
    lady's purity, the lady's innocence,
Paid for, certified, and restored.

Crawled amorously into bed. Felt among the maggots for the
    mouldering lips. The crumbled arms. Found them.
Tumult of cheers. Music and prayer by the YMCA. Horns,
    rockets. Spotlight.
The child was nursed on government bonds. Cut its teeth on
    a hand grenade. Grew fat on shrapnel. Bullets. Barbed
    wire. Chlorine gas. Laughed at the bayonet through its
    heart.

These are the things you saw and heard, these are the things
    you did, this is your record,
You.

X MINUS X

Even when your friend, the radio, is still; even when her
    dream, the magazine, is finished; even when his life, the
    ticker, is silent; even when their destiny, the boulevard,
    is bare;
And after that paradise, the dance-hall, is closed; after that
    theater, the clinic, is dark,

Still there will be your desire, and hers, and his hopes and
    theirs,
Your laughter, their laughter,
Your curse and his curse, her reward and their reward, their
    dismay and his dismay and her dismay and yours—

Even when your enemy, the collector, is dead; even when
    your counsellor, the salesman, is sleeping; even when
    your sweetheart, the movie queen, has spoken; even
    when your friend, the magnate, is gone.

DIVIDENDS

This advantage to be seized; and here, an escape prepared
      against an evil day;
So it is arranged, consummately, to meet the issues.
      Convenience and order. Necessary murder and divorce.
      A decent repute.

Such are the plans, in clear detail.
She thought it was too soon but they said no, it was too late.
      They didn't trust the other people.
Sell now.
He was a fool to ignore the market. It could be explained, he
      said. With the woman, and after the theater she made a
      scene. None of them felt the crash for a long time.

(But what is swifter than time?)

So it is resolved, upon awakening. This way it is devised,
      preparing for sleep. So it is revealed, uneasily, in strange
      dreams.
A defense against gray, hungry, envious millions. A veiled
      watch to be kept upon this friend.
Dread that handclasp. Seek this one. Smile.
They didn't trust the others. They were wary. It looked
      suspicious. They preferred to wait, they said.

Gentlemen, here is a statement for the third month,
And here, Mildred, is the easiest way.
Such is the evidence, convertible to profit. These are the
      dividends, waiting to be used.
Here are the demands again, considered again, and again the
      endless issues are all secure.
Such are the facts. Such are the details. Such are the proofs.

Almighty God, these are the plans,
These are the plans until the last moment of the last hour of
  the last day,
And then the end. By error or accident.
Burke of cancer. Jackson out at the secret meeting of the
  board. Hendricks through the window of the
  nineteenth floor.
Maggots and darkness will attend the alibi.

Peace on earth. And the finer things.
So it is all devised.
Thomas, the car.

DEAR BEATRICE FAIRFAX:
*Is it true that Father Coughlin and Miss Aimee Semple
McPherson and Mr. H.L. Mencken and Peter Pan?*

Foolproof baby with that memorized smile,
Burglarproof baby, fireproof baby with that rehearsed appeal,
Reconditioned, standardized, synchronized, amplified, best-
by-test baby with those push-the-button tears,

Your bigtime sweetheart worships you and you alone,
Your goodtime friend lives for you, only you,
He loves you, trusts you, needs you, respects you, gives for
you, fascinated, mad about you,
All wrapped up in you like the accountant in the trust, like
the banker trusts the judge, like the judge respects
protection, like the gunman needs his needle, like the
trust must give and give—

He's with you all the way from the top of the bottle to the
final alibi,
From the handshake to the hearse, from the hearse to the
casket,
To the handles on the casket, to the nails, to the hinges, to
the satin, to the flowers, to the music, to the prayer, to
the graveyard, to the tomb,

But just the same, baby, and never forget,
It takes a neat, smart, fast, good, sweet doublecross
To doublecross the gentleman who doublecrossed the
gentleman who doublecrossed
Your doublecrossing, doublecrossing, doublecross friend.

AMERICAN RHAPSODY (2)

She said did you get it, and he said did you get it,
    at the clinic, at the pawnshop, on the breadline, in jail,
    shoes and a roof and the rent and a cigarette and bread
        and a shirt and coffee and sleep—

Reaching at night for a bucket of coal among the B & O flats
        in the B & O yards,
    they said there's another one, get him they said,
    or staring again at locked and guarded factory gates; or
        crouched in a burglarproof loft, hand around a gun;
        or polite, urgent, face before a face behind a
        steelbarred cage:

All winter she came there, begging for milk. So we had the
        shacks along the river destroyed by police. But at the
        uptown exhibit a rich, vital sympathy infused the
        classic mood. When the muriatic acid in the whiskey
        failed, and running him down with an auto failed,
        and ground glass failed, we finished the job by
        shoving a gastube down his throat.
    Next year, however, we might have something definite,

Mountains or plains, crossroads, suburbs, cities or the sea,
    did you take it, was it safe, did you buy it, did you beg it,
        did you steal it, was it known,

Name, address, relatives, religion, income, sex, bank account,
        insurance, health, race, experience, age,
    out beyond the lunatic asylum, on the city dump; on the
        junkheap past the bank, past the church, past the
        jungle, past the morgue,

where rats eat the crusts and worms eat the satins and
    maggots eat the mould
and fire eats the headlines, eats the statements and the
    pictures, eats the promises and proofs, eats the rind of
    an orange and a rib and a claw and a skull and an eye,

Did you find it, was it there, did they see you, were they
    waiting, did they shoot, did they stab, did they burn,
    did they kill—
one on the gallows and one on the picketline and one in
    the river and one on the ward and another one slugged
    and another one starved and another insane and
    another by the torch.

SUNDAY TO SUNDAY

Unknown to Mabel, who works as cook for the rich and
      snobbish Aldergates,
The insured, by subway suicide, provides for a widow and
      three sons;
Picked from the tracks, scraped from the wheels, identified,
      this happy ending restores the nation to its heritage: A
      Hearst cartoon.

Meanwhile it is infant welfare week, milk prices up, child
      clinics closed, relief curtailed,
The Atlantic and Pacific fleets in full support off Vera Cruz,
In court, sentence suspended, Rose Raphael dispossessed of a
      Flatbush packingbox,
Jim Aldergate in love with Mabel, but unaware she has been
      married to Zorrocco the gangster,

An envoy bearing again an after-luncheon wreath to the tomb
      of the patriot dead,
Stocks firmer, meanwhile, on rumors of drought and war,
And Zorrocco, not knowing Mabel loves Jim, has returned to
      use her for his criminal schemes; but in a motor crash
      he is killed, Mabel winning at last to happiness in Jim's
      arms,
Directed by Frederick Hammersmith and produced by
      National,

As hundreds, thousands, millions search the want ads, search
      the factories, search the subways, search the streets,
      search to sleep in missions, jungles, depots, parks, sleep
      to wake again to gutters, scrapheaps, breadlines, jails,
Unknown to the beautiful, beautiful, beautiful Mabel;

unknown to the deathray smile of politician or priest;
unknown to Zorrocco, Jim, or the unknown soldier;
unknown to WGN and the bronze, bronze bells of
Sunday noon.

NO CREDIT

Whether dinner was pleasant, with the windows lit by
    gunfire, and no one disagreed; or whether, later, we
    argued in the park, and there was a touch of vomit-gas
    in the evening air;
Whether we found a greater, deeper, more perfect love, by
    courtesy of Camels, over NBC; whether the comics
    amused us, or the newspapers carried a hunger death
    and a White House prayer for Mother's Day;
Whether the bills were paid or not, whether or not we had
    our doubts, whether we spoke our minds at Joe's, and
    the receipt said "Not Returnable," and the cash-register
    rang up "No Sale,"
Whether the truth was then, or later, or whether the best had
    already gone—

Nevertheless, we know; as every turn is measured; as every
    unavoidable risk is known;
As nevertheless, the flesh grows old, dies, dies in its only life,
    is gone;
The reflection goes from the mirror; as the shadow, of even a
    rebel, is gone from the wall;
As nevertheless, the current is thrown and the wheels revolve;
    and nevertheless, as the word is spoken and the wheat
    grows tall and the ships sail on—

None but the fool is paid in full; none but the broker, none
    but the scab is certain of profit;
The sheriff alone may attend a third degree in formal attire;
    alone, the academy artists multiply in dignity as a
    trooper's bayonet guards the door;
Only Steve, the side-show robot, knows content; only Steve,

the mechanical man in love with a photo-electric beam,
remains aloof; only Steve, who sits and smokes or stands
in salute, is secure;

Steve, whose shoebutton eyes are blind to terror, whose
painted ears are deaf to appeal, whose welded breast will
never be slashed by bullets, whose armature soul can
hold no fear.

ESCAPE

Acid for the whorls of the fingertips; for the face, a surgeon's
     knife; oblivion to the name;
Eyes, hands, color of hair, condition of teeth, habits, haunts,
     the subject's health;
Wanted or not, guilty or not guilty, dead or alive, did you see
     this man

Walk in a certain distinctive way through the public streets or
     the best hotels,
Turn and go,
Escape from collectors, salesmen, process-servers, thugs; from
     the landlord's voice or a shake of the head; leave an
     afternoon beer; go from an evening cigar in a well-
     known scene,
Walk, run, slip from the earth into less than air?—

Gone from the teletype, five-feet ten; lost from the headlines,
     middle-aged, gray, posed as a gentleman;
A drawling voice in a blue serge suit, fled from the radio,
     forehead scarred,

Tear up the letters and bury the clothes, throw away the keys,
     file the number from the gun, burn the record of birth,
     smash the name from the tomb, bathe the fingers in
     acid, wrap the bones in lime,
Forget the street, the house, the name, the day;

But something must be saved from the rise and fall of the
     copper's club; something must be kept from the
     auctioneer's hammer; something must be guarded from
     the rats and the fire on the city dump;

Something, for warmth through the long night of death;
    something to be saved from the last parade through
    granite halls and go, go free, arise with the voice that
    pleads not guilty,
Go with the verdict that ascends forever beyond steelbarred
    windows into blue, deep space,

Guilty of vagrancy, larceny, sedition, assault,
Tried, convicted, sentenced, paroled, imprisoned, released,
    hunted, seized,
Under what name and last seen where? And in what disguise
    did the soiled, fingerprinted, bruised, secondhand,
    worn-down, scarred, familiar disguise escape?

No name, any name, nowhere, nothing, no one, none.

DIRGE

1-2-3 was the number he played but today the number came
    3-2-1;
Bought his Carbide at 30 and it went to 29; had the favorite
    at Bowie but the track was slow—

O executive type, would you like to drive a floating-power,
    knee-action, silk-upholstered six? Wed a Hollywood
    star? Shoot the course in 58? Draw to the ace, king,
    jack?
O fellow with a will who won't take no, watch out for three
    cigarettes on the same, single match; O democratic
    voter born in August under Mars, beware of liquidated
    rails—

Denouement to denouement, he took a personal pride in the
    certain, certain way he lived his own, private life,
But nevertheless, they shut off his gas; nevertheless, the bank
    foreclosed; nevertheless, the landlord called;
    nevertheless, the radio broke,

And twelve o'clock arrived just once too often,
Just the same he wore one gray tweed suit, bought one straw
    hat, drank one straight Scotch, walked one short step,
    took one long look, drew one deep breath,
Just one too many,

And wow he died as wow he lived,
Going whop to the office and blooie home to sleep and biff
    got married and bam had children and oof got fired,
Zowie did he live and zowie did he die,

With who the hell are you at the corner of his casket, and
    where the hell're we going on the right-hand silver
    knob, and who the hell cares walking second from the
    end with an American Beauty wreath from why the hell
    not,

Very much missed by the circulation staff of the New York
    Evening Post; deeply, deeply mourned by the B.M.T.

Wham, Mr. Roosevelt; pow, Sears Roebuck; awk, big dipper;
    bop, summer rain;
Bong, Mr., bong, Mr., bong, Mr., bong.

WHAT IF MR. JESSE JAMES SHOULD SOME DAY DIE?

Where will we ever again find food to eat, clothes to wear, a
    roof and a bed, now that the Wall Street plunger has
    gone to his hushed, exclusive, paid-up tomb?
How can we get downtown today, with the traction king
    stretched flat on his back in the sun at Miami Beach?
And now that the mayor has denounced the bankers, now
    that the D.A. denies all charges of graft, now that the
    clergy have spoken in defense of the home,

O dauntless khaki soldier, O steadfast pauper, O experienced
    vagrant, O picturesque mechanic, O happy hired man,
And you still unopened skeleton, you tall and handsome
    target, you neat, thrifty, strong, ambitious, brave
    prospective ghost,
Is there anything left for the people to do, is there anything at
    all that remains unsaid?

But who shot down the man in the blue overalls? Who
    stopped the milk? Who took the mattress, the table, the
    birdcage, and piled them in the street? Who drove tear
    gas in the picket's face? Who burned the crops? Who
    killed the herd? Who leveled the walls of the
    packingbox city? Who held the torch to the Negro
    pyre? Who stuffed the windows and turned on the gas
    for the family of three?

No more breadlines. No more blackjacks. And save us from
    the sheriffs, the G-men and the scabs.
No more heart-to-heart shakedowns. No more Ku Klux Klan.
    No more trueblue, patriotic, doublecross leagues.

No more gentlemen of the old guard, commissioned to
 safeguard, as chief commanding blackguard in the
 rearguard of the home guard, the 1 inch, 3 inch, 6 inch,
 10 inch, 12 inch,
No more 14, 16, 18 inch shells.

$2.50

But that dashing, dauntless, delphic, diehard, diabolic cracker
    likes his fiction turned with a certain elegance and wit;
    and that anti-anti-anti-slum-congestion clublady prefers
    romance;
Search through the mothballs, comb the lavender and lace;
Were her desires and struggles futile or did an innate fineness
    bring him at last to a prouder, richer peace in a world
    gone somehow mad?

We want one more compelling novel, Mr. Filbert Sopkins
    Jones,
All about it, all about it,
With signed testimonials to its stark, human, while-u-wait,
    iced-or-heated, taste-that-sunshine tenderness and
    truth;
One more comedy of manners, Sir Warwick Aldous Wells,
    involving three blond souls; tried in the crucible of war,
    Countess Olga out-of-limbo by Hearst through the
    steerage peerage,
Glamorous, gripping, moving, try it, send for a 5 cent, 10
    cent sample, restores faith in the flophouse, workhouse,
    warehouse, whorehouse, bughouse life of man,
Just one more long poem that sings a more heroic age, baby
    Edwin, 58,

But the faith is all gone,
And all the courage is gone, used up, devoured on the first
    morning of a home relief menu,
You'll have to borrow it from the picket killed last Tuesday
    on the fancy knitgoods line;
And the glamor, the ice for the cocktails, the shy appeal, the
    favors for the subdeb ball? O.K.,

O.K.,
But they smell of exports to the cannibals,
Reek of something blown away from the muzzle of a twenty-
    inch gun;

Lady, the demand is for a dream that lives and grows and
        does not fade when the midnight theater special pulls
        out on track 15;
Cracker, the demand is for a dream that stands and quickens
        and does not crumble when a General Motors dividend
        is passed;
Lady, the demand is for a dream that lives and grows and
        does not die when the national guardsmen fix those
        cold, bright bayonets;
Cracker, the demand is for a dream that stays, grows real,
        withstands the benign, afternoon vision of the clublady,
        survives the cracker's evening fantasy of honor, and
        profit, and grace.

DENOUEMENT

1

Sky, be blue, and more than blue; wind, be flesh and blood;
    flesh and blood, be deathless;
Walls, streets, be home;
Desire of millions, become more real than warmth and breath
    and strength and bread;
Clock, point to the decisive hour and, hour without name
    when stacked and waiting murder fades, dissolves, stay
    forever as the world grows new—

Truth, be known, be kept forever, let the letters, letters,
    souvenirs, documents, snapshots, bills be found at last,
    be torn away from a world of lies, be kept as final
    evidence, transformed forever into more than truth;
Change, change, rows and rows and rows of figures, spindles,
    furrows, desks, change into paid-up rent and let the
    paid-up rent become South Sea music;
Magic film, unwind, unroll, unfold in silver on that million
    mile screen, take us all, bear us again to the perfect
    denouement—

Where everything lost, needed, each forgotten thing, all that
    never happens,
Gathers at last into a dynamite triumph, a rainbow peace, a
    thunderbolt kiss,
For you, the invincible, and I, grown older, and he, the
    shipping clerk, and she, an underweight blonde
    journeying home in the last express.

2

But here is the body found lying face down in a burlap sack,
    strangled in the noose jerked shut by these trussed and
    twisted and frantic arms;
But here are the agents, come to seize the bed;
But here is the vase holding saved-up cigar-store coupons, and
    here is a way to save on cigars and to go without meat;
But here is the voice that strikes around the world, "My
    friends . . . my friends," issues from the radio and
    thunders "My friends" in newsreel close-ups, explodes
    across headlines, "Both rich and poor, my friends,
    must sacrifice," re-echoes, murmuring, through
    hospitals, death-cells, "My friends . . . my friends . . .
    my friends . . . my friends . . ."

And who, my friend, are you?
Are you the one who leaped to the blinds of the cannon-ball
    express? Or are you the one who started life again with
    three dependents and a pack of cigarettes?—

But how can these things be made finally clear in a post-
    mortem scene with the lips taped shut and the blue eyes
    cold, wide, still, blind, fixed beyond the steady glare of
    electric lights through the white-washed ceiling and the
    cross-mounted roof, past the drifting clouds?—

Objection, over-ruled, exception, proceed:—

Was yours the voice heard singing one night in a fly-blown,
    soot-beamed, lost and forgotten Santa Fe saloon? Later
    bellowing in rage? And you boiled up a shirt in a
    Newark furnished room? Then you found another job,

and pledged not to organize, or go on strike?—

We offer this union book in evidence. We offer these rent
 receipts in evidence. We offer this vacation card
 marked, "This is the life. Regards to all."—

You, lodge member, protestant, crossborn male, the placenta
 discolored, at birth, by syphilis, you, embryo four
 inches deep in the seventh month,
Among so many, many sparks struck and darkened at
 conception,
Which were you,
You, six feet tall on the day of death?—

Then you were at no time the senator's son? Then you were
 never the beef king's daughter, married in a storm of
 perfume and music and laughter and rice?
And you are not now the clubman who waves and nods and
 vanishes to Rio in a special plane?
But these are your lungs, scarred and consumed? These are
 your bones, still marked by rickets? These are your
 pliers? These are your fingers, O master mechanic, and
 these are your cold, wide, still, blind eyes?—

The witness is lying, lying, an enemy, my friends, of Union
 Gas and the home:—

But how will you know us, wheeled from the icebox and
 stretched upon the table with the belly slit wide and the
 entrails removed, voiceless as the clippers bite through
 ligaments and flesh and nerves and bones,
How will you know us, attentive, strained, before the director's
 desk, or crowded in line in front of factory gates,

How will you know us through ringed machinegun sights as
     we run and fall in gasmask, helmet, flame-tunic,
     uniform, bayonet, pack,
How will you know us, crumbled into ashes, lost in air and
     water and fire and stone,
How will you know us, now or any time, who will ever know
     that we have lived or died?—

And this is the truth? So help you God, this is the truth? The
     truth in full, so help you God? So help you God?
But the pride that was made of iron and could not be broken,
     what has become of it, what has become of the faith
     that nothing could destroy, what has become of the
     deathless hope,

You, whose ways were yours alone, you, the one like no one
     else, what have you done with the hour you swore to
     remember, where is the hour, the day, the achievement
     that would never die?—

Morphine. Veronal. Veronal. Morphine. Morphine.
     Morphine. Morphine.

        3

Leaflets, scraps, dust, match-stubs strew the linoleum that
     leads upstairs to the union hall, the walls of the
     basement workers' club are dim and cracked and above
     the speaker's stand Vanzetti's face shows green, behind
     closed doors the committeeroom is a fog of smoke—

Who are these people?—

All day the committee fought like cats and dogs and twelve of
	Mr. Kelly's strongarm men patrolled the aisles that
	night, them blackjack guys get ten to twenty bucks a
	throw, the funds were looted, sent to Chicago, at the
	meeting the organizer talked like a fool, more scabs
	came through in trucks guarded by police,
Workers of the world, workers of the world, workers of the
	world—

Who are these people and what do they want, can't they be
	decent, can't they at least be calm and polite,
Besides the time is not yet ripe, it might take years, like Mr.
	Kelly said, years—

Decades black with famine and red with war, centuries on
	fire, ripped wide—

Who are these people and what do they want, why do they
	walk back and forth with signs that say "Bread Not
	Bullets," what do they mean "They Shall Not Die" as
	they sink in clouds of poison gas and fall beneath clubs,
	hooves, rifles, fall and do not arise, arise, unite,
Never again these faces, arms, eyes, lips—

Not unless we live, and live again,
Return, everywhere alive in the issue that returns, clear as
	light that still descends from a star long cold, again alive
	and everywhere visible through and through the scene
	that comes again, as light on moving water breaks and
	returns, heard only in the words, as millions of voices
	become one voice, seen only in millions of hands that
	move as one—

Look at them gathered, raised, look at their faces, clothes,
      who are these people, who are these people,
What hand scrawled large in the empty prison cell "I have
      just received my sentence of death: Red Front," whose
      voice screamed out in the silence "Arise"?—

And all along the waterfront, there, where rats gnaw into the
      loading platforms, here, where the wind whips at
      warehouse corners, look, there, here,
Everywhere huge across the walls and gates "Your comrades
      live,"
Where there is no life, no breath, no sound, no touch, no
      warmth, no light but the lamp that shines on a trooper's
      drawn and ready bayonet.

AS THE FUSE BURNS DOWN

What will you do when the phone rings and they say to you:
    What will you do?
What will you say, when the sun lights all the avenue again,
    and the battle monument still reads: These dead did not
    die in vain?
When night returns, when the clock strikes one, the clock
    strikes two, three, four, when the city sleeps, awakes,
    when day returns, what will you say, feel, believe, do,

Do with the culture found in a tabloid, what can be done
    with a Lydia Pinkham ad?
What reply can you give to the pawnclerk's decent bid for
    your silverware?
How are you to be grateful as "Thrift" glares out, in a
    hundred thousand watts, across the ghetto nights;
    reassured, as the legless, sightless one extends his cup;
    who can be surprised, why, how, as the statesman
    speaks for peace and moves for war?
Then, when they tell you the executioner does the best that
    he can, what can you say? What then?

Or they come to you, as human fingers comb the city's refuse,
    and say, Look, you have been saved;
When they tell you: See, you were right, and it is the day the
    utilities evidence has been destroyed;
And the state is saved again (three dead, six shot), and they
    tell you, Look, you have survived, the reward is yours,
    you have won—What then? What then?

What will you say and where will you turn?
What will you do? What will you do? What will you do?

AMERICAN RHAPSODY (3)

Before warmth and sight and sound are gone,
And some time the evening lights spring up, as always, but
     not for you and not for me,
Before the sky is lost, before the clouds are lost, before their
     slow, still shadows are lost from the hills,

Shall we meet at 8 o'clock and kiss and exclaim and arrange
     another meeting, as though there were love,
Pretend, even alone, we believe the things we say,
Laugh along the boulevard as though there could be laughter,
Make our plans and nourish hope, pretending, what is the
     truth, that we ourselves are fooled?

You can be a princess and I'll be the beggar; no, you can be
     the beggar, and I'll be king;
You be the mother and go out and beg for food; I'll be a
     merchant, the man you approach, a devoted husband,
     famous as a host; the merchant can be a jobless clerk
     who sleeps on subway platforms then lies dead in
     potter's field; the clerk can be a priest, human, kindly,
     one who enjoys a joke; the priest can be a lady in jail for
     prostitution and the lady can be a banker who has his
     troubles, too;
Let the merchant be grieved, let the priest be stirred, let the
     banker be moved, let the red-squad copper be a patron
     of the arts;
You be a rat; I'll be the trap; or we both can be maggots in the
     long black box;
Murder can be comic and hunger can be kind.

LULLABY

Wide as this night, old as this night is old and young as it is
     young, still as this, strange as this;
Filled as this night is filled with the light of a moon as gray;
Dark as these trees, heavy as this scented air from the fields,
     warm as this hand;
As warm, as strong;

Is the night that wraps all the huts of the south and folds the
     empty barns of the west;
Is the wind that fans the roadside fire;
Are the trees that line the country estates, tall as the lynch
     trees, as straight, as black;
Is the moon that lights the mining towns, dim as the light
     upon tenement roofs, gray upon the hands at the bars
     of Moabit, cold as the bars of the Tombs.

TWENTIETH-CENTURY BLUES

What do you call it, bobsled champion, and you, too,
      Olympic roller-coaster ace,
High-diving queen, what is the word,
Number one man on the Saturday poker squad, motion-
      picture star incognito as a home girl, life of the party or
      you, the serious type, what is it, what is it,

When it's just like a fever shooting up and up and up but
      there are no chills and there is no fever,
Just exactly like a song, like a knockout, like a dream, like a
      book,

What is the word, when you know that all the lights of all the
      cities of all the world are burning bright as day, and you
      know that some time they all go out for you,
Or your taxi rolls and rolls through streets made of velvet,
      what is the feeling, what is the feeling when the radio
      never ends, but the hour, the swift, the electric, the
      invisible hour does not stop and does not turn,
What does it mean, when the get-away money burns in
      dollars big as moons, but where is there to go that's just
      exactly right,
What have you won, plunger, when the 20-to-1 comes in;
      what have you won, salesman, when the dotted line is
      signed; irresistible lover, when her eyelids flutter shut at
      last, what have you really, finally won;
And what is gone, soldier, soldier, step-and-a-half marine who
      saw the whole world; hot-tip addict, what is always just
      missed; picker of crumbs, how much has been lost,
      denied, what are all the things destroyed,
Question mark, question mark, question mark, question mark,

And you, fantasy Frank, and dreamworld Dora and
      hallucination Harold, and delusion Dick, and
      nightmare Ned,

What is it, how do you say it, what does it mean, what's the
      word,
That miracle thing, the thing that can't be so, quote,
      unquote, but just the same it's true,
That third-rail, million-volt exclamation mark, that ditto,
      ditto, ditto,
That stop, stop, go.

PANTOMIME

She sleeps, lips round, see how at rest,
How dark the hair, unstrung with all the world;
See the desirable eyes, how still, how white, sealed to all faces,
    locked against ruin, favor, and every risk,

Nothing behind them now but a pale mirage,
Through which the night-time ragman of the street below
    moves in a stiff and slow ballet,
Rhythmic from door to door, hallway to curb and gutter to
    stoop, bat's eyes bright, ravenous, ravenous for the
    carrion found and brought by tireless fingers to unreal
    lips;

Her hand relaxed beside the enchanted head, mouth red,
    small,
See how at peace the human form can be, whose sister, whose
    sweetheart, daughter of whom, and now the adorable
    ears, coral and pink,
Deaf to every footfall, every voice,
Midnight threats, the rancor stifled in rented bedrooms,
    appeals urged across kitchen tables and the fury that
    shouts them down, gunfire, screams, the sound of
    pursuit,
All of these less than the thunderous wings of a moth that
    circles here in the room where she sleeps,

Sleeps, dreaming that she sleeps and dreams.

DEVIL'S DREAM

But it could never be true;
How could it ever happen, if it never did before, and it's not
    so now?

But suppose that the face behind those steel prison bars—
Why do you dream about a face lying cold in the trenches
    streaked with rain and dirt and blood?
Is it the very same face seen so often in the mirror?
Just as though it could be true—

But what if it is, what if it is, what if it is, what if the thing
    that cannot happen really happens just the same,
Suppose the fever goes a hundred, then a hundred and one,
What if Holy Savings Trust goes from 98 to 88 to 78 to 68,
    then drops down to 28 and 8 and out of sight,
And the fever shoots a hundred two, a hundred three, a
    hundred four, then a hundred five and out?

But now there's only the wind and the sky and sunlight and
    the clouds,
With everyday people walking and talking as they always have
    before along the everyday street,
Doing ordinary things with ordinary faces and ordinary voices
    in the ordinary way,
Just as they always will—

Then why does it feel like a bomb, why does it feel like a target,
Like standing on the gallows with the trap about to drop,
Why does it feel like a thunderbolt the second before it strikes,
    why does it feel like a tight-rope walk high over hell?

Because it is not, will not, never could be true
That the whole wide, bright, green, warm, calm world goes:
CRASH.

LONGSHOT BLUES

What if all the money is bet on the odd;
Maybe the even wins,
What if odd wins, but it wins too late,

Whoever, wherever,
Ever knows who will be just the very one
This identical day at just this very, very, very, very hour,

Whose whole life falls between roto-press wheels moving
        quicker than light, to reappear, gorgeous and calm, on
        page eighteen—
Who reads all about it: *Prize-winning beauty trapped, accused,*

Who rides, and rides, and rides the big bright limited south,
        or is found, instead, on the bedroom floor with a
        stranger's bullet through the middle of his heart,
Clutching at a railroad table of trains to the south while the
        curtains blow wild and the radio plays and the sun
        shines on, and on, and on, and on,
Never having dreamed, at 9 o'clock, it would ever, at 10
        o'clock, end this way,

Forever feeling certain, but never quite guessing just exactly
        right,
As no man, anywhere, ever, ever, ever, ever, ever knows for
        sure—

Who wins the limousine, who wins the shaving cup, who
        nearly wins the million-dollar sweeps,
Who sails, and sails, and sails the seven seas,
Who returns safe from the fight at the mill gates, or wins, and

wins, and wins, and wins the plain pine coffin and a
union cortege to a joblot grave?—

With that long black midnight hour at last exploding into
      rockets of gold,
With every single cloud in the sky forever white and every
      white cloud always the winner in its race with death,
With every pair of eyes burning brighter than the diamonds
      that burn on every throat,
With every single inch of the morning all yours and every
      single inch of the evening yours alone, and all of it
      always, always, altogether new.

LUNCH WITH THE SOLE SURVIVOR

Meaning what it seems to when the day's receipts are counted
    and locked inside the store and the keys are taken
    home;
Feeling as it does to drive a car that rides and rides like a long,
    low, dark, silent streak of radio waves;
Just the way the hero feels in a smash-hit show;
Exactly like the giant in a Times Square sign making love
    across the sky to a lady made of light;

And then as though the switch were thrown and all of the
    lights went out;
Then as though the curtain fell and then they swept the aisles
    and then it's someone's turn to go,
Smoke the last cigarette, drink the last tall drink, go with the
    last long whistle of the midnight train as it fades among
    the hills—

Meaning what it seems to mean but feeling the way it does,
As though the wind would always, always blow away from
    home.

[MOA MOA MUNE]

Moa moa mune.

Piece puss Popple pie poon.

Noa.

BULLETIN

It comes to this,
To this and no other crisis or deadlock at the unforeseen hour,
No longer disguised,
With none above the hazards, nor anywhere away,

Comes to this, as armies march and cities burn,
Perhaps as checkerboards of light rise quietly, here, to the
      evening sky—
That every hazard comes, at last, to an end,

And it comes to this: The scalpel or the grave,
Rags, or music, or an unforeseen change
To this and no other role in a different city at a different hour,

Filled with life where there was no life before,
Death where there had been so much life;
Still reliving yesterday's coup and obeying, still, decrees long
      revoked;
How many times, hearing the heart beat, again aware that the
      heart beats just so many times,
(How many times?)

Then it comes to this:
This, the reward and this, the exchange,
This in return for the much or little so often planned;

Lock the windows, it comes to this,
Nothing bid for the dreams, nothing asked for the faith, it
      comes to this,
Foreclose upon the living, sublet the future and sue the dead,
      it comes to this,

As time, time, time still slips between the fingers and flows
       through the heart,
Time after time it comes to this,
Comes to this, it is a question of time,

Time after time,
This,
This and no other unforeseen way.

EN ROUTE

No violence,
Feeling may run high for a time, but remember, no violence,
And hurry, this moment of ours may not return.

But we will meet again? Yes, yes, now go,
Take only the latest instruments, use trained men in
    conservative tweeds who know how to keep their
    mouths shut,
The key positions must be held at all costs,
Bring guns, ropes, kerosene, it may be hard to persuade our
    beloved leader there must be no violence, no violence,

No violence, nothing left to chance, no hysteria and above all,
    no sentiment,
The least delay, the slightest mistake means the end, yes, the
    end—
Why, are you worried?

What is there to be worried about? It's fixed, I tell you, fixed,
    there's nothing to it, listen:
We will meet across the continents and years at 4 A.M. outside
    the Greek's when next the barometer reads 28.28 and
    the wind is from the South South-East bringing rain
    and hail and fog and snow;
Until then I travel by dead reckoning and you will take your
    bearings from the stars;

I cannot tell you more, except this: When you give the sign
    our agent will approach and say, "Have you seen the
    handwriting?" Then your man is to reply, "We have
    brought the money";

So we will make ourselves known to each other,
And it will be the same as before, perhaps even better, and we
     will arrange to meet again, as always, and say good-bye
     as now, and as we always will, and it will be O.K.; now
     go—

But what if the police find out? What if the wires are down?
     What if credit is refused? What if the banks fail? What
     if war breaks out? What if one of us should die?
What good can all of this be to you, or to us, or to anyone?
     Think of the price—

What are you trying to do, be funny? This is serious;
Hurry;
We must be prepared for anything, anything, anything.

HOLD THE WIRE

If the doorbell rings, and we think we were followed here; or
    if the bell should ring but we are not sure—
How can we decide?

IF IT'S ONLY THE GAS-MAN it may be all right,
IF HE'S AN AUTHORIZED PERSON IN A DOUBLE-BREASTED
    SUIT we'd better get it over with,
IF HE'S SOME NOBODY it may be good news,
But it might mean death IF THE SAMPLES ARE FREE,

HOW DO WE KNOW YOU'RE THE PERSON THAT YOU
    SAY?

Decide, decide,
We'd better be certain, if we live just once, and the sooner the
    better if we must decide,

BUT NOT IF IT'S WAR,
Not until we've counted the squares on the wallpaper over
    again, and added up the circles, and the circles match
    the squares—
Shall we move to the Ritz if rails go up, or live in potter's field
    if the market goes down?
If they sign for peace we return to the city, if they burn and
    bomb the city we will go to the mountains—
Who will kill us, if they do, and who will carry on our work?

Who are you, who are you, you have the right number but
    the connection's very poor;
We can hear you well enough, but we don't like what you're
    saying;

Yes, the order was received, but we asked for something else—

Are you the inventor who wants to sell us an invisible man?
WE'D CERTAINLY LIKE TO BUY HIM BUT WE HAVEN'T
    GOT THE PRICE;
Are you someone very famous from the Missing Persons
    Bureau but you can't recall the name?
COME AROUND NEXT AUGUST, WE'RE BUSY AS HELL
    TODAY;
If it's another bill collector there is no one here at all;

If it's Adolf Hitler, if it's the subway gorilla, if it's Jack the
    Ripper,
SEND HIM IN, SEND HIM IN, IF IT'S JOLLY JACK THE
    RIPPER IN A DOUBLE-BREASTED SUIT AND THE
    SAMPLES ARE FREE.

A DOLLAR'S WORTH OF BLOOD, PLEASE

With the last memo checked: *They will sign, success*; with the
    phone put down upon the day's last call; then with the
    door locked at last,
Wait; think;
What should the final memo be?

SAY THE LAST WORD,
SAY THE LAST WORD ADDING ALL WE'VE MADE AND
    LOST,
SAY THE LAST WORD THAT WEIGHS THE TRIUMPH
    SEALED IN INK AGAINST THE DEBT PRESERVED IN
    STONE AND THE PROFIT LOCKED IN STEEL,

One final word that the doorman knows, too, and the lawyer,
    and the drunk,
That the clerk knows, too, sure of tomorrow's pleasant
    surprise,
And the stranger, who knows there is nothing on earth more
    costly than hope and nothing in all the world held one-
    half so cheap as life,

One final word that need never be changed,
One final word to prove there is a use for the hard-bought
    distrust and the hard-won skill,
One final word that stands above and beyond the never-
    ending weakness and the never-failing strength,

SAY THE LAST WORD, YOU LONG STRAIGHT STREETS,
SAY THE LAST WORD, YOU WISE GUY, DUMB GUY, SOFT
    GUY, RIGHT GUY, FALL GUY, TOUGH GUY,
SAY THE LAST WORD, YOU BLACK SKY ABOVE.

PORTRAIT (2)

The clear brown eyes, kindly and alert, with 12-20 vision,
        give confident regard to the passing world through R.K.
        Lampert & Company lenses framed in gold;
His soul, however, is all his own;
Arndt Brothers necktie and hat (with feather) supply a touch
        of youth.

With his soul his own, he drives, drives, chats and drives,
The first and second bicuspids, lower right, replaced by
        bridgework, while two incisors have porcelain crowns;

(Render unto Federal, state, and city Caesar, but not unto
        time;
Render nothing unto time until Amalgamated Death serves
        final notice, in proper form;

The vault is ready;
The will has been drawn by Clagget, Clagget, Clagget & Brown;
The policies are adequate, Confidential's best, reimbursing
        for disability, partial or complete, with double
        indemnity should the end be a pure and simple
        accident)

Nothing unto time,
Nothing unto change, nothing unto fate,
Nothing unto you, and nothing unto me, or to any other
        known or unknown party or parties, living or deceased;

But Mercury shoes, with special arch supports, take much of
        the wear and tear;
On the course, a custombuilt driver corrects a tendency to slice;

Love's ravages have been repaired (it was a textbook case) by
    Drs. Schultz, Lightner, Mannheim, and Goode,
While all of it is enclosed in excellent tweed, with Mr.
    Baumer's personal attention to the shoulders and the
    waist;

And all of it now roving, chatting amiably through space in a
    Plymouth 6,
With his soul (his own) at peace, soothed by Walter
    Lippmann, and sustained by Haig & Haig.

A PATTERN

The alarm that shatters sleep, at least, is real;
Certainly the razor is real, and there is no denying the need
    for coffee and an egg;
Are there any questions, or is this quite clear, and true?

Surely it is morning, and in the mail the chainstore people
    offer a new Fall line;
There is a bill for union dues, a request for additional
    support;
Then the news: somewhere a million men are on the march
    again, elsewhere the horror mounts; and there are
    incidental leprosies—
(Briefly, here, the recollection of some old, imagined
    splendor, to be quickly dropped and crushed
    completely out.)

Are there any questions?
Has anyone any objections to make?
Can a new political approach or a better private code evolve
    from this?
Does it hold any premise based on faith alone?

Or are you, in fact, a privileged ghost returned, as usual, to
    haunt yourself?
A vigorous, smiling corpse come back to tour the morgues?
To inspect the scene of the silent torture and the invisible
    death, and then to report?

And if to report, are there any different answers now, at last?

TAKE A LETTER

Would you like to live, yourself, the way that other people do,
Would you like to be the kind of man you've always dreamed
  you'd be,
Do you know that tax consultants get very good pay,
Or would you rather become a detective, and trap your man,

ARREST HIM, ARREST HIM
How do you know you can't compose
ARREST THAT MAN
Would you like to have poise, speak Russian, Spanish,
  French,

ARREST THAT MAN, HE FITS THE DESCRIPTION
  PERFECTLY
Maybe you, too, can paint,
I KNOW HIM FROM HIS PICTURE, IT WAS IN THE
  MORNING PAPERS
Want to stop the tobacco habit, like to study aviation, own a
  genuine diamond ring,

I TELL YOU, IT'S HIM
Do you crawl with crazy urges,
Get those wild, wild feelings that you can't control,
IT'S HIM, IT'S HIM, HE'S HERE AGAIN, HE'S WANTED,
  IT'S HIM

Feel a big, strange, jumpy, weird, crazy new impulse,
Want to own your own home and wear the very best clothes,
Would you like to live and love and learn as other people do,

STOP HIM, HE SOUNDS JUST EXACTLY LIKE THE

MISSING BOSTON HEIR
HOLD HIM, HE MIGHT EVEN BE THE SENATOR FROM
   THE SOUTH WHOSE MIND WENT BLANKER STILL
ARREST THAT MAN, HE FITS THE HUMAN GIRAFFE
   FROM A TO Z

But he never could be you,
The most impressive bankrupt in the most exclusive club,
Or the mildest, coolest madman on the whole Eastern coast.

C STANDS FOR CIVILIZATION

They are able, with science, to measure the millionth of a
    millionth of an electron-volt,
THE TWENTIETH CENTURY COMES BUT ONCE
The natives can take to caves in the hills, said the British
    M.P., when we bomb their huts,
THE TWENTIETH CENTURY COMES BUT ONCE

Electric razors;
I am the law, said Mayor Hague;
The lynching was televised, we saw the whole thing from
      beginning to end, we heard the screams and the crackle
      of flames in a soundproof room,
THE TWENTIETH CENTURY COMES BUT ONCE

You are born but once,
You have your chance to live but once,
You go mad and put a bullet through your head but once,

THE TWENTIETH CENTURY COMES BUT ONCE
Once too soon, or a little too late, just once too often,

But zooming through the night in Lockheed monoplanes the
      witches bring accurate pictures of the latest disaster
      exactly on time,
THE TWENTIETH CENTURY COMES BUT ONCE
ONLY ONCE, AND STAYS FOR BUT ONE HUNDRED
    YEARS.

AMERICAN RHAPSODY (4)

Tomorrow, yes, tomorrow,
There will suddenly be new success, like Easter clothes, and a
    strange and different fate,
And bona-fide life will arrive at last, stepping from a non-stop
    monoplane with chromium doors and a silver wing and
    straight white staring lights.

There will be the sound of silvery thunder again to stifle the
    insane silence;
A new, tremendous sound will shatter the final unspoken
    question and drown the last, mute, terrible reply;
Rockets, rockets, Roman candles, flares, will burst in every
    corner of the night, to veil with snakes of silvery fire the
    nothingness that waits and waits;
There will be a bright, shimmering, silver veil stretched
    everywhere, tight, to hide the deep, black, empty,
    terrible bottom of the world where people fall who are
    alone, or dead,

Sick or alone,
Alone or poor,
Weak, or mad, or doomed, or alone;

Tomorrow, yes, tomorrow, surely we begin at last to live,
With lots and lots of laughter,
Solid silver laughter,
Laughter, with a few simple instructions, and a bona-fide
    guarantee.

LITERARY

I sing of simple people and the hardier virtues, by Associated
Stuffed Shirts & Company, Incorporated, 358 West
42d Street, New York, brochure enclosed;
Of Christ on the Cross, by a visitor to Calvary, first class;
Art deals with eternal, not current verities, revised from last
week's Sunday supplement;
Guess what we mean, in *The Literary System*; and a thousand
noble answers to a thousand empty questions, by a
patriot who needs the dough.

And so it goes.
Books are the key to magic portals. Knowledge is power. Give
the people light.
Writing must be such a nice profession.
Fill in the coupon. How do you know? Maybe you can be a
writer, too.

SOS

It is posted in the clubrooms,
It is announced in bright electric lights on all the principal
      streets, it is rumored, proclaimed, and radio'd out to sea,
SOS, SOS,
That her hair is a dark cloud and her eyes are deep blue;

Total strangers on the buses, at the beaches, in the parks,
Argue and discuss, as though they really knew,
Whether she prefers cork tips, likes a sweet or dry sherry,
      takes lemon with her tea,
SOS, SOS,

But they all agree that her hats, that her gowns, that her
      slippers, that her gloves, that her books, that her
      flowers,
And her past, and her present, and her future as stated in the
      cards, and as written in the stars,

Are all about right,
All dead right and dead against the law,

But her eyes are blue,
Blue for miles and miles and miles,
SOS, SOS,
Blue across the country and away across the sea.

AD

WANTED: Men;
Millions of men are WANTED AT ONCE in a big new field;
NEW, TREMENDOUS, THRILLING, GREAT.

If you've ever been a figure in the chamber of horrors,
If you've ever escaped from a psychiatric ward,
If you thrill at the thought of throwing poison into wells,
     have heavenly visions of people, by the thousands,
     dying in flames—

YOU ARE THE VERY MAN WE WANT
We mean business and our business is YOU
WANTED: A race of brand-new men.

Apply: Middle Europe;
No skill needed;
No ambition required; no brains wanted and no character
     allowed;

TAKE A PERMANENT JOB IN THE COMING PROFESSION
Wages: DEATH.

RADIO BLUES

Try 5 on the dial, try 10, 15;
Just the ghost of an inch, did you know, divides Japan and Peru?
20, 25;
Is that what you want, static and a speech and the fragment of
    a waltz, is that just right?
Or what do you want at twelve o'clock, with the visitors gone,
    and the Scotch running low?

30, 35, 35 to 40 and 40 to 50;
Free samples of cocoa, and the Better Beer Trio, and
    hurricane effects for a shipwreck at sea,
But is that just right to match the feeling that you have?

From 60 to 70 the voice in your home may be a friend of yours,
From 70 to 80 the voice in your home may have a purpose of
    its own,
From 80 to 90 the voice in your home may bring you love, or
    war,
But is that what you want?

100, 200, 300, 400;
Would you like to tune in on the year before last?
500, 600,
Or the decade after this, with the final results of the final
    madness and the final killing?

600, 700, 800, 900;
What program do you want at midnight, or at noon, at three
    in the morning,
At 6 A.M. or at 6 P.M.,
With the wind still rattling the windows, and shaking the blinds?

Would you care to bring in the stations past the stars?
Would you care to tune in on your dead love's grave?

1000, 2000, 3000, 4000;
Is that just right to match the feeling that you want?
5000, 6000;
Is that just right?
7000, 8000;
Is that what you want to match the feeling that you have?
9000, 10,000;
Would you like to tune in upon your very own life, gone
       somewhere far away?

THE PROGRAM

ACT ONE, Madrid-Barcelona,
ACT TWO, Paris in springtime, during the siege,
ACT THREE, London, Bank Holiday, after an air raid,
ACT FOUR, a short time later in the U.S.A.

EAT ZEPHYR CHOCOLATES
(Do not run for the exits in case of fire;
The Rome-Berlin theater has no exits)
SUZANNE BRASSIERES FOR PERFECT FORM

CAST, IN THE ORDER OF DISAPPEARANCE:
Infants,
Women and children,
Soldiers, sailors, miscellaneous crowds—

With 2,000 wounded and 1,000 dead,
10,000 wounded and 5,000 dead,
100,000 wounded and 50,000 dead,
10,000,000 wounded and 5,000,000 dead

(Scenes by the British ruling caste,
Costumes, Bonnet, Laval, et al.,
Spanish embargo by the U.S. Congress,
Music and lighting by Pius XI)

SMOKE EL DEMOCRACIES,
TRY THE NEW GOLGOTHA FOR COCKTAILS AFTER THE
        SHOW.

MEMO

Is there still any shadow there, on the rainwet window of the
    coffee pot,
Between the haberdasher's and the pinball arcade,
There, where we stood one night in the warm, fine rain, and
    smoked and laughed and talked.

Is there now any sound at all,
Other than the sound of tires, and motors, and hurrying feet,
Is there on tonight's damp, heelpocked pavement somewhere
    the mark of a certain toe, an especial nail, or the butt of
    a particular dropped cigarette?—

(There must be, there has to be, no heart could beat if this
    were not so,
That was an hour, a glittering hour, an important hour in a
    tremendous year)

Where we talked for a while of life and love, of logic and the
    senses, of you and of me, character and fate, pain,
    revolution, victory and death,

Is there tonight any shadow, at all,
Other than the shadows that stop for a moment and then
    hurry past the windows blurred by the same warm,
    slow, still rain?

HAPPY NEW YEAR

Speak as you used to;
Make the drinks and talk while you mix them, as you have so
        many times before;

IF IT IS TRUE THAT THE WORLD IS FOR SALE

Then say it, say it once and forget it, drop it, tell how it was
        at bridge or the grocer's,
Repeat what you said, what the grocer said, what the errand
        boy said, what the janitor said,
Say anything at all,

BUT IF IT IS TRUE THAT THE NERVE AND BREATH AND
PULSE ARE FOR SALE

Tell how it was in some gayer city or brighter place, speak of
        some bloodier, hungrier, more treacherous land,
Any other age, any far land,

BUT IF IT IS TRUE

Forget the answers that give no reason, forget the reasons that
        do not explain;
Do you remember the day at the lake, the evening at Sam's,
        the petrified forest, would you like to see London in
        June once more?

BUT IF IT IS TRUE, IF IT IS TRUE THAT ONLY LIARS
LOVE TRUTH

Pour the cocktails,
It is late, it is cold, it is still, it is dark;
Quickly, for time is swift and it is late, late, later than you
    think,
With one more hour, one more night, one more day
    somehow to be killed.

Q & A

Where analgesia may be found to ease the infinite, minute
    scars of the day;
What final interlude will result, picked bit by bit from the
    morning's hurry, the lunch-hour boredom, the fevers of
    the night;
Why this one is cherished by the gods, and that one not;
How to win, and win again, and again, staking wit alone
    against a sea of time;
Which man to trust and, once found, how far—

Will not be found in Matthew, Mark, Luke, or John,
Nor Blackstone, nor Gray's, nor Dun & Bradstreet, nor
    Freud, nor Marx,
Nor the sage of the evening news, nor the corner astrologist,
    nor in any poet,

Nor what sort of laughter should greet the paid
    pronouncements of the great,
Nor what pleasure the multitudes have, bringing lunch and
    the children to watch the condemned be plunged into
    death,

Nor why the sun should rise tomorrow,
Nor how the moon still weaves upon the ground, through the
    leaves, so much silence and so much peace.

FLOPHOUSE

Out of the frailest texture, somehow, and by some means
    from the shabbiest odds and ends,
If that is all there is;
In some way, of even the shaken will,

If, now, there is nothing else left,
Now and here in the pulse and breath,
Locked, somewhere, in the faded eyes, careful voice, graying
    hair, impassive face—

Out of the last remnants of skill and the last fragments of
    splendor,
If nothing else, now, remains,
Somehow there must be another day,
One more week, month, season to be pieced together,
Yet one more year must be raised, even from the ashes, and
    fanned to warmth and light,

Out of so much fantastic knowledge,
Surgeon, engineer, or clerk,
From the rags and scraps of dismembered life;

And if now there is nothing, nothing, nothing,
From even the fatigue sealed deep in the bones,
From even the chill in the oldest wound.

DEBRIS

The windows, faintly blue and gold in the sun's first light;
The mirages of the night suddenly replaced by the familiar room;
There is the empty bottle again, and the shattered glass (do
      you remember?);
Once more the light left burning in the lamp, and again the
      cluttered table-top (do you remember that?).

Do the faces and the words come back to you;
Do all the things the drinking and the talk once more blotted
      out come back to you now,
With bitter cigarettes in the morning air?

It strikes and strikes, insane but true: This life, this life, this
      life, this life;
While mist rises from the cool valleys,
And somewhere in fresh green hills there is the singing of a bird.

TOMORROW

Now that the others are gone, all of them, forever,
And they have your answer, and you have theirs, and the
    decision is made,
And the river of minutes between you widens to a tide of
    hours, a flood of days, a gulf of years and a sea of
    silence;

If, now, there are any questions you would like to ask of the
    shapes that still move and speak inaudibly in the empty
    room,
If there are any different arrangements you would like to
    suggest,

Make them to the riverboats, whose echoing whistle will be a
    clear reply,
Speak to the seagulls, their effortless flight will provide any
    answer you may wish to hear,
Ask the corner chestnut vendor, ask the tireless hammer and
    pulse of the subway,
Speak to the family on the illuminated billboard, forever
    friendly, or to the wind, or to the sign that sways and
    creaks above the stationer's door.

REQUIEM

Will they stop,
Will they stand there for a moment, perhaps before some
      shop where you have gone so many times
(Stand with the same blue sky above them and the stones, so
      often walked, beneath)

Will it be a day like this—
As though there could be such a day again—

And will their own concerns still be about the same,
And will the feeling still be this that you have felt so many
      times,
Will they meet and stop and speak, one perplexed and one
      aloof,

Saying: Have you heard,
Have you heard,
Have you heard about the death?

Yes, choosing the words, tragic, yes, a shock,
One who had so much of this, they will say, a life so filled
      with that,
Then will one say that the days are growing crisp again, the
      other that the leaves are turning,
And will they say good-bye, good-bye, you must look me up
      sometime, good-bye,
Then turn and go, each of them thinking, and yet, and yet,

Each feeling, if it were I, instead, would that be all,
Each wondering, suddenly alone, if that is all, in fact—

And will that be all?
On a day like this, with motors streaming through the fresh
    parks, the streets alive with casual people,
And everywhere, on all of it, the brightness of the sun.

IF MONEY

Why do you glance above you, for a moment, before you stop
    and go inside,
Why do you lay aside the book in the middle of the chapter
    to rise and walk to the window and stare into the street,
What do you listen for, briefly, among the afternoon voices,
    that the others do not,
Where are your thoughts, when the train whistles or the
    telephone rings, that you turn your head,
Why do you look, so often, at the calendar, the clock?

What rainbow waits, especially, for you,
Who will call your number, that angel chorales will float
    across the wire,
What magic score do you hope to make,
What final sweeps do you expect to win that the sky will drop
    clusters of stars in your hair and rain them at your feet,
What do you care whose voice, whose face, what hour, what
    day, what month, what year?

DANCE OF THE MIRRORS

You,
You at night and you in the sun,
You, farther than the pylons that walk, charged with light,
      across the fields of wheat and vanish through the hills,
You, invincible to change, and vulnerable to every wind that
      breathes upon these singing wires,
You, and the clouds above the wires, and the sky above the
      hills,

Yes, you,
Everywhere you, driving, laughing, arranging the day,
      efficient at the desk and brisk across the phone,
Telegrams and you, cocktails and you,
You and the image in the glass, and the knock at the door,
      then the second image, and the embrace, the kiss,
You, yes,
You, beneath the sculptured slab and raised mound, lost with
      the echo of Handel among cathedral beams—

You,
And all of the things that the world ignores, all of the things
      that the world has forgotten or never known,
You and the glow-worm, you and the rainbow, and the desert
      mirage, and the Northern Lights,
You, the footstep, you, the drumbeat and the dance, you, the
      trigger, the bullet, the target, and the shield.

MANHATTAN

Deep city,
Tall city, worn city, switchboard weaving what ghost horizons
      (who commands this cable, who escapes from this net,
      who shudders in this web?), cold furnace in the sky,
Guardian of this man's youth, graveyard of the other's, jailer
      of mine,
Harassed city, city knowing and naive, gay in the theaters,
      wary in the offices, starved in the tenements,
City ageless in the hospital delivery rooms and always too old
      or too young in the echoing morgues—

City for sale, for rent:
Five rooms, the former tenant's mattress, still warm, is leaving
      on the van downstairs;
Move in;
Here are the keys to the mailbox, the apartment, and the
      outside door,
It is yours, all yours, this city, this street, this house designed
      by a famous architect, you would know the name at
      once,
This house where the suicide lived, perhaps this floor, this
      room that reflects the drugstore's neon light;
Here, where the Wall Street clerk, the engineer, the socialist,
      the music teacher all lived by turns,
Move in,
Move in, arrange the furniture and live, live, go in the
      morning to return at night,
Relax, plan, struggle, succeed, watch the snow fall and hear
      the rain beat, know the liner's voice, see the evening
      plane, a star among stars, go west at the scheduled hour,
Make so many phone calls in the foyer again, have so many

business talks in the livingroom, there will be cocktails,
    cards, and the radio, adultery again (downtown), vomit
    (again) in the bath,
Scenes, hysterics, peace,
Live, live, live, and then move out,
Go with the worn cabinets and rugs all piled on the curb
    while the city passes and the incoming tenant
    (unknown to you) awaits,
Yes, go,
But remember, remember that, that year, that season—

Do you, do you, do you,
City within city, sealed fortress within fortress, island within
    enchanted island,
Do you, there outside the stationer's shop, still hear gunfire
    and instant death on winter nights,
Still see, on bright Spring afternoons, a thin gray figure
    crumple to the walk in the park
(Who stared, who shrugged and went home, who stayed and
    shivered until the ambulance arrived?—
Let the spirit go free, ship the body west),
Do you remember that, do you,
Do you remember the missing judge, the bigshot spender and
    the hundred dollar bills (did he do three years?),
The ballgame of ballgames (the fourth in the series, or was
    that the sixth?),
The reform party and the gambling clean-up (a ten-day
    laugh), the returning champion (what about it?), the
    abortion (so what?), the rape (who cares?),
The paralyzed newsboy, the taxi-driver who studied
    dramatics, the honest counterman, the salesman in love
    with the aviator's wife, the day at the zoo, the evening
    in the park, the perfect girl, the funny little guy with the

funny little face—

City, city, city,
Eye without vision, light without warmth, voice without
     mind, pulse without flesh,
Mirror and gateway, mirage, cloud against the sun,
Do you remember that, that year, that day, that hour, that
     name, that face,
Do you remember:

Only the day, fulfilled, as it burns in the million windows of
     the west,
Only the promise of the day, returning, as it flames on the
     roofs and spires and steeples of the east.

SCHEHERAZADE

Not the saga of your soul at grips with fate, bleedingheart, for
    we have troubles of our own,
Nor the inside story of the campaign scandal, wise-guy, for
    we were there ourselves, or else we have forgotten it
    years ago;
Not all the answers, oracle, to politics and life and love; you
    have them, but your book is out of date;
No, nor why you are not a heel, smooth baby, for that is a lie, nor
    why you had to become one, for that is much too true,
Nor the neighborhood doings five years ago, rosebud, nor the
    ruined childhood, nor the total story of friendship
    betrayed,
Nor how cynical you are, rumpot, and why you became so;

Give us, instead (if you must), something that we can use,
    like a telephone number,
Or something we can understand, like a longshot tip on
    tomorrow's card,
Or something that we have never heard before, like the
    legend of Ruth.

HOW DO I FEEL?

Get this straight, Joe, and don't get me wrong.
Sure, Steve, O.K., all I got to say is, when do I get the dough?

Will you listen for a minute? And just shut up? Let a guy
     explain?
Go ahead, Steve, I won't say a word.

Will you just shut up?
O.K., I tell you, whatever you say, it's O.K. with me.

What's O.K. about it, if that's the way you feel?
What do you mean, how I feel? What do you know, how I
     feel?

Listen, Joe, a child could understand, if you'll listen for a
     minute without butting in, and don't get so sore.
Sure, I know, you got to collect it first before you lay it out, I
     know that; you can't be left on a limb yourself.

Me? On a limb? For a lousy fifty bucks?
Take it easy, Steve, I'm just saying—

I'm just telling you—
Wait, listen—

Now listen, wait, will you listen for a minute? That's all I ask.
     Yes or no?
O.K., I only—

Yes or no?
O.K., O.K.

168

O.K., then, and you won't get sore? If I tell it to you straight?
Sure, Steve, O.K., all I got to say is, when do I get the dough?

ENGAGEMENTS FOR TOMORROW

Business of forcing a showdown.
Hit this hard, and take no excuses.
(Stuff about expenses. Business about the risks. Stuff about
    overhead.)

If the bank should call, stall them off.
Don't say yes or no, but it has to sound good. Maybe gone
    for the week.
Yes, left no word, but had hoped to be back, regret the delay
    and so forth and so on, will definitely return on such-
    and-such a date.

Lunch with so-and-so.
One highball, no more. Two at most. A walk to clear the
    head.

And stuff for all the other deals, for every possible turn and
    twist.
Wallop it hard. Keep them guessing. And naturally, no
    mistakes.
Cheerful stuff. Personality stuff. Courteous stuff.
Tough, if necessary, and rough. But careful.
Give it the business. All of it. The works.

And finally the big stuff.
(Make a note of this, must think it all out.)
Stuff about the reason for all the other stuff.
Business about loyalty (the need for, and so forth), brains
    (stuff, stuff), and something about the breaks.
Business about what it is that makes the whole business go
    round without any beginning and without any end, like

the wind or like the ocean, a feeling to tear the heart out of a wooden Indian's breast.

Straight stuff. Real stuff. True stuff. The McCoy.
Sometime. Soon. Before it's too late.
Because, after all.
And so on, and so on, and so on, and so on.

THE DOCTOR WILL SEE YOU NOW

This patient says he is troubled by insomnia, and that one
      finds it difficult to stay awake.
Miss A confides a fear of narrow places. Mr. B, in Wall Street,
      is everywhere pursued by a secret agent, and by a certain
      X-ray eye that transmits his business secrets to a rival
      clique.
Practice, in general, is good. The patients are of all classes. In
      every case the problem is to exorcise these devils. And to
      adjust.

To adjust the person to his gods, and to his own estate, and to
      the larger group.
Adjust to the conventions and the niceties. That is, by
      inference, to the Chamber of Commerce, to the local
      police, to the Society of Ancient Instruments, and to
      the West Side Bicycle Club.
Adjust the kleptomaniac to modes of safer intercourse. The
      bigamist to the canons of the church, and to the
      criminal code.
(And all of these, perhaps, to him.)
Adjust the devils to the saints. The saints to the smiling
      devils. The martyrs to the renegades, and each of them,
      alike, to the hearty fools.

Adjust to the present, and to a longer view.
To cities shining in the sky tonight, and smoking in the dust
      tomorrow.
Adjust the mothers. And the husbands. And the fathers. And
      the wives.
Adjust to the sons, once resolute, now dead. And to the
      daughters, living but mad.

Adjust to the morning crucifixion and the evening calm.
Adjust them all. And then adjust them to this new
     perspective. Adjust.

Mr. X believes that tall brunettes can bring him only grief.
     Mrs. Y walks backward to escape the evil eye. Mr. Z
     hears voices.
They have nothing new to communicate, but he is disturbed.

Madness, never obsolete, grows fashionable.
Do its canons, unlike those of any other pursuit, seem to
     make unreasonable demands upon the patient?
Or require of the practitioner, himself, adjustments too
     fantastic, perhaps too terrible to reach?

READINGS, FORECASTS, PERSONAL GUIDANCE

It is not—I swear it by every fiery omen to be seen these
       nights in every quarter of the heavens, I affirm it by all
       the monstrous portents of the earth and of the sea—
It is not that my belief in the true and mystic science is
       shaken, nor that I have lost faith in the magic of the
       cards, or in the augury of dreams, or in the great and
       good divinity of the stars—
No, I know still whose science fits the promise to the
       inquirer's need, invariably, for a change: Mine. My
       science foretells the wished-for journey, the business
       adjustment, the handsome stranger. (Each of these is
       considered a decided change.)
And I know whose skill weighs matrimony, risks a flier in
       steel or wheat against the vagaries of the moon—
(Planet of dreams, of mothers and of children, goddess of
       sailors and of all adventurers, forgive the liberty. But a
       man must eat.) My skill,
Mine, and the cunning and the patience. (Two dollars for the
       horoscope in brief and five for a twelve months' forecast
       in detail.)

No, it is this: The wonders that I have seen with my own eyes.

It is this: That still these people know, as I do not, that what
       has never been on earth before may still well come to
       pass,
That always, always there are new and brighter things beneath
       the sun,
That surely, in bargain basements or in walk-up flats, it must
       be so that still from time to time they hear wild angel
       voices speak.

It is this: That I have known them for what they are,
Seen thievery written plainly in their planets, found greed and
    murder and worse in their birth dates and their
    numbers, guilt etched in every line of every palm,
But still a light burns through the eyes they turn to me, a
    need more moving than the damned and dirty dollars
    (which I must take) that form the pattern of their larger
    hopes and deeper fears.

And it comes to this: That always I feel another hand, not
    mine, has drawn and turned the card to find some
    incredible ace,
Always another word I did not write appears in the spirit
    parchment prepared by me,
Always another face I do not know shows in the dream, the
    crystal globe, or the flame.

And finally, this: Corrupt, in a world bankrupt and corrupt,
    what have I got to do with these miracles?
If they want miracles, let them consult someone else.
Would they, in extremity, ask them of a physician? Or expect
    them, in desperation, of an attorney? Or of a priest? Or
    of a poet?

Nevertheless, a man must eat.
Mrs. Raeburn is expected at five. She will communicate with
    a number of friends and relatives long deceased.

NET

Surely, surely, whether broken on the wheel, or burned at the
     stake, or nailed to the cross,
Or brought to death by rack, bowstring, strappado, screw,
By bludgeon, pike, lance, javelin, mace, scimitar, arrow, sword,
Bayonet, bullet, shrapnel, shell, grenade, bomb, or gas,

It is as certain as the fall of summer rain,
Sure as the return of winter snow and certain as the symmetry
     of every flake that falls,

That the flesh of infidel, heretic, and faithful is equally weak
     and fails, falls, dies, rots,
Certain that each is forever doomed and lost, and there where
     he lies is forever damned, and damned, and damned,
     and damned.

AGENT NO. 174 RESIGNS

The subject was put to bed at midnight, and I picked him up
    again at 8 A.M.
I followed, as usual, while he made his morning rounds.
After him, and like him, I stepped into taxis, pressed elevator
    buttons, fed tokens into subway turnstiles, kept him
    under close surveillance while he dodged through heavy
    traffic and pushed through revolving doors.

We lunched very pleasantly, though separately, for $1.50,
    plus a quarter tip. (Unavoidable expense.)
Then we resumed. For twenty minutes on the corner the
    subject watched two shoeshine boys fish for a dime
    dropped through a subway grate. No dice.
And then on. We had a good stare into a window made of
    invisible glass.
Another hour in a newsreel movie—the usual famine, fashions,
    Florida bathing, and butchery. Then out again.
I realized, presently, that the subject was following a blonde
    dish in blue he had seen somewhere around.
(Nothing, ultimately, came of this.)
And shortly after that a small black pooch, obviously lost,
    attached himself to your agent's heels.
Does he fit into this picture anywhere at all?
It doesn't matter. In any case, I resign.

Because the situation, awkward to begin with, swiftly
    developed angles altogether too involved.
Our close-knit atomic world (night would disperse it) woven
    of indifference (the blonde's), of love (the subject's), of
    suspicion (my province), and of forlorn hope (the
    dog's), this little world became a social structure, and
    then a solar system with dictates of its own.

We had our own world's fair in a pinball arcade. The blonde
    had her picture taken in a photomat.
And so (whether by law, or by magnetism) did we.
But still there was nothing, in any of this, essentially new to
    report.

Except, I began to think of all the things the subject might
    have done, but he did not do.
All the exciting scenes he might have visited but failed to visit,
    all the money I might have watched him make or
    helped him spend, the murders he might have
    committed, but somehow he refrained.
What if he met a visiting star from the coast? And she had a
    friend?
Or went to Havana, or the South Sea Isles?
Did my instructions, with expenses, cover the case?
But none of this happened. Therefore, I resign.

I resign, because I do not think this fellow knew what he was
    doing.
I do not believe the subject knew, at all clearly, what he was
    looking for, or from what escaping.
Whether from a poor man's destiny (relief and the Bellevue
    morgue), or a middle-class fate (always the same job
    with a different firm), or from a Kreuger-Musica
    denouement.
And then, whose life am I really leading, mine or his? His or
    the blonde's?

And finally because this was his business, all of it, not mine.
Whatever conscience, boredom, or penal justice he sought to
    escape, it was his business, not mine in the least. I want

no part of it.

I have no open or concealed passion for those doors we opened together, those turnstiles we pushed, those levers, handles, knobs.

Nor for the shadow of a bathing beauty on a screen, nor the picture of a ruined village. Nor any interest in possible defects shown by invisible glass.

I mean, for instance, I do not (often) feel drawn toward that particular type of blonde in that particular shade of blue.

And I have no room to keep a dog.

Therefore, this resignation.

Whether signed in a Turkish bath, with a quart of rye, or in a good hotel, sealed with a bullet, is none of your business. None at all.

There is no law compelling any man on earth to do the same, second hand.

I am tired of following invisible lives down intangible avenues to fathomless ends.

Is this clear?

Herewith, therefore, to take effect at once, I resign.

JACKPOT

Having weighed, as a man must weigh, having measured for
      precision, as a person must, having tested, as one must
      test, for safety, for convenience, and for strength,
Today, finally, the equipment and the power and the controls
      all check; today the records tally and your accounts
      balance, at last;
Now, on this day that you have dreamed about so often but
      had scarcely hoped would come to pass,
You have, then, this incredible moment of victory.
(Incredible, for there were times when faith alone was not
      enough. When neither skill, nor wit, nor nerve sufficed,
      and luck ruled all.)

That others failed where you did not, you are aware. You
      know, too, that many lost much. Some even died.
(The man who invented this, today's household necessity, is
      on home relief.
He who sold these luxury products made millions, and lost
      them, and made them again. And is blind, did you
      know?
This one inherited a kingdom, cruises the Caribbean in
      winter, collects bottle-caps, knits ties and sweaters, does
      basket-weaving, consults his chiropractor before daring
      to breathe.
This idol of the stage and screen regularly visits an insane
      son.)

Is it, then, a gift, or a curse? And what do you care? Now?

Now, with the final edition ready (you have discovered life on
      Mars) and the presses set to roll.

Now, with the harvest in, at last, and the moon finally new
and full, the tide at its height.
Now, with the motors warm, the direct wire open, the
weather clear and the track fast.
Now, O.K., you can write your own ticket, straight down the
line it is all yours.

PACT

It is written in the skyline of the city (you have seen it, that
    bold and accurate inscription), where the gray and gold
    and soot-black roofs project against the rising or the
    setting sun,
It is written in the ranges of the farthest mountains, and
    written by the lightning bolt,
Written, too, in the winding rivers of the prairies, and in the
    strangely familiar effigies of the clouds,

That there will be other days and remoter times, by far, than
    these, still more prodigious people and still less credible
    events,
When there will be a haze, as there is today, not quite blue
    and not quite purple, upon the river, a green mist upon
    the valley below, as now,

And we will build, upon that day, another hope (because
    these cities are young and strong),
And we will raise another dream (because these hills and fields
    are rich and green),

And we will fight for all of this again, and if need be again,
And on that day, and in that place, we will try again, and this
    time we shall win.

YES, THE AGENCY CAN HANDLE THAT

You recommend that the motive, in Chapter 8, should be
    changed from ambition to a desire, on the heroine's
    part, for doing good; yes, that can be done.
Installment 9 could be more optimistic, as you point out, and
    it will not be hard to add a heartbreak to the class
    reunion in Chapter 10.
Script 11 may have, as you say, too much political intrigue of
    the sordid type; perhaps a diamond-in-the-rough
    approach would take care of this. And 12 has a
    reference to war that, as you suggest, had better be
    removed; yes.
This brings us to the holidays, that coincide with our prison
    sequence. With the convicts' Christmas supper, if you
    approve, we can go to town.

Yes, this should not be difficult. It can be done. Why not?

And script 600 brings us to the millennium, with all the
    fiends of hell singing Bach chorales.
And in 601 we explore the Valleys of the Moon (why not?),
    finding in each of them fresh Fountains of Youth.

And there is no mortal ill that cannot be cured by a little
    money, or lots of love, or by a friendly smile; no.
And few human hopes go unrealized; no.
And the rain does not ever, anywhere, fall upon corroded
    monuments and the graves of the forgotten dead.

HOMAGE

They said to him, "It is a very good thing that you have done,
    yes, both good and great, proving this other passage to
    the Indies. Marvelous," they said. "Very. But where,
    Señor, is the gold?"
They said: "We like it, we admire it very much, don't
    misunderstand us, in fact we think it's almost great. But
    isn't there, well, a little too much of this Prince of
    Denmark? After all, there is no one quite like you in
    your lighter vein."
"Astonishing," they said. "Who would have thought you had
    it in you, Orville?" They said, "Wilbur, this machine of
    yours is amazing, if it works, and perhaps some day we
    can use it to distribute eggs, or to advertise."

And they were good people, too. Decent people.
They did not beat their wives. They went to church. And
    they kept the law.

ANY MAN'S ADVICE TO HIS SON

If you have lost the radio beam, then guide yourself by the
    sun or the stars.
(By the North Star at night, and in daytime by the compass
    and the sun.)
Should the sky be overcast and there are neither stars nor a
    sun, then steer by dead reckoning.
If the wind and direction and speed are not known, then trust
    to your wits and your luck.

Do you follow me? Do you understand? Or is this too
    difficult to learn?
But you must and you will, it is important that you do,
Because there may be troubles even greater than these that I
    have said.

Because, remember this: Trust no man fully.
Remember: If you must shoot at another man squeeze, do not
    jerk the trigger. Otherwise you may miss and die,
    yourself, at the hand of some other man's son.
And remember: In all this world there is nothing so easily
    squandered, or once gone, so completely lost as life.

I tell you this because I remember you when you were small,
And because I remember all your monstrous infant boasts
    and lies,
And the way you smiled, and how you ran and climbed, as no
    one else quite did, and how you fell and were bruised,
And because there is no other person, anywhere on earth,
    who remembers these things as clearly as I do now.

DISCUSSION AFTER THE FIFTH OR SIXTH

Now, about that other one, the sober one
(To be objective, for a change, about one's public self. After
    all, each of us has that stupider side),
Yes, you have seen him around, that self-appointed Dr. Jekyll
    who shares (reluctantly) by day this name and being
    with his Mr. Hyde (as he would put it) of the night,

Yes, him,
That fellow with this face, this voice, and even (by some
    crashing magic we will not go into now) possessed with
    a few of the same superficial traits,
That one whose first awakening voice is a hoarse, barbaric
    blast (you know against whom), who damns the excess
    (however moderate), deplores the extravagance and
    winces (as he reaches for the aspirin) at the smallest
    memory,
That fellow with the curdled eyes and not quite steady hands
    (poor guy, he must be slipping), to say nothing of a
    disposition that is really a wonderful, wonderful thing
    in itself,

Yes, well, now that you have the picture, take him,
And all his pathetic protests and his monumental vows to
    abstain, totally, forthwith (these need not concern us here)
(Two more of the same)
But, more especially, his pious recantations and denials, his
    ceaseless libel of one who is (why dodge the issue?) his
    mental, physical, and yes, moral superior—
But do you begin to see the point?

Because the point is this (he talks of self-respect, and decency
    is a favorite word of his), the point is this:
Does he think that he is the only one?
Does he think that he is the only man on earth who has felt
    this thing?
The only person ever to sit and watch the rain drive against
    the lighted windows, revolving at once some private
    trouble and knowing, for everything that breathes, a
    cold impersonal dismay?

From which (drinking, he says, is just an escape) he searches
    daily, down a thousand familiar avenues, for an escape
    that simply does not exist
(Those Chinese dreams he palms as reality, those childish
    ambitions, and then that transparent guile of his),
That fool (who must, it seems, be suffered) (but not gladly),
    that bore (and who has tolerated most? Has overlooked
    most? Which of us has forgiven most), that fool in love
    with some frowsy fate that plays with him as a cat plays
    with a mouse,
That fool (and this, at last, is the question), what would his
    decency amount to, but for the simple decency of this
    escape?

And if this is not true,
If this is not the final truth, then no one here is drunk, drunk
    as a lord of ancient France,
If this is not the inescapable truth, then the night is not dark
    but bright as day, and the lights along the street are not
    really made of burning pearls and rubies dipped in
    liquid fire,
If this is not true, the truth itself, as hard as hell and stronger

than death,
Then time does not fly but life grows younger by the hour,
    and the rain is not falling, falling, everywhere falling,
And there are not, here, only pleasant sights and sounds and a
    pleasant warmth.

PAY-OFF

Do you, now, as the news becomes known,
And you have the telegram still in your hand, here in the
      familiar room where there is no sound but the ticking
      of the clock,
Or there on the street, where you see the first headlines, and
      it is true this time, really true, actual as the green and
      red of the traffic lights, as real as the fruit vendor's
      rhythmic cry,

Do you recall any being other than this, before your world
      suddenly shook and settled to this new, strange axis
      upon which it will turn, now, always while you live?
Does it seem possible, now, you were ever bored? Or drunk
      and confident? Or sober and afraid?
Will the sound of the clock ever fade, or the voice of the
      vendor sometime stop?

FIVE A.M.

Street by street the lights go out, and the night turns gray,
    bringing respite to this and to all other agencies,
With the gears of commerce unmeshed and stopped, the
    channels of communication slowed and stilled
(Radio, ticker, and spirit control)—

Bringing peace, briefly, to the members of the board and
    bench and staff,
Sleep, for a space, to the journeymen of the switchboard and
    the dictaphone,
Rest to the lieutenants of steel, and wool, and coal, and
    wheat,
And to the envoys from abroad (Her Majesty's, His
    Excellency's, and the mysterious Mr. X),
And to the representatives of the people (both houses), and to
    the vicars of the Lord (conformist and dissident)
And to the inspectors of the arson, forgery, bomb, and
    homicide squads—

While the crated shipments of this agency (with those of
    others) stand in guarded sheds at Quebec,
Wait for release on rainswept wharves of Shanghai and the Rio,
Move, slowly, from a dark siding in Butte.

190

PAYDAY IN THE MORGUE

Go ahead, will you, see who's there, knocking at the door.
Knocking? Wasn't that a voice? Or the telephone ringing? Or
    a piano being played somewhere upstairs?

It may have been a voice, but there is no phone or piano in
    the place.
On the radio, I meant. A sort of a concert from very far away.

Radio? Where do you see any radio in here? Go ahead, will
    you, see who it is, we'll save the hand, and you can trust
    us with your chips.
I can, can I? How do I know I can? I never saw any of you
    people before tonight. Besides, how do I know whose is
    the body, and whose the voice? It might even be the
    future, and if it is, then what?

You would say that.
Well, it could be, couldn't it?

Don't mention that word. Don't even think the thought. Just
    answer the door.
Answer it yourself. These are the first decent cards I held all
    evening. Let them go ahead and knock. Some one,
    somewhere has to die, tonight, but some other person
    might be lucky as hell.

Maybe it's the wagon from the morgue, that's all, bringing
    somebody cold and dripping from the river, or bloody
    from the street. And that would be O.K., they were all
    square guys before the curtains went down.
Maybe it's Thunderbolt again, the Iroquois chief, with

another message from some one long departed, and
who's afraid of him?
Maybe they're the things Mr. Johnson's always seeing in
dreams. Or a few of Mrs. Edwards' remote controls. Or
the tiny bouncing men in Mr. Brown's DTs. And they
aren't so bad, just crazy, that's all.

Yes, but wouldn't they come in by themselves, if it's them?
Walls wouldn't stop them. Not a little wood, and stone,
and steel.
Maybe we should ask. I guess we'd better.

Is that you, Mr. Johnson, in Coffin Compartment 404? Did
you ring, Mrs. Edwards, in Compartment 13? Are you
haunted, Mr. Brown, by the torso murder baby? Are
you haunted again by the man without a name?
Mr. Johnson? Mrs. Edwards? Mr. Brown? Mr. Brown?

*They must be deaf in there. Deaf and blind. Deafer than ashes
and blinder than dust.*

Deafer than ashes, is that what I heard?
Did you hear those voices, did you hear them, too?
I wouldn't answer that, not if I were you. Like something
straight from the Age of Ice.
Or something from the future like I said, didn't I say?

Now don't get excited. We'll just keep quiet and deal the
cards and whoever it is they'll get tired and go away.
How many for you?
One.
Two cards here, and I'm in with a dollar.
I'll just see that, and I raise you three.
Up another five.

Gentlemen, aren't the stakes a little too high, or is the sky the
     limit?

I'd answer the door, but you know how it is. A fellow with a
     family.
Sure.
It's either them or us, see what I mean?
Or you could put it like this, either them or some one else.
Either millions of men with feet like lizards and the heads of
     rats, or gods made of music bathed in blinding light.

CLASS REUNION

And Steve, the athlete, where is he?
And Clark, the medico who played Chopin and quoted
      Keats, where is he now?
And Dale, who built that bridge (so often shown in the
      rotogravures) taming a veritable Styx on some fabulous
      continent?
Elvira, who dealt in nothing less than truths that were
      absolute?
And Henderson, law student who floated a financial empire,
      is it true he died in jail?

And true that Steve is bald, and broke, and fat?
And true that Dale's long bridge is a tangle of junk, destroyed
      by dynamite in a great retreat?

Perhaps the empire of credit was not, after all, so shrewd or
      bold.
Perhaps Clark did much better in drygoods, to tell the truth,
      than he would have with surgery or Keats.
Perhaps Dale's bridge was not, really, a towering miracle. Or
      it may be such miracles are not so important, after all.
It may be Elvira came as close to the thing, with her
      absolutes, as anyone else. She's the mother of five.

White mice, running mazes in behavior tests, have never
      displayed more cunning than these, who arrived by
      such devious routes at such incredible ends.

For it is the end, surely? We knew the story to be working
      toward an end, and this, then, is in fact the end?
And there is no chance we will be met tonight, or tomorrow

night, or any other night, by destiny moving in still
another direction?
As one might meet a figure on a dark street, and hear from
the shadows a familiar but unwelcome voice:

"Hello, remember me? We had an appointment, but you
broke it to attend a class reunion.
You can forget that, now. Tonight something new is coming up.
Let's go."

PORTRAIT OF A COG

You have forgotten the monthly conference. Your four
        o'clock appointment waits in the ante-room. The
        uptown bureau is on the wire again.
Most of your correspondence is still unanswered, these bills
        have not been paid, and one of your trusted agents has
        suddenly resigned.
And where are this morning's reports? They must be filed at
        once, at once.

It is an hour you do not fully understand, a mood you have
        had so many times but cannot quite describe,
It is a fantastic situation repeated so often it is commonplace
        and dull,
It is an unlikely plot, a scheme, a conspiracy you helped to
        begin but do not, any longer, control at all.

Perhaps you are really in league with some maniac partner
        whom you have never met, whose voice you have never
        heard, whose name you do not even know.
It is a destiny that is yours, yours, all yours and only yours, a
        fate you have long ago disowned and disavowed.

When they dig you up, in a thousand years, they will find you
        in just this pose,
One hand upon the buzzer, the other reaching for the phone,
        eyes fixed upon the calendar, feet firmly on the office rug.

Shall you ask the operator for an outside wire? And then
        dictate this memo:
No (overwhelming) passions. No (remarkable) vices. No
        (memorable) virtues. No (terrific) motives.

Yes, when they dig you up, like this, a thousand years from
    now,
They will say: Just as he was in life. A man typical of the
    times, engaged in typical affairs.
Notice the features, especially, they will say. How self-assured
    they are, and how serene.

AMERICAN RHAPSODY (5)

First you bite your fingernails. And then you comb your hair
    again. And then you wait. And wait.
(They say, you know, that first you lie. And then you steal,
    they say. And then, they say, you kill.)

Then the doorbell rings. Then Peg drops in. And Bill. And
    Jane. And Doc.
And first you talk, and smoke, and hear the news and have a
    drink. Then you walk down the stairs.
And you dine, then, and go to a show after that, perhaps, and
    after that a night spot, and after that come home again,
    and climb the stairs again, and again go to bed.

But first Peg argues, and Doc replies. First you dance the
    same dance and you drink the same drink you always
    drank before.
And the piano builds a roof of notes above the world.
And the trumpet weaves a dome of music through space. And the
    drum makes a ceiling over space and time and night.
And then the table-wit. And then the check. Then home
    again to bed.
But first, the stairs.

And do you now, baby, as you climb the stairs, do you still
    feel as you felt back there?
Do you feel again as you felt this morning? And the night
    before? And then the night before that?

(They say, you know, that first you hear voices. And then you
    have visions, they say. Then, they say, you kick and
    scream and rave.)

198

Or do you feel: What is one more night in a lifetime of
    nights?
What is one more death, or friendship, or divorce out of two,
    or three? Or four? Or five?
One more face among so many, many faces, one more life
    among so many million lives?

But first, baby, as you climb and count the stairs (and they
    total the same), did you, sometime or somewhere, have
    a different idea?
Is this, baby, what you were born to feel, and do, and be?

A LA CARTE

Some take to liquor, some turn to prayer,
Many prefer to dance, others to gamble, and a few resort to
      gas or the gun.
(Some are lucky, and some are not.)

Name your choice, any selection from one to twenty-five:
Music from Harlem? A Viennese waltz on the slot-machine
      phonograph at Jack's Bar & Grill? Or a Brahms
      Concerto over WXV?
(Many like it wild, others sweet.)

Champagne for supper, murder for breakfast, romance for
      lunch and terror for tea,
This is not the first time, nor will it be the last time the world
      has gone to hell.
(Some can take it, and some cannot.)

GENTLEMAN HOLDING HANDS WITH GIRL

Of you, both the known and unknown quantities, but more
    especially, of those unknown,
Of the mysteries of the arches and the ligaments, the question
    of the nerves and muscles, the haunting riddle of the
    joints,
Of jetblack eyes and nutbrown hair,
Of the latest movie star, and Hollywood, and of a job that
    pays real dough, and then of debts, current and past.
    The past?

Of the distant past. Of nutbrown eyes and jetblack hair. Of
    blue eyes, and of yellow hair. Red hair and hazel eyes.
    Gray eyes.
Of perfection: Can it ever be obtained?
Of time and change and chance. Right now, returning from
    Arcturus, of you.

Of the crazy hats and negligées in the shops along the avenue,
    of perfume and of lace;
A startling fragment abruptly, here, shoots to the surface out
    of early youth;
Of Freud, and of Krafft-Ebing for a moment. Of Havelock
    Ellis (must read, some day, in full).

Is it like stepping into a looking-glass, or like flying through
    space?

Of the indubitable beginning of life, and of its indubitable end,
Of the mirage within a mirage,
With all of the daughters of all the daughters summed up, at
    last, in you.

LOVE, 20¢ THE FIRST QUARTER MILE

All right, I may have lied to you, and about you, and made a
     few pronouncements a bit too sweeping, perhaps, and
     possibly forgotten to tag the bases here or there,
And damned your extravagance, and maligned your tastes,
     and libeled your relatives, and slandered a few of your
     friends,
O.K.,
Nevertheless, come back.

Come home. I will agree to forget the statements that you
     issued so copiously to the neighbors and the press,
And you will forget that figment of your imagination, the
     blonde from Detroit;
I will agree that your lady friend who lives above us is not
     crazy, bats, nutty as they come, but on the contrary
     rather bright,
And you will concede that poor old Steinberg is neither a
     drunk, nor a swindler, but simply a guy, on the
     eccentric side, trying to get along.
(Are you listening, you bitch, and have you got this straight?)

Because I forgive you, yes, for everything,
I forgive you for being beautiful and generous and wise,
I forgive you, to put it simply, for being alive, and pardon
     you, in short, for being you.

Because tonight you are in my hair and eyes,
And every street light that our taxi passes shows me you again,
     still you,
And because tonight all other nights are black, all other hours
     are cold and far away, and now, this minute, the stars
     are very near and bright.

Come back. We will have a celebration to end all
    celebrations.
We will invite the undertaker who lives beneath us, and a
    couple of the boys from the office, and some other
    friends,
And Steinberg, who is off the wagon, by the way, and that
    insane woman who lives upstairs, and a few reporters, if
    anything should break.

STATISTICS

Sixty souls, this day, will arrange for travel to brighter lands
    and bluer skies.
At sunset, two thousand will stop for a moment to watch
    birds flying south.
In five thousand rooms the shades will be drawn, with the
    lamps adjusted, the tables prepared, and the cards
    arranged for solitaire.
This day, ninety-four will divorce, while thirty-three persons
    meet great, though unexpected, financial success.
Twenty-one, on this day, will elect to die.

These are the figures, incontrovertibly; such are the facts.
Sixty, two thousand, five thousand, ninety-four, thirty-three,
    twenty-one.

Actuary of actuaries, when these ordained numbers shall have
    been fulfilled at the scheduled hour,
What shall be done to prove and redeem them, to explain and
    preserve them?
How shall these accounts be balanced, otherwise than in
    personal flesh and blood?

By cold addition or subtraction? And on what fiery
    comptometer?
Because the need for an answer that is correct is very great.

SUBURBAN SUNSET, PRE-WAR, OR WHAT ARE WE MISSING?

These models (they were the very last word) arrived in the
    morning.
(The stock jobs came in three sizes: Small, medium, and
    rather huge)
Throughout breakfast, they absorbed every child in the
    village.
By noon, the wives and widows of the county declared
    themselves ravished.
Then in the evening the gentlemen returned from the city, to
    digest this affair. And were, in their turn, consumed.

Perhaps, to give a clearer picture of what transpired, one
    should describe a single, typical case.
Mr. Hone (his was the medium, in robin's egg blue) plugged
    in as directed and gave it the juice.
When nothing went, except a hissing from the tank of Just-
    right Air, he shook the cabinet, reread the instructions,
    then called Mr. Ballard of Mountain View Road.
Trying again with the lever at Maximum Force he turned on
    the current and stood back to watch.
Newark came in, and two city stations, but without much
    volume. And with none of the advertised results at all.
Mr. Hone then kicked the model (about where the knees
    would be) and threw a book-end at the instrument
    panel.
Still nothing. Nothing but an oblong stare from the
    shatterproof full-view lens.
Swearing, Mr. Hone retired to the kitchen, made himself a
    highball, went out to the porch and stretched full
    length in a steamer chair.

Well, Mrs. Hone pointed out, he was perspiring freely, just as
   the company claimed he would be.
And his mind was fully occupied, exactly as guaranteed.

Nevertheless, night descended upon the county about as
   always.
Fragrantly. As damply as ever, but no damper. Neither more
   nor less quiet than the evening before.

BEWARE

Someone, somewhere, is always starting trouble,
Either a relative, or a drunken friend, or a foreign state.
Trouble it is, trouble it was, trouble it will always be.
Nobody ever leaves well enough alone.

It begins, as a rule, with an innocent face and a trivial remark:
"There are two sides to every question," or "Sign right here,
      on the dotted line,"
But it always ends with a crash of glass and a terrible shout—
No one, no one lets sleeping dragons sleep.

And it never happens, when the doorbell rings, that you find
      a troupe of houris standing on your stoop.
Just the reverse.
So beware of doorbells. (And beware, beware of houris, too)
And you never receive a letter that says: "We enclose,
      herewith, our check for a million."
You know what the letter always says, instead.
So beware of letters. (And anyway, they say, beware of great
      wealth)

Be careful of doorbells, be cautious of telephones, watch out
      for genial strangers, and for ancient friends;
Beware of dotted lines, and mellow cocktails; don't touch
      letters sent specifically to you;
Beware, especially, of innocent remarks;
Beware of everything,
Damn near anything leads to trouble,
Someone is always, always stepping out of line.

THIRTEEN O'CLOCK

Why do they whistle so loud, when they walk past the
    graveyard late at night?
Why do they look behind them when they reach the gates?
    Why do they have any gates? Why don't they go
    through the wall?
But why, O why do they make that horrible whistling sound?

GO AWAY, LIVE PEOPLE, STOP HAUNTING THE DEAD.

If they catch you, it is said, they make you rap, rap, rap on a
    table all night,
And blow through a trumpet and float around the room in
    long white veils,
While they ask you, and ask you: Can you hear us, Uncle
    Ted?
Are you happy, Uncle Ted? Should we buy or should we sell?
    Should we marry, Uncle Ted?
What became of Uncle Ned, Uncle Ted, and is he happy, and
    ask him if he knows what became of Uncle Fred?

KEEP AWAY, LIVE PEOPLE, KEEP FAR AWAY,
STAY IN THE WORLD'S OTHER WORLD WHERE YOU
    REALLY BELONG, YOU WILL PROBABLY BE MUCH
    HAPPIER THERE.

And who knows what they are hunting for, always looking,
    looking, looking with sharp bright eyes where they
    ought to have sockets?
Whoever saw them really grin with their teeth?
Who knows why they worry, or what they scheme, with a brain
    where there should be nothing but good, damp air?

STAY AWAY, LIVE PEOPLE, STAY AWAY, STAY AWAY,
YOU MEAN NO HARM, AND WE AREN'T AFRAID OF YOU,
    AND WE DON'T BELIEVE SUCH PEOPLE EXIST,
BUT WHAT ARE YOU LOOKING FOR? WHO DO YOU
    WANT?
WHO? WHO? WHO? O WHO?

CRACKED RECORD BLUES

If you watch it long enough you can see the clock move,
If you try hard enough you can hold a little water in the palm
      of your hand,
If you listen once or twice you know it's not the needle, or
      the tune, but a crack in the record when sometimes a
      phonograph falters and repeats, and repeats, and
      repeats, and repeats—

And if you think about it long enough, long enough, long
      enough, long enough then everything is simple and you
      can understand the times,
You can see for yourself that the Hudson still flows, that the
      seasons change as ever, that love is always love,
Words still have a meaning, still clear and still the same;
You can count upon your fingers that two plus two still
      equals, still equals, still equals, still equals—
There is nothing in this world that should bother the mind.

Because the mind is a common sense affair filled with
      common sense answers to common sense facts,
It can add up, can add up, can add up, can add up
      earthquakes and subtract them from fires,
It can bisect an atom or analyze the planets—
All it has to do is to, do is to, do is to, do is to start at the
      beginning and continue to the end.

CONTINUOUS PERFORMANCE

The place seems strange, more strange than ever, and the
     times are still more out of joint;
Perhaps there has been some slight mistake?

It is like arriving at the movies late, as usual, just as the story
     ends:
There is a carnival on the screen. It is a village in springtime,
     that much is clear. But why has the heroine suddenly
     slapped his face? And what does it mean, the sequence
     with the limousine and the packed valise? Very strange.
Then love wins. Fine. And it is the end. O.K.
But how do we reach that carnival again? And when will that
     springtime we saw return once more? How, and when?

Now, where a moment ago there was a village square, with
     trees and laughter, the story resumes itself in arctic
     regions among blinding snows. How can this be?
What began in the long and shining limousine seems closing
     now, fantastically, in a hansom cab.
The amorous business that ended with happiness forever after
     is starting all over again, this time with a curse and a
     pistol shot. It is not so good.

Nevertheless, though we know it all and cannot be fooled,
     though we know the end and nothing deceives us,
Nevertheless we shall stay and see what it meant, the mystery
     of the packed valise,
Why curses change at last to kisses and to laughter in a
     limousine (for this is fixed, believe me, fixed),
How simply and how swiftly arctic blizzards melt into
     blowing trees and a village fair.

And stay to see the Hydra's head cut off, and grown again,
    and incredibly multiplied,
And observe how Sisyphus fares when he has once more
    almost reached the top,
How Tantalus again will nearly eat and drink.
And learn how Alph the sacred river flows, in Xanadu, forever
    to a sunless sea,
How, from the robes of simple flesh, fate emerges from new
    and always more fantastic fate.

Until again we have the village scene. (And now we know the
    meaning of the packed valise)
And it is a carnival again. In spring.

PUBLIC LIFE

Then enter again, through a strange door, into a life again all
    strange,
Enter as a rich man, or perhaps a poor man,
Enter as beggarman or thief, doctor or lawyer or merchant or
    chief,
Enter, smiling, enter on tiptoe, enter blowing kisses, enter in
    tears,

But enter, enter,
Enter in overalls, mittens, sweater and cap, grime and grit and
    grease and gear,
Exit, then, exit and change, quick change and return,
Return in spats and pinstripe trousers, white bow tie and high
    silk hat, studs and tails,

Return as the villain: "The mortgage is due." (A role you
    never thought would be yours)
Enter as Nell (this comes with a shock): "You cur, you fiend."
Enter the hero: "Gold is your God and may he serve you
    well." (Can it possibly be this is you again?)

Enter Pa and Ma, strangers, stragglers, a miscellaneous crowd.
Enter Jane disguised as Du Barry, exit Du Barry disguised as
    Jane,
Come in with gun and mask and murderous intent,
Leave with bloodless hands and a silent prayer, in peace,

Exit to thunder and lightning and clouds and the night,
Enter on the following morning in sunshine, to the sound of
    birds,

Enter again to a different scene,
Enter again, through a strange door, into a life again all new
and strange.

ELEGY IN A THEATRICAL WAREHOUSE

They have laid the penthouse scenes away, after a truly
     phenomenal run,
And taken apart the courtroom, and the bright, shiny office,
     and laid them all away with the cabin in the clearing
     where the sun slowly rose through a smashing third act,
And the old family mansion on the road above the mill has
     been gone a long time,
And the road is gone—
The road that never did lead to any mill at all.

The telephone is gone, the phone that rang and rang, and
     never did connect with any other phone,
And the great steel safe where no diamonds ever were,
They have taken down the pictures, portraits of ancestors lost
     and unclaimed, that hung on the massive walls,
And taken away the books that reached to the study ceiling,
The rows and rows of books bound in leather and gold with
     nothing, nothing, nothing inside—

And the bureaus, and the chests, that were empty to the brim,
And the pistols that brought down so many, many curtains
     with so many, many blanks—

Almost everything is gone,
Everything that never held a single thing at all.

CERTIFIED LIFE

The neighborhood athlete is in love again, staring about him
      with sightless eyes, and that, for him, is the same as
      having a patent on life;
The corner druggist can judge a person by his face, a talent as
      good as smuggled jewels, and that fixes everything, or
      nearly everything, for him;
Corporal Towne believes that he believes in Fate, a
      partnership Fate has never denied, and that takes care of
      Corporal Towne;
End problems in chess absorb the postman, and in this way
      he is taken care of, too—

And so, in some way, all people everywhere, all, all, all of us
      have our special but adequate arrangements made,
We hold the right tickets to the right destinations,
Have extra buttons which we use, when we must, to cloak us
      more tightly against the heavier storms,
Own magic lamps that we rub to change the darkest night
      into sunrise and then to perpetual noon,
Go everywhere with confidence, knowing our passports have
      been visa'd by a certain influential friend we happen to
      have in heaven—

And no man on earth, given three wishes, could possibly be at
      a loss for his first, or second, or final wish;
There is no man whose papers, even for an hour, have not
      been completely in order;
No one has ever forgotten the password, or totally lost his
      ticket;
Or arrived at the familiar address of an ancient firm, to find it
      no longer in business, and only vaguely known;

No one, no one ever waits for a bus, long after midnight, on a rainy corner where the busline does not run at all.

KING JUKE

The juke-box has a big square face,
A majestic face, softly glowing with red and green and lights.
Have you got a face as bright as that?

BUT IT'S A PROVEN FACT, THAT A JUKE-BOX HAS NO
    EARS.

With its throat of brass, the juke-box eats live nickels raw;
It can turn itself on or shut itself off;
It has no hangovers, knows no regrets, and it never feels the
    need for sleep.
Can you do that?
What can you do that a juke-box can't, and do it ten times
    better than you?

And it hammers at your nerves, and stabs you through the
    heart and beats upon your soul—
But can you do that to the box?

Its resourceful mind, filled with thoughts that range from love
    to grief, from the gutter to the stars, from pole to pole,
Can seize its thoughts between fingers of steel,
Begin them at the start and follow them through in an
    orderly fashion to the very end.
Can you do that?
And what can you say that a juke-box can't, and say it in a
    clearer, louder voice than yours?
What have you got, a juke-box hasn't got?

Well, a juke-box has no ears, they say.
The box, it is believed, cannot even hear itself.
IT SIMPLY HAS NO EARS AT ALL.

218

CONFESSION OVERHEARD IN A SUBWAY

You will ask how I came to be eavesdropping, in the first place.
The answer is, I was not.
The man who confessed to these several crimes (call him John
      Doe) spoke into my right ear on a crowded subway
      train, while the man whom he addressed (call him
      Richard Roe) stood at my left.
Thus, I stood between them, and they talked, or sometimes
      shouted, quite literally straight through me.
How could I help but overhear?
Perhaps I might have moved away to some other strap. But
      the aisles were full.
Besides, I felt, for some reason, curious.

"I do not deny my guilt," said John Doe. "My own, first, and
      after that my guilty knowledge of still further guilt.
I have counterfeited often, and successfully.
I have been guilty of ignorance, and talking with conviction.
      Of intolerable wisdom, and keeping silent.
Through carelessness, or cowardice, I have shortened the lives
      of better men. And the name for that is murder.
All my life I have been a receiver of stolen goods."

"Personally, I always mind my own business," said Richard
      Roe. "Sensible people don't get into those scrapes."

I was not the only one who overheard this confession.
Several businessmen, bound for home, and housewives and
      mechanics, were within easy earshot.
A policeman sitting in front of us did not lift his eyes, at the
      mention of murder, from his paper.
Why should I be the one to report these crimes?

You will understand why this letter to your paper is
  anonymous. I will sign it: Public-Spirited Citizen, and
  hope that it cannot be traced.
But all the evidence, if there is any clamor for it, can be
  substantiated.
I have heard the same confession many times since, in
  different places.
And now that I come to think of it, I had heard it many times
  before.

"Guilt," said John, "is always and everywhere nothing less
  than guilt.
I have always, at all times, been a willing accomplice of the
  crass and the crude.
I have overheard, daily, the smallest details of conspiracies
  against the human race, vast in their ultimate scope,
  and conspired, daily, to launch my own.
You have heard of innocent men who died in the chair. It was
  my greed that threw the switch.
I helped, and I do not deny it, to nail that guy to the cross,
  and shall continue to help.
Look into my eyes, you can see the guilt.
Look at my face, my hair, my very clothing, you will see guilt
  written plainly everywhere.
Guilt of the flesh. Of the soul. Of laughing, when others do
  not. Of breathing and eating and sleeping.
I am guilty of what? Of guilt. Guilty of guilt, that is all, and
  enough."

Richard Roe looked at his wristwatch and said: "We'll be
  twenty minutes late.
After dinner we might take in a show."

Now, who will bring John Doe to justice for his measureless
     crimes?
I do not, personally, wish to be involved.
Such nakedness of the soul belongs in some other province,
     probably the executioner's.
And who will bring the blunt and upright Richard Roe to the
     accuser's stand, where he belongs?
Or will he deny and deny his partnership?

I have done my duty, as a public-spirited citizen, in any case.

ART REVIEW

Recently displayed at the Times Square Station, a new
      Vandyke on the face-cream girl.
(Artist unknown. Has promise, but lacks the brilliance shown
      by the great masters of the Elevated age)
The latest wood carving in a Whelan telephone booth, titled
      "O Mortal Fools WA 9-5090," shows two winged
      hearts above an ace of spades.
(His meaning is not entirely clear, but this man will go far)
A charcoal nude in the rear of Flatbush Ahearn's Bar & Grill,
      "Forward to the Brotherhood of Man," has been boldly
      conceived in the great tradition.
(We need more, much more of this)
Then there is the chalk portrait, on the walls of a waterfront
      warehouse, of a gentleman wearing a derby hat:
      "Bleecker Street Mike is a doublecrossing rat."
(Morbid, but powerful. Don't miss)

Know then by these presents, know all men by these signs
      and omens, by these simple thumbprints on the throat
      of time,
Know that Pete, the people's artist, is ever watchful,
That Tuxedo Jim has passed among us, and was much
      displeased, as always,
That George the Ghost (no man has ever seen him) and Billy
      the Bicep boy will neither bend nor break,
That Mr. Harkness of Sunnyside still hopes for the best, and
      has not lost his human touch,
That Phantom Phil, the master of them all, has come and
      gone, but will return, and all is well.

THE JOYS OF BEING A BUSINESSMAN

Enter the proprietor of the Riviera Cafe;
Remarks, "It is a wonderful morning," as in fact it always is,
    for him;
Glances at the cash-register with marked disinterest, first,
    then at the morning man behind the bar, and at the
    early customers in front;
Disappears into the kitchen and at once returns, hangs up his
    coat;
Straightens the service flag in the window, and tests a
    Venetian blind;
States: "I was looking at the bills since ten o'clock, already;"
    (it is now about 11 A.M.)
Picks up a frond of palm leaves from the vase inside the door
    and inspects the stem, the leaves, the veins of the leaves;
Drinks coffee at the bar, peering steadily through the window
    at the street;
Queries, "Joe been here, yet?" And listens to the answer, Joe
    has not.

Puts on his coat and departs for a shave, returns, hangs up his
    coat;
Asserts: "Hot today. Another scorcher."
Studies the menu, frowns, shrugs in executive resignation,
    and puts it down; no comment;
Has a glass of vermouth on the stroke of noon.

Declares: "Tell Joe I'll be back tonight," and puts on his coat;
Gives a final, disapproving survey, filled with the cares of the
    High Command;
Austerely, but forgivingly departs.

TRAVELOGUE IN A SHOOTING-GALLERY

There is a jungle, there is a jungle, there is a vast, vivid, wild,
    wild, marvelous, marvelous, marvelous jungle,
Open to the public during business hours,
A jungle not very far from an Automat, between a hat store
    there, and a radio shop.

There, there, whether it rains, or it snows, or it shines,
Under the hot, blazing, cloudless, tropical neon skies that the
    management always arranges there,
Rows and rows of marching ducks, dozens and dozens and
    dozens of ducks, move steadily along on smoothly-oiled
    ballbearing feet,
Ducks as big as telephone books, slow and fearless and out of
    this world,
While lines and lines of lions, lions, rabbits, panthers,
    elephants, crocodiles, zebras, apes,
Filled with jungle hunger and jungle rage and jungle love,
Stalk their prey on endless, endless rotary belts through never-
    ending forests, and burning deserts, and limitless veldts,
To the sound of tom-toms, equipped with silencers, beaten
    by thousands of savages there.

And there it is that all the big game hunters go, there the
    traders and the explorers come,
Leanfaced men with windswept eyes who arrive by streetcar,
    auto or subway, taxi or on foot, streetcar or bus,
And they nod, and they say, and they need no more:
"There . . . there . . .
There they come, and there they go."

And weighing machines, in this civilized jungle, will read
     your soul like an open book, for a penny at a time, and
     tell you all,
There, there, where smoking is permitted,
In a jungle that lies, like a rainbow's end, at the very end of
     every trail,
There, in the only jungle in the whole wide world where
     ducks are waiting for streetcars,
And hunters can be psychoanalyzed, while they smoke and
     wait for ducks.

AFTERNOON OF A PAWNBROKER

Still they bring me diamonds, diamonds, always diamonds,
Why don't they pledge something else for a change, if they
      must have loans, other than those diamond clasps and
      diamond rings,
Rubies, sapphires, emeralds, pearls,
Ermine wraps, silks and satins, solid gold watches and silver
      plate and violins two hundred years old,
And then again diamonds, diamonds, the neighborhood
      diamonds I have seen so many times before, and shall
      see so many times again?

Still I remember the strange afternoon (it was a season of
      extraordinary days and nights) when the first of the
      strange customers appeared,
And he waited, politely, while Mrs. Nunzio redeemed her
      furs, then he stepped to the counter and he laid down a
      thing that looked like a trumpet,
In fact, it was a trumpet, not mounted with diamonds, not
      plated with gold or even silver, and I started to say: "We
      can't use trumpets—"
But a light was in his eyes,
And after he was gone, I had the trumpet. And I stored it
      away. And the name on my books was Gabriel.

It should be made clear my accounts are always open to the
      police, I have nothing to conceal,
I belong, myself, to the Sounder Business Principles League,
Have two married daughters, one of them in Brooklyn, the
      other in Cleveland,
And nothing like this had ever happened before.
How can I account for my lapse of mind?

All I can say is, it did not seem strange. Not at the time. Not
    in that neighborhood. And not in that year.

And the next to appear was a man with a soft, persuasive
    voice,
And a kindly face, and the most honest eyes I have ever seen,
    and ears like arrows, and a pointed beard,
And what he said, after Mrs. Case had pledged her diamond
    ring and gone, I cannot now entirely recall,
But when he went away I found I had an apple. An apple, just
    an apple.
"It's been bitten," I remember that I tried to argue. But he
    smiled, and said in his quiet voice: "Yes, but only
    twice."
And the strangest thing is, it did not seem strange. Not
    strange at all.

And still those names are on my books.
And still I see listed, side by side, those incongruous, and not
    very sound securities:
(1) Aladdin's lamp (I must have been mad), (1) Pandora's
    box, (1) Magic carpet,
(1) Fountain of youth (in good condition), (1) Holy Grail,
    (1) Invisible man (the only article never redeemed, and
    I cannot locate him), and others, others, many others,
And still I recall how my storage vaults hummed and
    crackled, from time to time, or sounded with music, or
    shot forth flame,
And I wonder, still, that the season did not seem one of
    unusual wonder, not even different—not at the time.

And still I think, at intervals, why didn't I, when the chance
    was mine, drink just once from that Fountain of youth?

Why didn't I open that box of Pandora?
And what if Mr. Gabriel, who redeemed his pledge and went
    away, should some day decide to blow on his trumpet?
Just one short blast, in the middle of some busy afternoon?

But here comes Mr. Barrington, to pawn his Stradivarius.
And here comes Mrs. Case, to redeem her diamond ring.

MONOGRAPH ON INTERNATIONAL PEACE

Someone, a dissatisfied customer, has thrown a brickbat
        through the plate-glass window of the Riviera Café
(The sound and the fury left nothing to be desired)
And somebody else has stolen another customer's brand-new
        overcoat.

The fifty surviving patrons are in complete agreement;
Such things are neither nice nor reasonable, and yet there are,
        you will always find, in any group of people, a few like
        that.
(How often have you wished you had the nerve?)

But even as peace returns, and the lady nearest the window
        brushes a splinter from her escort's sleeve, she says,
"Brother of yours or not, I won't take that from nobody. So
        what are you going to do about it, Al?"
And somebody's elbow upsets somebody else's beer,
There is a dispute about whose nickel came first in the juke
        box—the Tchaikovsky nickel or the Grieg—
While two 4-F's accuse each other of simple, multiple, and
        compound crimes
(Their verbal combat is the bloodiest the neighborhood has
        ever known),

And love, flourishing in a booth at the rear, is plainly turning
        sour in one at the front;
The little neutral beside the cigarette machine defends his
        assertion that the new pennies do not look like dimes,
Even as an aggressor elbows him aside, looking for a foot of
        Lebensraum at the bar.

In the phone booth, you can hear the manager of the next-
     door funeral parlor swear to his wife that he is calling
     from a client's home.

And if neither Grieg nor the rumba is conducive to rectitude,
If neither rye, nor Scotch, nor beer, nor brandy, nor wine can
     produce some measure of harmony here, on this little
     block,
What chance have presidents, prime ministers, marshals,
     kings and queens?

While races and nations grope their way toward a lasting
     peace,
We on this small but crowded front have settled nothing,
     nothing, nothing at all;
Minute by minute we continue to have our wavering victories
     and our own staggering but temporary defeats.

Regarding the brotherhood of man, here is the latest
     communiqué:
Somebody has stolen an overcoat,
Someone has shattered a plate-glass window with a brick.

MODEL FOR A BIOGRAPHY

Years in sporting goods, rich in experience, were followed by
      years in soda, candy, and cigars.
(If there is some connection, you might point it out here)
A real estate venture, resulting in ruin, prepared this man for
      his later triumph in the hardware game.
(If there is no connection, or if the logic seems weak, his is
      not the first life that failed to make sense—
You had better play it safe, and stick to one point):

HE WAS EXPERIENCED. HE WAS PREPARED.

And years of marriage (a happy, happy marriage) prepared
      him for years and years of divorce.
(O happy divorce)
(But you'd better not say that. Think of the relatives. And the
      public, by and large, would not believe you, or if they
      did, would not understand)
Then what can you say? You have to say something that
      makes a little sense:

HE WAS EXPERIENCED. HE WAS PREPARED.

He was kind, without fail, to other people's mothers;
Reprieved from insurance, he was sentenced to a bank, but
      made a daring, spectacular daylight escape;
Rejected by the Marines, he was welcomed by the
      Quartermaster Corps with open arms,
And when it is over, well, when it is over:

HE WILL BE EXPERIENCED. HE WILL BE PREPARED.

PIANO TUNER

It is the sound of a cat like no cat ever seen before walking
      back and forth on ivory keys;
No note on this board, however the wires are tightened, can
      be tuned to any other note;
The instrument cannot be played, not correctly,
Not by any players known today, not from the scores and
      arrangements that now exist—

Somehow this wire, however strung, always returns a sound
      with an overtone, and always in the overtone the sound
      of distant gunfire can be plainly heard,
Another, however loose or taut, echoes as though to fingers
      tapping not music but bulletins despatched from
      remote time and space,
Then there are chords, neither minor chords nor discords, in
      some way filled with a major silence—

And it cannot be, it is not according to the standard scale;
Some wholly new and different kind of scale, perhaps, with
      unknown values, or no values, or values measured by
      chance and change—

This key responds with something not even sound at all,
      sometimes a feeling, and the feeling is anguish,
Sometimes a sense, like the touch of a hand,
Or a glimpse of familiar rooftops wrapped first in summer
      sunlight and then in falling snow—

As though the instrument were devil'd by melodies not
      written yet,
Or possessed by players not yet born.

RECEPTION GOOD

Now, at a particular spot on the radio dial, "—in this corner,
  wearing purple trunks,"
Mingles, somehow, with the news that "—powerful enemy
  units have been surrounded in the drive—"
And both of these with the information that "—there is a way
  to avoid having chapped and roughened hands."

Such are the new and complex harmonies, it seems, of a
  strange and still more complex age;
It is not that the reception is confused or poor, but rather it is
  altogether too clear and good,

And no worse, in any case, than that other receiving set, the
  mind,
Forever faithfully transmitting the great and little impulses that
  arrive, however wavering or loud, from near and far:
"It is an ill wind—" it is apt to report, underscoring this with
  "—the bigger they are the harder they fall," and
  simultaneously reminding, darkly, that "Things are
  seldom as they seem,"

Reconciling, with ease, the irreconcilable,
Piecing together fragments of a flashing past with clouded
  snapshots of the present and the future,
("Something old, something new," its irrelevant announcer
  states. "Something borrowed, something blue.")

Fashioning a raw, wild symphony of a wedding march, a
  drinking song, and a dirge,
Multiplying enormous figures with precision, then raising the
  question: But after all, what is a man?

Somehow creating hope and fresh courage out of ancient
     doubt.

"Both boys are on their feet, they're going to it," the radio
     reports,
"—the sinking was attended by a heavy loss of life—"
"—this amazing cream for quick, miraculous results."

How many pieces are there, in a simple jigsaw puzzle?
How many phases of a man's life can crowd their way into a
     single moment?
How many angels, actually, can dance on the point of a pin?

END OF THE SEERS' CONVENTION

We were walking and talking on the roof of the world,
In an age that seemed, at that time, an extremely modern age,
Considering a merger, last on the agenda, of the Seven Great
      Leagues that held the Seven True Keys to the Seven
      Ultimate Spheres of all moral, financial, and occult life.

"I foresee a day," said one of the delegates, an astro-analyst
      from Idaho, "when men will fly through the air, and
      talk across space;
They will sail in ships that float beneath the water;
They will emanate shadows of themselves upon a screen, and
      the shadows will move, and talk, and seem as though
      real."

"Very interesting, indeed," declared a Gypsy delegate.
"But I should like to ask, as a simple reader of tea-leaves and
      palms:
How does this combat the widespread and growing evil of the
      police?"

The astrologer shrugged, and an accidental meteor fell from
      his robes and smoldered on the floor.
"In addition," he said, "I foresee a war,
And a victory after that one, and after the victory, a war again."

"Trite," was the comment of a crystal-gazer from Miami
      Beach.
"Any damn fool, at any damn time, can visualize wars, and
      more wars, and famines and plagues.
The real question is: How to seize power from entrenched
      and organized men of Common Sense?"

"I foresee a day," said the Idaho astrologer, "when human
    beings will live on top of flag-poles,
And dance, at some profit, for weeks and months without any
    rest,
And some will die very happily of eating watermelons, and
    nails, and cherry pies."

"Why," said a bored numerologist, reaching for his hat, "can't
    these star-gazers keep their feet on the ground?"
"Even if it's true," said a Bombay illusionist, "it is not, like
    the rope-trick, altogether practical."

"And furthermore and finally," shouted the astrologer, with
    comets and halfmoons dropping from his pockets, and
    his agitated sleeves,
"I prophesy an age of triumph for laziness and sleep, and
    dreams and utter peace.
I can see couples walking through the public parks in love,
    and those who do not are wanted by the sheriff.
I see men fishing beside quiet streams, and those who do not
    are pursued by collectors, and plastered with liens."

"This does not tell us how to fight against skepticism,"
    muttered a puzzled mesmerist, groping for the door.
"I think," agreed a lady who interpreted the cards, "we are all
    inclined to accept too much on faith."

A sprinkling of rain, or dragon's blood,
Or a handful of cinders fell on the small, black umbrellas they
    raised against the sky.

FINALE

How cold, how very cold is the wind that blows out of
    nowhere into nowhere,
Winding across space and uncalendar'd time,

Filled with the sound of living voices, as it winds through the
    ears that once were Stephen's ears,
Charged with the scent of fields and forests, as it blows
    through the nostrils that once were Jane's,

Winding through the sockets that once were David's eyes,
Weaving again, as she used to do, the soft brown hair that
    once was Mary's hair,
Bringing again the words that once were Stephen's and David's
    and Mary's words into and out of their deaf ears,
Scattering the worlds that once were theirs, and yours, and mine,
Bearing away to nowhere and to no place the very especial
    sins and virtues that once were ours,

How cold, how extremely cold is this wind.

A TRIBUTE, AND A NIGHTMARE

You wonder, sometimes, but more often worry, and feel
    dismayed in a world of change,
Seeing landmarks vanish, old bastions fall, and you frequently
    question what Fate may have in store for you—
But you really need not—
Whatever else it holds, it holds the changeless and eternal
    Martin Dies.

Will the world be bright, and filled with laughter?
You will hear all about it from Congressman Dies (Chairman
    of the Committee to Investigate Gloom).

Will the world be grim, inhabited by wolves with long, sharp
    teeth?
It will not go unchampioned. See Martin Dies, President of
    the Anti-Grandma League.

Will the people of the earth be nudists, eventually, and largely
    vegetarian?
Be especially wary of Dies, Martin, spinach crusader, the
    Kiddies' Kandidate unanimously acclaimed by Martin
    Dies.
Will the planet be Red with revolution (you hope) from the
    tropics to the poles?
You will have to deal (you fear, and rightly) with Commissar
    Dies, Chairman of the Committee to Probe Versive
    Activity.

Stranger, whoever you are, and whatever your final
    destination may be,
I give you, freely, a name to conjure with:

In heaven: Martin Dies, Chairman of the Membership
    Committee,
In hell: Martin Dies, President of United Coke & Coal.

[SOMEBODY'S WAR BONDS]

Somebody's War Bonds aren't going to be worth a damn.

Somebody's War Bonds are going to be worth exactly the
   paper they are printed on—no more.

They will be used to start the fire in the stove some cold
   morning.
They will be used to paper the walls, and stop up a chink in
   the window frames.

We all hope this happens to the enemy's bonds, not ours.

But it might be ours.

We are already in this so deep we had better make sure the
   enemy's bonds, not ours, are finally and irrevocably
   valueless. There is only one way to do that. We will
   have to get in deeper still.

BUY MORE BONDS!

SHERLOCK SPENDS A DAY IN THE COUNTRY

The crime, if there was a crime, has not been reported as yet;
The plot, if that is what it was, is still a secret somewhere in
      this wilderness of newly fallen snow;
The conference, if it was a conference, has been adjourned,
      and now there is nothing in this scene but pine trees,
      and silence, and snow, and still more snow.

Nevertheless, in spite of all this apparent emptiness, notice
      the snow;
Observe how it literally crawls with a hundred different
      signatures of unmistakable life.
Here is a delicate, exactly repeated pattern, where, seemingly,
      a cobweb came and went,
And here some party, perhaps an acrobat, walked through
      these woods at midnight on his mittened hands.
Thimbles, and dice tracks, and half moons, these trademarks
      lead everywhere into the hills;
The signs prove some amazing fellow on a bicycle rode
      straight up the face of a twenty-foot drift,
And someone, it does not matter who, walked steadily
      somewhere on obviously cloven feet.

Let us ourselves adjourn to the village bar, Watson (not
      saying very much when we get there),
To consider this mighty, diversified army, and what grand
      conspiracy of conspiracies it hatched,
What conclusions it reached, and where it intends to strike,
      and when,
Being careful to notice, as we go and return, the character and
      number of our own tracks in the snow.

4 A.M.

It is early evening, still, in Honolulu, and in London, now, it
      must be well past dawn,
But here in the Riviera Café, on a street that has been lost and
      forgotten long ago, as the clock moves steadily toward
      closing time,
The spark of life is very low, if it burns at all—

And here we are, four lost and forgotten customers in this
      place that surely will never again be found,
Sitting, at ten-foot intervals, along this lost and forgotten bar
(Wishing the space were further still, for we are still too close
      for comfort),
Knowing that the bartender, and the elk's head, and the
      picture of some forgotten champion
(All gazing at something of interest beyond us and behind us,
      but very far away),
Must somehow be aware of us, too, as we stare at the cold
      interior of our lives reflected in the mirror beneath and
      in back of them—

Hear how lonely the radio is, as its voice talks on and on,
      unanswered,
How its music proves again that one's life is either too
      humdrum or too exciting, too empty or too full, too
      this, too that;
Only the cat that has been sleeping in the window, now
      yawning and stretching and trotting to the kitchen to
      sleep again,
Only this living toy knows what we feel, knows what we are,
      really knows what we merely think we know—

And soon, too soon, it will be closing time, the door will be
     locked,
Leaving each of us alone, then, with something too ravaging
     for a name
(Our golden, glorious futures, perhaps)—
Lock the door now and put out the lights, before some
     terrible stranger enters and puts, to each of us, a
     question that must be answered with the truth—

They say the Matterhorn at dawn, and the Northern Lights of
     the Arctic, are things that should be seen;
They say, they say—in time, you will hear them say anything,
     and everything;
What would the elk's head, or the remote bartender say, if
     they could speak?
The booth where last night's love affair began, the spot where
     last year's homicide occurred, are empty now, and still.

SPOTLIGHT

The hour that was bleak, as he worked, does not betray itself
     in the gem that the craftsman has polished;
Nor do the facets of the stone, however they sparkle, give
     evidence of the hour that, to him, was gay;
The day that was overlong, perhaps because of household
     demands, is not apparent here in these swiftly changing
     lights;
None of this shows at all in the rare thing set in the finished
     clasp—

Nor is there any hint that the maker was either young, or old;
Whether happily married, or often distraught;
No suggestion that he was concerned, as he cut and ground
     and polished, by the thought of uninvited relatives, or a
     welcome face;
No clue that he lived in a certain house, on a certain street,
That possibly the neighbors were a nuisance, the street too
     slovenly, the children a few too many in the daytime
     and the traffic too loud at night—

You, wearing this perfect stone, will have no inkling of these
     things at all;
You will understand that the spotlight, in fact, falls elsewhere;
You, and you alone, will know the hour that is really grim,
     and the truly magic face.

MUSEUM

And now you see the artificial sun come up, everywhere
    suffusing a marvelously painted sky;
It is dawn, revealing leagues of earth, and a taxidermist's
    frozen version of the actual life—

There is the Executive in his office; he is serious, but pleasant;
    a man of great importance in and to his day
(See the telephone? And the ashtray and the desk pad, to the
    very life);
Here is the smiling Junior Clerk; the Typist;
And that one is the Salesman, laughing as he seems about to
    light a fresh cigar—

HABITAT: N. AMERICA, it says,
And as the light grows clear and gold, there are the bridges,
    towers, railways, docks
(Exactly scaled to one one-thousandth size, it says),
And there a tiny crane unloads a perfect ship—

The activity increases (for the day, too, is only one one-
    thousandth size);
A ticker races, and soon, very soon, a bell will ring;
See the mail truck leave with letters bound for the utmost
    horizons of this empire limited only by the telephone,
    the radio, and the mail;
In a moment, that toy elevator will reach the top; a signal
    block will fall;
And pretty soon, there will be a silvery bell—

In those adjoining rooms, likewise equipped with phones and
    desks and miniature lights

(The scene is indescribably real, and this is a gay, casual little
        tableau),
Sit the Switchboard Girl, the jovial Attorney—
But there is the bell—success, success—

And we must go, for there is still so much to see in a single
        afternoon;
All the exhibits that follow this: the Second Age of Innocence,
        the Era of the Torrents, the Third Age of Fire—

But before we leave we must watch the measured sun go
        down, and see the miniature trains light up,
Winding their way through moonlit hills toward distant cities
        that we know are blazing with lights, with electric signs
        where giants walk and mermaids swim—

Knowing, also, that somewhere in the darkness behind us the
        Typist is still busily polishing her fingernails,
The Executive, though the office is darkened, is still poised
        for action, and the laughing Salesman still clings to his
        long cigar,
Each of them comfortable and secure as in life, each mulling
        some personal problem,
Each confidently waiting for the sun that will surely rise.

ONCE UPON A TIME

Ever, ever, ever, ever, ever so long ago,
In a land very far, terribly far, very, very, very far away—

Youth was bolder, and age more just,
Love was everlasting, not the matter of caprice it is today,
(Ask any dean of college, pulpit, radio, or newspaper, he will
      tell you the same)—

Learning was respected then, the arts were truly glorious in
      those mightier times
(Even the youngest student, today, will say this is true)
Leaves were greener in springtime than they are now, and
      redder in autumn, while in winter the trees were
      straighter and taller and whiter with snow,
Laughter was the rule, then, rather than the exception, and
      tragedy, when it befell, transfigured simple grief
(No one ever argues these familiar facts)—

And why should this be even sadder than it sounds?—

It was such a long, long, long, long, long time ago,
In a place that was so far, so very far, so terribly far away.

M.D.

We cough. We shiver. We have seizures of pain, and
    weakness. Often there is blood.
We are not as strong as we thought ourselves to be—

Doctor, we urge you, help us—

Our throats are simply throats, not as good as the least of our
    amplifiers made of bright and lasting steel,
Our minds are not as swift and sure as the machines that add,
    subtract, divide in the twinkling of an eye,
Our eyes themselves are subject to strange fatigues, less discerning
    than the many magic eyes that we have made,
There is a certain amount of fear that we ourselves shall never
    be able to compete—

Yes, it is the fear. And also the blood. Always the blood.
No, it is the muscles. Or something in the bones. Perhaps in
    the very heart itself.
If you could see us as we are in the morning, shivering in that
    dread—

Understanding death, but knowing something worse than
    death is there, present in the blood.
Or in the unsteady tendons. Or is it the nerves? The joints.
The teeth. The hair. The clumsy limbs. Perhaps the soul—

We have had so much contact with one another, each has
    been so often exposed to each,
The dangers of this contamination are so very great, so
    terrible—

O Doctor, Doctor, Doctor—

BRYCE & TOMLINS

Every need analyzed, each personal problem weighed,
      carefully, and solved according to the circumstance of
      each
(No investment too great. No question too small)
In confidence, at no cost, embarrassment, or obligation to
      you—

Offering maximum safety
(At 5%)
Full protection against change and chance, rust, moths, and
      the erratic flesh
(Trusts in perpetuity. Impartial executors of long-range wills)
Year after year, security in spite of the treacherous currents of
      impulse, yours and others',
Despite the swiftest tide of affairs—

Rails, chemicals, utilities, steel,
Listed or unlisted, let these stand guard through the shadowy
      times to be,
The heavy parchment with its exact phrases proof you shall
      walk this day's path, identically, tomorrow,
That as long as you wish you may see these streets and parks
      with the same eyes,
The same mood as today—

As though your features, yours, were stamped on the wind,
      yet more lasting than bronze,
The voice, free as always, yet recorded forever,
Your being, yours, still with its problems stronger than even
      the chemicals or the steel—

Decades of experience behind each portfolio can protect that
    future,
Filled with its unfinished business, incomplete desire, and still
    with the stubborn will to protect that future—

All of this, plus 5% of this, until the end of time.

THE FACE IN THE BAR ROOM MIRROR

Fifteen gentlemen in fifteen overcoats and fifteen hats holding
      fifteen glasses in fifteen hands,
Staring and staring at fifteen faces reflected in the mirror
      behind the polished bar,
Tonight, as last night,
And the night before that, and night after night, after night,
      after night—

What are they dreaming of,
Why do they come here and when will it happen, that thing
      for which they return and return,
To stand and wait, and wait, and wait, and wait—

What fifteen resolves are growing clear and hard, between
      cryptic remarks, in those fifteen living silences,
What crystal stairs do they climb or descend into fifteen
      unseen heavens or hells,
What fifteen replies do they give the single question, does
      anything on earth ever change, or stay?—

Before the shot rings out, the mirror shatters, the floor gapes
      open and the heavens fall,
And they go at last on their fifteen separate, purposeful ways—

Fifteen magicians,
Masters of escape from handcuff and rope, straitjacket,
      padlock, dungeon and chain,
Now planning escapes still more dazzling,
And fifteen times more terrible than these.

THE JUKE-BOX SPOKE AND THE JUKE-BOX SAID:

A few of them, sometimes, choose record number 9,
Or sometimes number 12,
And once in a while someone likes selection 5,
But the voice they really crave, all of them, everywhere and
      always, from the hour the doors open until the hour
      they close,
Repeated and repeated like a beating human heart,
Echoing in the walls, the ceiling, shaking the tables, the
      chairs, the floor—

OVER AND OVER, IT IS SELECTION NUMBER 8—

Whispered and chuckling, as though it arose from the bottom
      of the earth,
Or sometimes exploding like thunder in the room,
Not quite a curse and not exactly a prayer,
Eternally the same, but different, different, different every
      time—

THE WORDS OF NUMBER 8, THE MELODY OF NUMBER 8,
    THE SOUL OF NUMBER 8

Saying the simple thing they cannot say themselves,
Again and again, voicing the secret that they must reveal, and
      can never tell enough,
Yet it never quite gets told—

Sometimes number 9, or 12,
Or 5—

BUT ALWAYS NUMBER 8, AND ONCE AGAIN NUMBER 8,
TIME AFTER TIME, JUST ONCE MORE NUMBER 8. . . 8. . . 8. . .

NEWSPAPERMAN

This charge was laid upon me long ago: Do not forget;
Remember these lives, that the world in turn will not
       forget—

Big John Marino, the terror of his district,
Where none were as strong as he, none as handsome, as
       cunning, as cruel,
Saying, before the state destroyed him:
"Tell them the truth. Tell them everything, so they will
       always know."
Know always, therefore, the great, the ruthless and bold, the
       one and only Big John—

Do not forget the fabulous bankrupt, and the vivid fortunes
       that somewhere, surely, the years still guard;
Keep the memory of an heiress, flashlit favorite in a season
       that cannot fade;
Never let fade, altogether, the programs identifying those
       others, miscellaneous members of the cast—

Each of them unique, though now the names, faces, and
       stories are obscured,
Each saying in words, or underneath the words, and some
       with their sealed eyes and cold lips
(But even so they were sure of themselves, still sure)
Urging always: "It is vital;
You must remember the fateful beginning, fully to
       understand the end
(Though of course there can be no real end);
To grasp the motives, fully, it is vital to remember the stamp
       of the mind,

Vital to know even the twist of the mind. . . ."

You will remember me?
Do not forget a newspaperman who kept his word.

THE PEOPLE v. THE PEOPLE

I have never seen him, this invisible member of the panel, this
      thirteenth juror, but I have certain clues;
I know, after so many years of practice, though I cannot
      prove I know;
It is enough to say, I know that I know.

He is five feet nine or ten, with piercing, bright, triumphant eyes;
He needs glasses, which he will not wear, and he is almost
      certainly stone deaf.
(Cf. Blair v. Gregg, which he utterly ruined.)
He is the juror forever looking out of the window, secretly
      smiling, when you make your telling point.
The one who is wide awake when you think he is asleep. The
      man who naps with his eyes wide open.
Those same triumphant eyes.
He is the man who knows. And knows that he knows.

His hair is meager and he wears wash ties, but these are not
      important points.
He likes the legal atmosphere, that is plain, because he is
      always there.
It is the decent, the orderly procedure that he likes.
He is the juror who arrived first, though you thought he was
      late; the one who failed to return from lunch, though
      you had not noticed.
Let me put it like this: He is the cause of your vague
      uneasiness when you glance about and see that the
      other twelve are all right.

I would know him if I were to see him, I could swear to his
      identity, if I actually saw him once;

I nearly overheard him, when I was for the defense: "They
 never indict anyone unless they are guilty;"
And when I was the State: "A poor man (or a rich man)
 doesn't stand a chance."
Always, before the trial's end, he wants to know if the sergeant
 knew the moon was full on that particular night.

And none of this matters, except I am convinced he is the unseen
 juror bribed, bought, and planted by The People,
An enemy of reason and precedent, a friend of illogic,
Something, I now know, that I know that I really know—

And he or anyone else is welcome to my Blackstone, or my
 crowded shelves of standard books,
In exchange for the monumental works I am convinced he
 has been writing through the years:
"The Rules of Hearsay;" "The Laws of Rumor;"
"An Omnibus Guide to Chance and Superstition," by One
 Who Knows.

CASTAWAY

I know your neckties where they line the rack, orderly from
  day to day, from year to year,
And the clothing, except for the suit you wear, unwrinkled on the
  hangers, with each thing perfect in its perfect place—

O CASTAWAY, BEWARE—

You, a trifle anxious in this impersonal place, a little worried
  in these fiery times, but holding securely to your solid
  reef,
Certain you will arise upon the morning as strong and young
  as you are today—

O CASTAWAY, O CASTAWAY—

Send messages now, press many buttons and make phone
  calls, seek the best advice and speed, speed the telegrams
  for aid,
You do not want to meet the same fate as those others who
  have been cast out, and cast so far away—

Not one of those marooned here in some quiet office, park, or
  decent hotel,
The dreamers, or those too careful, the silent, or one of those
  who abruptly shouts aloud on some busy street,
Anarchist and time-server, timid and self-assured alike—

Each showing in his eyes, in the way he flexes his fingers, in
  the very way he speaks,
Each proving that he also recalls,
Remembers how the elders were all abandoned here, and

knows that the young may fail in confusion, too—

Therefore, while the long sun rises, and still there is no sign,
But before the pale sun sets again, and then it will be too late—

O CASTAWAY, O CASTAWAY, O CASTAWAY, BEWARE.

STRANGER AT CONEY ISLAND

Not here, but a little farther, after we have passed through the
    hall of mirrors,
Seeing ourselves as ogres, devils, zombies, diplomats,
And after we have entered the dragon's jaws, drifting in our
    wooden boat down a silent river between white, gaping,
    enormous teeth,
Floating in darkness through grottos of ogres, then plastic
    devils stoking the painted flames of a gospel hell,
Coming safely again into sunlight, and the sound of a band—

To a cavern of echoes, where we hear the fun as strangers
    rehearse and rehearse the surprise they shall give
    themselves tomorrow,
Watch the signs flash red, and gold, and blue, and green,
"Eat" "Drink" "Be Merry" "At Mike's,"
Where there is no score, in any game, less than a million
    magic bells and a billion electric lights—

Beyond the highest peak of the steepest roller-coaster, in the
    company of persons we do not know,
Through arcades where anyone, even hermits can have their
    fortunes told by iron gypsies sealed behind plateglass
    walls,
Into and beyond the bazaars where every prize is offered, dolls
    and vases, clocks and pillows, miniature closets for the
    family skeleton,
Given freely, with no questions asked, to any, any winner at all—

Until we emerge, safe at last, upon that broad and crowded
    beach,
To cry aloud: Is there a stranger here?

The stranger we have come so far, and through so many
        dangers, to find?
That one who, alone, can solve these many riddles we have
        found so difficult:—

Who, among us all, is the most popular person?
Whom shall we vote the handsomest, the wittiest, most likely
        to succeed?
What is the name, and the mission, of the embryo so long
        preserved in a jar of alcohol?
How may we ever distinguish between an honest, and a
        criminal face?—

Is this stranger somewhere among you?
Perhaps sprawled beneath a striped umbrella, asleep in the
        sand, or tossing a rubber ball to a child,
Or even now awaiting us, aware of our needs, knowing the
        day and the hour.

HIGHER MATHEMATICS

So many asteroids speed and flash and spin along the
      heavenly way where Francis L. Regan travels his regular
      rounds
(More at ease than you or I would be in a walk to the corner
      store),
Covering countless light-years in a single, lonely, brave patrol,
Seeking, and being sought by so many departed souls, legendary,
      half-remembered, or those now wholly lost—

Some of whom will be photographed, in their spectral beings,
      by Francis L. Regan,
The portraits to be displayed, later, in the window of the
      Psychic Institute
(Showing both Before, and After),
The spirit resembling the original features, except they are
      paler and more serene—

But among all these hosts, in so many eons and in so much
      space, there is only one Mr. Regan,
One photographer to the dead (by self-appointment), whose
      business hours, for mundane sittings, are from nine to five,
Who has a definite social security number, and whose lodge
      dues are paid to date,
Whose hobbies, habits, likes and dislikes are not noticeably
      strange,
Who lives in a solid house on a tangible street—

Whose own earthly presence is limited, no less than yours and
      mine,
But who could, if today he wished, return from the farthest
      reaches with a picture of the world's first man.

DECISION

With so much at stake, an inhuman risk for a prize until now
    beyond all grasp,
No longer another promise but this time a verdict, at last the
    judgment itself that cannot be fully understood, or
    borne,
Here, in the very shadow of the senses, where all things verge
    upon becoming real—

Do not be dismayed, be at ease, the assistant secretary will see
    you now,
Here and finally the right man, the assistant in the soft, thick,
    blue-carpeted room with the deep leather chairs at the
    proper end of the right marble hall,
The authoritative man with those powerful but delicate
    photo-electric eyes,
Perception like radar, a calculator mind—

And you will be cautious, with so much in the balance, be careful,
    recall what happened the last time you were here,
Remember certain rumours told you by a friend,
Do not forget, with a world at issue, you may not, must not
    commit yourself too far—

As he tells you, reviewing the case, that somewhere it seems a
    living nerve has been exposed,
Then initialing a memo, careful to leave no fingerprints, he
    explains that somewhere a mind, stripped of words, has
    clearly been brought face to face with doubt,
Long distance telephone wires have apparently been crossed,
That somehow, in spite of reason, a heart begins to beat
    against another heart—

Nor will you be dismayed when he admits that none of this is
    really in his province,
He would like to gamble, himself, but he is not in fact the
    right man to see—

For you will recognize this as merely the code of codes,
You have given the correct password, he the proper
    countersign,
And tomorrow will be a different, even more decisive day,
There, before another assistant secretary, in a leather-
    cushioned room at the other end of the other long,
    white, marble hall.

IRENE HAS A MIND OF HER OWN

In the small but crowded attic of Irene's mind there is room
      for everything except confusion, hesitancy, and doubt;
Breath-control was the issue for one whole day, last week
("Nobody recognized the food value of vegetable-tops, either,
      ten years ago")—

And to this attic, like a bird building a nest with bits of yarn,
      cardboard, and fragments of *The Reader's Digest,*
She brings ancient leaflets and modern radio hints,
      suggestions from strangers met on the train to Buffalo,
      volumes legally filched from the public library,
      telegrams intuitively received from the great beyond:
"Your Troubles—How to Enjoy Them," "The Power of
      Silence," "Ten Basic Errors of Contract Bridge"—

The neighboring artist is a guaranteed immortal
("Van Gogh was even more insane"),
While extra-sensory perception is already an indisputable fact
(The man who found Irene's purse returned her driver's
      license),
And the richest part of any food, Irene knows, is the natural
      skin in which it comes—

We, personally, no longer feel sure,
But looking at the paper in which the butter came, at the
      empty tins and bottles we are saving
(Just in case),
We only know, and give profound thanks, that Irene is on
      our side.

LANISTA

Behold the afternoon sun, how slowly it withdraws from the
     sand, those darker stains within the shadows, though
     they have been covered and covered again, growing
     darker still,
Behold the stone tiers, how empty now,
Behold this day, merely a day, but rumored it may be the last
     on which these simple games, our great sports are ever
     held—

I, Arius, trainer of the best, matched in my youth against the best,
And against them all,
The swordsmen of every province, the netmen, even the beasts—

Knowing no mother or father save this arena, and no other life,
Twenty-eight killed (more than fifty palms), four times
     spared (once by the Emperor, saved by the people
     thrice),
Sometimes still seeing my portrait on the lamps, the vases, the
     matrons' gems
(In addition to the jeweled chains, the helmets, purses, and
     other favors once given me),
And my name, that I have heard in song—

And knowing as well a certain midnight of the spirit that
     comes to all, when each, in his cell, must be chained
     against self-destruction,
Only to be scourged on the very next day, by whips and red-
     hot irons, to the dangerous fight—

Yet now I hear, with wonder, that none of this has been of
     any avail,

These combats have had no meaning and are in fact nothing
        less than nothing at all—

As though the fight between the women and the dwarfs had
        been for nothing,
And the combat between the crippled and the blind, had that
        no point?
Is it not good that the race shall ever behold itself with pride
        and disgust, horror and fright?—

So they say this may be the last of our little games—

Well,
We shall see.

ELEGY

Cherubs of stone, smiling, wait and watch above the grave of
 the Greenpoint child,
Arrowheads still lie at his hand, ready to serve the Dakota
 man, and bowls to refresh him after the long hunt,
Trusted sentinels, open-eyed and leaning on their spears,
 stand guard before the airless tomb of the immortal
 King of Egypt, Lord of the earth, favorite of the
 heavens—

But who still watch those very sparks that once arose at
 midnight from that fire, there beside the river's edge,
What now serves the resolve, molded in fever, taken by one
 who for the first time saw and measured the city's walls,
Who knows the gesture that brought a moment's laughter to
 one, alone, who caught it then on a crowded street—

And when will the King arise from his prolonged rest, to
 pursue the ancient enemy in his chariot once more,
When will the hunter again return from the chase, to seize his
 bowl,
When will the Greenpoint child once more go out, and
 attend to his serious play in the sun?

MINUTES FROM THE CHAMBER OF COMMERCE

Ten divisions of bacillus Z stand poised at strategic points
      along the last frontier,
Fully trained and equipped,
And we face the future with confidence—

PROVIDED THE FUTURE DOES NOT COME TODAY—

Another vintage ancestor has been dug up in Crete, thirty
      ruined cities beneath the ruins on top,
The archeologists are digging, still,
And we in this city are prepared to take whatever fate may
      offer—

PROVIDED THE OFFER IS SOUND—

We know that voice-recorders have been attached to the
      phones of certain business rivals,
We have heard a rumor there may be thought-recorders, too,
Whatever the facts, we look them squarely, calmly, soberly in
      the face—

BUT ONLY WITH A TALL, COLD DRINK OF RYE IN
      HAND.

THIS DAY

Now, in this moment that has no identical twin throughout
    all time,
Being yours, yours alone,
Intimate as the code engraved upon your fingertips, and as
    rare—

Marked as your own features, personal as the voice in which
    you conduct your daily affairs,
Complex as those affairs, growing always into a new and still
    more special crisis
(In each of which you have your particular skill at reading the
    omens and the signs),
Here, in this natural scene, in a numbered house on a street
    with a name—

Unique as the signature you find upon some letter you had
    long ago forgotten and mislaid,
Elusive as the mood that letter now recalls, the story and its
    end as briefly alive,
And now as wholly lost—

As though this long but crowded day, itself, could sometime
    fade,
Had in fact already slipped through the fingers and now were
    gone, gone, simply gone—

Leaving no one, least of all yourself, to enact the unfinished
    drama that you, alone, once knew so well,
No one to complete the triumph, to understand or even
    believe in the disaster that must be repaired,
No one to glimpse this plan that seemed, at one time, must,
    must, must be fulfilled.

LONG JOURNEY

With us, on this journey that begins in the green and chilly
      suburbs on a late Spring afternoon
(Rain streaking the windows of the bus)
And in addition to the passengers, the driver confidently
      seated at the wheel—

Goes Captain Wonder of "Macabre Comics," silently
      plunging through infinities of time and space, changing
      at will from man to God
(The young and cynical student of this magic, though
      spellbound, does not really believe)
Everywhere combating evil, at all times fearless, and never, for
      very long, deceived—

While an immortal of the diamond once more rounds third
      base for home,
Jogging easily at the side of one who hears neither the wet
      tires nor the exhaust,
Only the roar of thousands across a sunswept field—

And this, for another, is not an abandoned development we
      are passing now,
A place of ruined mansions and bypassed factories,
It is a giant hall of radio, filled with the instant laughter that
      follows every perfect response—

And now for a moment the sun comes out, on this journey
      that is part of a farther voyage still
(Long, long after Magellan)
With the home port long since forgotten, and the ultimate
      reaches not even guessed—

Then a flurry of snow, and after that night, and the last stop
(It is the ten thousandth trip, but no band is playing; there
      had been no champagne at the first)
The driver simply reverses his illumined signs,
Singly, the passengers descend and resume, resume their
      separate ways—

Disillusioned (and used to it), alone and self-absorbed,
Unaware that Sinbad the Sailor has descended with them, and
      that Cyclops, Cinderella, the Princess of the Diamond
      Isles in love with Captain Wonder,
And Jack the Giant Killer have all been companions of
      theirs—

And that each of these has still a long, much longer way to go.

MRS. FANCHIER AT THE MOVIES

If I could reply, but once, to these many new and kindly
      companions I have found
(Now that so many of the old are gone, so far and for so long)
Overhearing them on the radio or the phonograph, or here in
      the motion pictures, as now—

These electrical voices, so sure in the sympathy they extend,
Offering it richly through the long hours of the day and the
      longer hours of the night
(Closer at hand, and although automatic, somehow more
      understanding than a live friend)
Speaking sometimes to each other, but often straight at me—

Wishing I could reply, if only once,
Add somehow to the final burst of triumphant music, or even in
      tragedy mingle with the promise of the fading clouds—

But wondering, too, what it really was I at one time felt so
      deeply for,
The actual voice, or this muted thunder? These giant
      shadows, or the naked face?
Or something within the voice and behind the face?—

And wondering whether, now, I would have the courage to
      reply, in fact,
Or any longer know the words, or even find the voice.

FAMILY ALBUM (1)

The Pioneers

They lived with dangers they alone could see,
Aware of them, everywhere and always, with X-ray eyes for
      the graver and subtle risks of impending evil and future
      guilt,
Sorcerers of the newsroom, genii of the wide screen, brevet
      phrenologists of bureau, cabinet, and court,
Consultant wizards of the high, the low, and the middle
      mirage—

Our forbears, quaint and queer in these posed photographs,
      stiffly smiling, no hint of their martyrdom revealed,
(But for the diaries they commissioned, we would not know
      their heartaches, even now)—

Visionaries (but practical), when the guilty fled in long black
      limousines,
Found clever refuge in opera boxes, night clubs, art galleries
      and public parks,
Our elders pursued in 300 horsepower sportscars, disguised as
      playboys, undercover girls,
If the crisis required it, posed successfully as double or triple
      agents, maniacs, drunks—

For thus they freed that raw, mid-century chaos of little
      empires from the pestilence of false thought;
Helped write, and signed, so many of the Magna Cartas in
      use to this very day;
Issued the first crude registry of licensed Truth;
Sought (and received) patents for the better types of logic,

durable humour, authentic taste;
Chartered the standard modes of legal prayer, for lease on a
    yearly basis,
(Renewable, with the forms filled in and the stamps affixed,
    for a nominal fee;
This trifling charge scarcely covers the cost;
What matters, of course, is the thought)—

God sometimes spoke to them on sleepless nights (as they
    told us, often), and they took down every word,
Revised and edited the counsel in the morning, making sure
    the names and addresses were correct,
Then gave it to the world, stamped: *For Immediate Release*—

They were not Gods, nor did they claim to be;
They were human, and fallible, content to be just what they
    were:
God's public relations.

FAMILY ALBUM (2)

Granny

This is Grandmother Susan, in one of the few pictures taken
    by the press,
(*Think!* published this one, and here Grandma is leaving
    court, perhaps to gather evidence for the next case)
She is twenty-five, here, in a frock typical of those innocent
    but turbulent times,
And we cannot tell, from the picture, whether she is armed—

Armed and equipped to perfection with the weapon she gave
    the sorcery of her special art,
The recorder snuggled in its holster, the holster concealed in
    her handbag, her girdle, sometimes her brassiere,
(With the listening microphone hidden—where?
The guilty, for all their cunning, never dreamed)
While the steadily turning reels, winding in compact silence,
    caught every guilty nuance of every guilty phrase,
("How about it, babe?" reorganized Chemosene; a drug firm
    failed on a whisper)
Stored away the convincing background noise of ice in
    shakers, the sound of authentic laughter,
And trapped, beyond reasonable doubt, the blackest crimes
    ever committed in speech—

While Granny smiled and dimpled in sympathy:
"Hi-Fi Sue Scores Again,"
"Think! names this average, all-round girl America's
    sweetheart of the year"—

Though there were rumours, and slanders, and yes, many jokes;
Grandpa, they said, was a deafmute—

But where are these jokers now?

FAMILY ALBUM (3)

The Boat

Our scholars say of this latest find, the boat uncovered in the
    desert sands,
Distant from templed places, far from trade routes, remote
    from the sea,
(But seaworthy, preserved in its arid tomb, still perfect in
    every wrought detail)—

They claim that this one, too, is a funeral vessel, designed for
    passage throughout the farthest islands in the sky of death,
Not a landlocked memorial, merely, bound nowhere,
But a solar craft on phantom course (as the helm is fixed) for
    the royal ports of the Ptolemaic year,
Bearing the illustrious dead, in safety, everywhere about that
    planned and prudent empire of the dead,
Under orders sealed by monarchs centuries before, on errands
    of state the dead must observe—

And this accords, it is true, with the intricate innocence of
    that age,
For they reveled, as we know, in matters that were skilfully
    and lucidly deranged—

But some of our savants claim this boat is of later origin—
    indeed, very late;
These say it derives from a wholly different rite;
This bark, they say, was a test and trial of the atom's might as
    related, mystically, to the actual sea;
That the Idaho ship is not pagan, at all, and differs, in many
    ways, from that early vessel of the Nile.

FAMILY ALBUM (4)

The Investigators

WHO DO YOU, WHO DO YOU, WHO DO YOU, WHO?
WHO DO YOU KNOW, WHO DO YOU HEAR ABOUT,
    WHO DO YOU SEE AND MEET IN YOUR DREAMS
    AND DAYDREAMS?—

Look what we found when we almost caught him, and he
    nearly confessed again and again,
Stacks and heaps of flagons and flasks and tubes and coils,
"Secret" it says on the door,
(Whatever that means, whoever lost it here, or threw it away,
    or he just forgot)
Crystals and powders and serums and herbs, who's got a
    hairpin,
Where's a corkscrew,
How would the blue stuff go with a gallon of green?—

WHO, WHO, WHO?
WHAT WERE YOU WHEN, WHY WERE YOU WHAT,
    WHERE WERE YOU WHICH, EITHER HOW OR WHY?

Could it be, no doubt an alchemist lived here once,
(Whoever knows how, it's easy to transmute lead into pure,
    solid, genuine gold)
But why does it look so tasty,
Perhaps you don't rub it on, you drink it instead,
It must be the essence of eternal youth and truth, beauty and
    health and duty and wealth,
Or at least second sight,
What are we waiting for, how will we ever find out until
    somebody tries?—

278

WHERE DO YOU, WHEN DO YOU?
HOW DO YOU WHICH?
WHO'S IN IT FOR WHAT, WHAT'S IN IT FOR WHO?—

Close your eyes tight, turn around three times, reach and
      pour and stir,
(It says in the rules, one wish per man)
Whatever it is, this is bound to be something final and big,
Open the valve, who's got a match?—

HOW DO YOU, WHEN DO YOU, WHERE DO YOU WHAT?
WHO DO YOU WHO, WHO DO YOU WHO, WHO DO YOU
      WHO?

Notes on the Poems

Each note gives the publication history of the poem (or, for previously unpublished poems, the date, if known, and the location of the manuscript). Changes in titles are recorded. A few notes identify persons named in dedications, provide information about dates of composition, or explain potentially obscure terms and allusions. Except for poems not previously published, the texts in this edition are those of the last published versions.

Abbreviations Used in the Notes

AA   *Angel Arms*. New York: Coward McCann, 1929.

AP   *Afternoon of a Pawnbroker, and Other Poems*. New York: Harcourt Brace, 1943.

CP   *Collected Poems of Kenneth Fearing*. New York: Random House, 1940.

DR   *Dead Reckoning*. New York: Random House, 1938.

NSP   *New and Selected Poems*. Bloomington: Indiana UP, 1956.

P   *Poems*. New York: Dynamo, 1935.

SCI   *Stranger at Coney Island and Other Poems*. New York: Harcourt Brace, 1948.

page 1 "Testament." *Wisconsin Literary Magazine* 22 (Nov 1922): 45.

2 "Villanelle of Marvelous Winds." *Wisconsin Literary Magazine* 22 (Nov 1922): 50.

3 "Violence." *Wisconsin Literary Magazine* 22 (Dec 1922): 79.

4 "Ashes." *Wisconsin Literary Magazine* 22 (Dec 1922): 82.

5 "Scottwell." *Wisconsin Literary Magazine* 22 (Apr 1923): 182.

6 "Divan and Morris Chair." *Wisconsin Literary Magazine* 22 (Jun 1923): 194.

7 "Secret." *Wisconsin Literary Magazine* 22 (Jun 1923): 207.

8 "Blair and Blair's Friends." *Wisconsin Literary Magazine* 22 (Jun 1923): 207.

9 "Man Dead." *Shadowland* 8 (Jul 1923): 43.

10 "Bal Masque." *Shadowland* 9 (Oct 1923): 25.

11 "Moral (OP. 1)." *Wisconsin Literary Magazine* 23 (Oct 1923): 18, as "Moral"; *Double Dealer* 7 (Nov-Dec 1924): 46.

12 "Moral (OP. 2)." *Wisconsin Literary Magazine* 23 (Nov 1923): 24; *Double Dealer* 7 (Nov-Dec 1924): 46.

13 "Sonnet to a Prominent Figure on the Campus." *Wisconsin Literary Magazine* 23 (Jan 1924): 20. The "prominent figure" is a statue of Lincoln on the campus of the University of Wisconsin-Madison.

14 "Cannibal Love." Previously unpublished signed typescript, General Manuscripts Miscellaneous, C0140, Princeton University Library. A dedication below the poem reads: "Only the highest regard for Bill and Maggie elicits this crimson proof that I once knew how to write, really write." The phrase "once knew" implies that Fearing was transcribing a poem from the distant past, presumably from a time before he abandoned formal verse. Its placement here assumes a date of 1924-25.

15 "Butterfly Arras." *Commonweal* 6 May 1925: 706.

16 "Finale." *Voices* (May-Jun 1925): 205.

17 "Hell." *Voices* (May-Jun 1925): 205.

18 "To a Dying Man." *International Arts* 1 (Aug 1925): 19.

19 "Carmichael." *Nation* 121 (30 Sep 1925): 359.

20 "Medusa." *Reviewer* 4 (Oct 1925): 56.

21 "Old Story." *World Tomorrow* 8 (Oct 1925): 308.

22 "Jack Knuckles Falters (*But Reads Own Statement at His Execution While Wardens Watch*)." *This Quarter* 1 (1926): 79-80; *AA 23-24*; *CP* 11-12.

24 "Aphrodite Metropolis I." *This Quarter* 1 (1926): 83, as "Aphrodite Metropolis III"; *AA* 25, as "Aphrodite Metropolis I." The present edition adopts the order followed in *AA*.

25 "Aphrodite Metropolis II." *This Quarter* 1 (1926): 82, as "Aphrodite Metropolis I"; *AA* 26, as "Aphrodite Metropolis II"; *CP*, as "Aphrodite Metropolis (1)"; *NSP* 8, as "Aphrodite Metropolis."

26 "Aphrodite Metropolis III." *This Quarter* 1 (1926): 81, as "Aphrodite Metropolis II"; *AA*, 27, as "Aphrodite Metropolis III"; *CP* 14, as "Aphrodite Metropolis (2)."

27 "Aphrodite Metropolis IV." *This Quarter* 1 (1926): 84; *AA* 29.

28 "The Night of a Jew." *The Minaret* 5 (May-Jun 1926): 9.

29 "Business as Usual." *New Yorker* 18 Sep 1926: 72.

30 "Ballad of the Salvation Army." *New Masses* Sep 1926: 11, as "Ballade of the Salvation Army"; *AA* 43-44.

31 "St. Agnes' Eve." *New Masses* Sep 1926: 11, as "St. Agnes Eve"; *AA* 7-9; *CP* 3-4; *NSP* 1-2.

34 "Death and Transfiguration of Fourteenth Street." *New Masses* Sep 1926: 11.

35 "Jake." *New Masses* Sep 1926: 11; *AA* 30; *CP* 15.

36 "Reveille." *New Masses* Sep 1926: 11, as "Reveille—7th Avenue"; *AA* 33.

37 "The Drunken Fly." *Menorah Journal* 12 (Dec 1926): 589, as "Nathan Schaffrin"; *AA* 12-13. According to Margery Latimer, KF "retitled [poems] with Jewish names so he could get in" the *Menorah Journal*. See her letter to Carl Rakosi, [early 1927?], Harry Ransom Humanities Research Center, University of Texas at Austin.

38 "Louis Mendele." *Menorah Journal* 12 (Dec 1926): 589.

39 "Alan Strache." *Menorah Journal* 12 (Dec 1926): 590.

40 "Anton Rubin, Artist." *Menorah Journal* 12 (Dec 1926): 590.

41 "My Mermaid." *New York Herald Tribune Books* 12 Dec 1926: 7.

42 "Triumph." *Scribner's Magazine* 81 (Jun 1927): 657, dedicated to Wilson Follett. Follett, an editor at Knopf, had rejected a collection of Fearing's poems but recommended "Triumph" to Robert Bridges (not the British poet but the American journalist and editor) for publication in *Scribner's*. Fearing also sent Bridges another poem, now lost, titled "Marcella White" (see the exchange of letters among Follett, Bridges, and Fearing in the Charles Scribner's Sons Archive, Princeton University Library). "Triumph" was obviously written before late December 1926, when the correspondence begins. The word *triumph* in the title is used in its literal Latin sense of a formal victory procession of a general and his army into Rome, in this instance that of Titus, line 13, the Roman general (later emperor) who conquered Jerusalem in A.D. 70. The "high-decked" car is the chariot in which the general traditionally rode in the procession.

44 "Angel Arms." *New Masses* Apr 1927: 31; *AA* 62-64.

46 "Bracelet." *Nation* 25 May 1927: 586.

47 "Evening Song." *Transition* 2 (May 1927): 139-140; *AA* 57-59, *CP* 25-27. Dedicated in *AA* to H. R., almost certainly Harry Ross, Fearing's closest friend.

49 "Afternoon of Colonel Brady." *New Masses* Jun 1927: 24.

51 "Cultural Notes." *Transition* 4 (Jun 1927): 169-171; *AA* 16-18; *CP* 9-10; *NSP* 6-7. Line 9: Max Nordau (1849-1923), Hungarian-born German physician and author, argued in *Degeneration* (1895) that modern civilization is morally degenerate and that this degeneracy is most vividly reflected in works of art and literature, which reveal the depravities of their individual creators.

53 "The City Takes a Woman." *Poetry* 30 (Jul 1927): 190, dedicated to K. H. M., who has not been identified. A typescript of this poem, following

the text in *Poetry*, is in the collection of the Brown County Library, Green Bay, Wisconsin. The library has no information about the provenance of the document, but it appears to be from the manuscript of an anthology. Fearing's name is printed above the title of the poem, and the title *Poetry* appears below the last line. Cf. the notes on "Escape" and "Longshot Blues."

54 "Caricature of Felice Ricarro." *Poetry* 30 (Jul 1927): 191, dedicated to "M.," almost certainly Margery Latimer. Felice Ricarro has not been identified.

55 "Rain." *Poetry* 30 (Jul 1927): 192. Dedicated to Lura Blackburn, Fearing's high school English teacher. KF may have earlier published this poem, or another by the same title, in a lost journal called *Learning*. See Margery Latimer to Laurie B. Latimer, 24 Dec 1924, James Weldon Johnson Collection, The Beinecke Rare Book and Manuscript Library, Yale University.

56 "Old Men." *Poetry* 30 (Jul 1927): 193.

57 "Breakfast with Hilda." *Free Verse* Autumn 1927: 20; *AA* 52-53; *CP* 23.

58 "Lithographing." *Transition* 10 (Jan 1928): 102; *AA* 34-35. Line 15, "Claude": The poet Claude McKay (1890-1948). See M. L. Rosenthal, "Chief Poets of the American Depression," diss., NYU, 1949, 1: 275. Rosenthal had interviewed Fearing for the dissertation.

59 "The Drinkers." *New Masses* Jan 1928: 5; *AA* 31-32; *CP* 16.

61 "Andy and Jerry and Joe." *New Masses* Jul 1928: 10; *AA* 14; *CP* 5; *NSP* 4. Dedicated in *AA* and *CP* to "Sylvia," i.e., Sylvia Rogers, with whom Fearing had a brief affair following his break with Margery Latimer.

62 "George Martin." *New Masses* Jul 1928: 10.

64 "John Standish, Artist." *New Masses* Jul 1928: 10; *AA* 19-20; *CP* 8; *NSP* 5. Dedicated in *New Masses*, *AA*, and *CP* to "J. R. G.," who has not been identified.

65 "Now." *Menorah Journal* 14 (Jun 1928): 569, as "No War"; *AA* 45-46; *CP* 19; *NSP* 9.

66 "Saturday Night." *Menorah Journal* 14 (Jun 1928): 568-569; *AA* 54-56; *CP* 24-25. Dedicated in *AA* to "W. L. R[iver]," Oak Park friend, New York City roommate, and author of the novel *Death of a Young Man* (New York: Simon, 1927), the protagonist of which is modeled on Fearing.

68 "Minnie and Mrs. Hoyne." *Menorah Journal* 14 (Jun 1928): 569-570; *AA* 10-11; *CP* 5-6; *NSP* 3-4. Strophe 3, line 7, "Free milk for babies": The Free Milk Fund for Babies, a private charity, provided free milk to

sick children of the poor.

70 "Nocturne." *Menorah Journal* 14 (Jun 1928): 570; *AA* 50-51; *CP* 22. Dedicated in *AA* to Lura Blackburn, Fearing's high school English teacher.

71 "Portrait (1)." *AA* 36-37, as "Portrait"; *CP* 17-18.

73 "They Liked It." *AA* 21-22; *CP* 28-29. Line 3, "the red eye in the Metropolitan": From 10 p.m. till 7 a.m., a beacon at the top of the Metropolitan Life Insurance Building on Madison Avenue between 23rd and 24th Streets flashed red on the quarter hours.

75 "Green Light." *AA* 47-49; *CP* 20-21; *NSP* 10-11. Like "the Metropolitan's red eye" in the preceding poem, "the green light" may refer to a specific landmark. If so, it has yet to be identified. Though clearly not a traffic light, it may be intended to suggest motion, speed, unceasing activity. The association of green with "go" was familiar because of the color coding not only of automobile traffic lights, which first appeared in the U.S. in 1914, but also of railroad signal lights, in use since the middle of the nineteenth century, and of New York subway signal lights, in use since about 1904.

77 "Invitation." *AA* 60-61; *CP* 30-31; *NSP* 12.

79 "The Cabinet of Simplicity." *AA* 38-42. Final strophe, "Comrade, this is no poem, / Who touches this,": cf. Whitman, "So Long!": "Camerado, this is no book, / Who touches this touches a man,".

82 "Winner Take All." *Menorah Journal* 19 (Feb 1930): 138, as "You Are Innocent"; *P* 19-20; *CP* 37-38; *NSP* 15-16.

84 "Obituary." *New Freeman* 11 Jun 1930: 305; *P* 23-24; *CP* 41-42; *NSP* 19-20. Strophe 6, line 1, "Will Hays": Hays, president of the Motion Picture Producers and Distributors of America, administered the so-called "Hays Code," a form of self-censorship in the film industry. Ibid., "I.R.T.": Interborough Rapid Transit, a New York City subway line.

86 "Conclusion." *New Masses* Sep 1930: 11, as "In Conclusion"; *P* 17-18; *CP* 35-36; *NSP* 13-14.

88 "American Rhapsody (1)." *New Masses* Oct 1930: 7, as "American Rhapsody"; *P* 25-26; *CP* 43-44. Between 1930 and 1940, Fearing published five poems under the title "American Rhapsody," numbering them only when they appeared in book form. Rhapsodies 1, 2, and 3 were collected in *P*. However, the fourth Rhapsody appeared by itself in *DR*, confusingly numbered 5. A new Rhapsody, the fifth, was added in *CP*, but because the second was dropped, the third, fourth, and fifth became 2, 3 and 4. Only the fourth and fifth, numbered 1 and 2, survived in *NSP*.

In the present edition, the five poems are placed and numbered in the order of their first publication. Strophe 4, lines 1-3: In the preface to *For Launcelot Andrews* (1928), T. S. Eliot calls himself "a classicist in literature, a royalist in politics, and an Anglo-Catholic in religion." In *After Strange Gods: A Primer of Modern Heresy* (1934), he declares that "reasons of race and religion combine to make any large number of free-thinking Jews undesirable."

90 "[It Happened in Far Off Frozen Nome]." Previously unpublished holograph manuscript in the collection of William L. Allison of Allegan, Michigan. Fearing wrote the poem for Allison, then a student at Oak Park-River Forest High School, Oak Park, Illinois, sometime between Jan and Apr 1932. Allison submitted the poem as his own to his, and Fearing's former, English teacher, Lura Blackburn. She was not deceived.

92 "Resurrection." *New Review* 2 (Apr 1932): 4; *P* 21-22; *CP* 39-40; *NSP* 17-18.

94 "1933." *New Masses* May 1933: 14; *P* 30-32; *CP* 52-54. Strophe 3, line 3, "RFC": The Reconstruction Finance Corporation, which made loans to businesses, industries, and banks. It was proposed by Herbert Hoover and approved by Congress in January 1932. Ibid., line 4, "Lucky Strike Hour": Lucky Strike cigarettes sponsored one of the most popular radio programs of the 1932-33 season, a sixty-minute variety show starring the comedian Jack Pearl. It aired on NBC every Thursday at 10 p.m. Strophe 5, line 3: As the relation between Woodrow Wilson's "safe for democracy" (1917) and Dickens's character Little Nell (*The Old Curiosity Shop*, 1840) is only metaphorical, so too may be the relation between the other (and as yet unidentified) quotations and the persons associated with them in this line. The quotations, in fact, are probably Fearing's inventions. Pius VIII, an obscure and relatively moderate pope, served as Pontiff for less than two years (Mar 1829-Nov 1830); Nicholas II (1868-1918), the last of the tsars and a weak, incompetent autocrat, was executed by the Bolsheviks; Louis Adolphe Thiers (1797-1877), French historian and statesman, crushed the Paris Commune of 1871.

97 "X Minus X." *Dynamo* 1 (Jan 1934): 12, as "Rialto Equation"; *P* 29; *CP* 51; *NSP* 23.

98 "Dividends." *Dynamo* 1 (Jan 1934): 13; *P* 27-28; *CP* 45-46; *NSP* 21-22.

100 "Dear Beatrice Fairfax: *Is it true that Father Coughlin and Miss Aimee Semple McPherson and Mr. H. L. Mencken and Peter Pan?*" *New Masses* 6 Mar 1934, as "Dear Beatrice Fairfax: Is it true that Bishop Manning

and Miss Aimee Semple McPherson and General Hugh Johnson and Mrs. Barbara Mdivani and Mr. Samuel Insull and Miss Greta Garbo and Mr. Prince Mike Romanoff?"; *P* 33, as in *New Masses*; *CP* 55. Beatrice Fairfax was the pseudonym used by the authors of a syndicated column of advice to the lovelorn, primarily by its originator, Marie Manning (1873?-1945), who wrote the first column in 1898. Charles Coughlin (1891-1979), known as the "radio priest," broadcast on political subjects to a wide audience on Sunday afternoons. Beginning as a populist, he grew increasingly anti-semitic and pro-fascist. Aimee Semple McPherson (1890-1944), a Canadian-born American evangelist and faith-healer, founded the Church of the Foursquare Gospel, which controlled 400 branch churches and a radio station.

101 "American Rhapsody (2)." *New Masses* 31 Jul 1934: 11, as "American Rhapsody"; *P* 35-36.

103 "Sunday to Sunday." *New Masses* 18 Sep 1934: 20; *P* 37-38; *CP* 56. Final strophe, "WGN": A Chicago radio station.

105 "No Credit." *Partisan Review* 1 (Sep-Oct 1934): 48; *P* 41-42; *CP* 58-59; *NSP* 25.

107 "Escape." *New Republic* 28 Nov 1934: 75; *P* 47-48; *CP* 58-59; *NSP* 25-26. A typescript of this poem, following the text in the *New Republic*, is in the collection of the Brown County Library, Green Bay, Wisconsin. The library has no information about the provenance of the document, but it appears to be from the manuscript of an anthology. Fearing's name is printed above the title of the poem, and the title *New Republic* appears below the last line. Cf. the notes on "The City Takes a Woman" and "Longshot Blues."

109 "Dirge." *New Masses* 18 Dec 1934: 14; *P* 43-44; *CP* 60-61; *NSP* 27-28. Strophe 1, line 2, "Bowie": a race track in Maryland. Strophe 2, line 2, "watch out for three cigarettes on the same, single match": The superstition that it is bad luck to light three cigarettes on one match is said to have originated in the trenches of World War I, when lighting three cigarettes on one match at night would give enemy marksmen time to zero in. Strophe 7, line 1, "B.M.T.": Brooklyn-Manhattan Transit System, a New York City subway line.

111 "What If Mr. Jesse James Should Some Day Die?" *New Masses* 18 Dec 1934: 14, as "Mr. Jesse James Will Some Day Die"; *P* 45-46; *CP* 47-48.

113 "$2.50." *Monthly Review* 1 (Dec 1934): 25; *P* 49-50; *CP* 62-63. "Cracker": killer-diller, hot stuff, ace. See entry 29.2, "Something Excellent," Lester V. Beney and Melvin Van den Bork, *The American*

Thesaurus of Slang (New York: Crowell, 1942).

115 "Denouement." *Dynamo* 2 (May-Jun 1935): 3-6, as "Denoument"; *P* 57-62, as "Denoument"; *CP* 68-72; *NSP* 31-35. A carbon of Fearing's typescript of the poem, with "Denouement" misspelled, is in the Kenneth Fearing Collection, Memorial Library, University of Wisconsin. The typescript of *P*—bound as a gift to the printer, Walter Frank, and signed by Fearing, Edward Dahlberg, and Sol Funaroff—is in the collection of the present editor. Part 2, line 4, "My friends . . .": Alludes to Franklin Roosevelt, who frequently used this phrase in political speeches and "fireside chats."

121 "As the Fuse Burns Down." *Kosmos* 4 (Jul-Aug 1935): 16; *P* 39-40; *CP* 57; *NSP* 24. Strophe 2, line 1, "Lydia Pinkham ad": Lydia Pinkham's Vegetable Compound, a patent medicine first marketed in 1875, was one of the most heavily advertised products in America.

122 "American Rhapsody (3)." *Partisan Review* 2 (Jan-Feb 1935): 29, as "American Rhapsody"; *P* 51; *CP* 64, as "American Rhapsody (2)."

123 "Lullaby." *Partisan Review* 2 (Jan-Feb 1935): 30; *P* 52; *CP* 65. Line 8: The Tombs (New York) and Moabit (Berlin) are prisons, the latter used by the Nazis for holding Communists condemned to death.

124 "Twentieth-Century Blues." *P* 53-54, as "20th Century Blues"; *CP*, 66-67; *NSP* 29-30.

126 "Pantomime." *American Spectator* 7 (Sep 1935): 14; *DR* 27; *CP* 86; *NSP* 47.

127 "Devil's Dream." *Partisan Review* 3 (Mar 1936): 14, as "Never, Never, Never"; *DR* 23-24; *CP* 81; *NSP* 42.

129 "Longshot Blues." *Poetry* 48 (Mar 1936): 68-69; *DR* 28-29; *CP* 47-48; *NSP* 48-49. A typescript of this poem, following the text in *Poetry*, is in the collection of the Brown County Library, Green Bay, Wisconsin. The library has no information about the provenance of the document, but it appears to be from the manuscript of an anthology. Fearing's name is printed above the title of the poem, and the title *Poetry* appears below the last line. Cf. the notes on "The City Takes a Woman" and "Escape."

131 "Lunch with the Sole Survivor." *Saturday Review of Literature* 26 Sep 1936: 7; *DR* 22; *CP* 102; *NSP* 59.

132 "[Moa moa mune]." Previously unpublished. A transcription by Rachel Landon, Fearing's first wife, is in the collection of the editor. Fearing composed the poem in 1937 in London using the vocabulary of his infant son Bruce. Translation: "More more music. / Piece [of bread] cat Popple [surname of neighbors] pie spoon. / No."

133 "Bulletin." *New Masses* 10 May 1938: 113, as "Your Move"; *DR* 38-39; *CP* 93-94.

135 "En Route." *New Republic* 11 May 1938: 10-11, as "Bulletin"; *DR* 16-17; *CP* 75-76; *NSP* 36-37.

137 "Hold the Wire." *Poetry* 52 (Jun 1938): 173-175; *DR* 25-26; *CP* 82-83; *NSP* 43-44.

139 "A Dollar's Worth of Blood, Please." *Poetry* 52 (Jun 1938): 175-176; *DR* 14-15; *CP* 78; *NSP* 39.

140 "Portrait (2)." *New Yorker* 27 Aug 1938: 47, as "Portrait"; *DR* 34-35, as "Portrait"; in *CP* 96-97, as "Portrait (2)"; *NSP* 53-54, as "Portrait."

142 "A Pattern." *Common Sense* 7 (Sep 1938): 25; *DR* 31; *CP* 90; *NSP* 51.

143 "Take a Letter." *Twentieth Century Verse* 12 (Sep-Oct 1938): 100; *DR* 46-47; *CP* 104-105; *NSP* 60. The original title of this poem, written at Yaddo in the summer of 1938, was "Hangover Blues." See the typescript of an early draft in the Kenneth Fearing Collection, Memorial Library, University of Wisconsin.

145 "C Stands for Civilization." *Twentieth Century Verse* 12 (Sep-Oct 1938): 101; *DR* 43-44; *CP* 101; *NSP* 58. Strophe 2, line 2, "Mayor Hague": Frank Hague (1876-1956) was mayor of Jersey City, New Jersey, from 1917 to 1947, the leader of a powerful Democratic political machine, and the most influential politician in the state. The use of the verb "televised" in strophe 2, line 3, may be the first ever in a poem.

146 "American Rhapsody (4)." *Poetry* 53 (Oct 1938): 12-13, as "American Rhapsody"; *DR* 33, as "(5)"; *CP* 92, as "(3)"; *NSP* 52, as "(1)."

147 "Literary." *Poetry* 53 (Oct 1938): 13, as "To a Daffodil, or Perhaps a Little Gossip About Flaubert"; *DR* 20; *CP* 79; *NSP* 40.

148 "SOS." *Poetry* 53 (Oct 1938): 14; *DR* 30; *CP* 89; *NSP* 50.

149 "Ad." *New Masses* 8 Nov 1938: 10; *DR* 45; *CP* 103.

150 "Radio Blues." *New Yorker* 26 Nov 1938: 24; *DR* 48-49; *CP* 106-107; *NSP* 61-62.

152 "The Program." *Salud!: Poems, Stories and Sketches of Spain by American Writers*, ed. Alan Calmer (New York: International, 1938): 37; *DR* 32; *CP* 91. Strophe 5, line 2: Georges Bonnet (1889-1973) and Pierre Laval (1883-1945), French politicians. Bonnet helped to draft the Munich Pact, and Laval proposed to end Mussolini's aggression in Ethiopia by ceding much of that country to Italy.

153 "Memo." *DR* 13; *CP* 77; *NSP* 38. Line 1, "coffee pot": coffee shop.

154 "Happy New Year." *DR* 18-19; *CP* 80; *NSP* 41.

156 "Q & A." *DR* 21; *CP* 85; *NSP* 46.

157 "Flophouse." *DR* 36; *CP* 95.

158 "Debris." *DR* 37; *CP* 99; *NSP* 55.

159 "Tomorrow." *DR* 40; *CP* 99; *NSP* 56.

160 "Requiem." *DR* 41-42; *CP* 100; *NSP* 57.

162 "If Money." *DR* 50; *CP* 109; *NSP* 63.

163 "Dance of the Mirrors." *DR* 51; *CP* 108.

164 "Manhattan." *DR* (dedicated to Alfred Hayes) 52-55; *CP* 110-112; *NSP* 64-66.

167 "Scheherazade." *DR* 55; *CP* 113; *NSP* 67.

168 "How Do I Feel?" *DR* 56; *CP* 84; *NSP* 45.

170 "Engagements for Tomorrow." *New Yorker* 4 Feb 1939: 24; *CP* 135; *NSP* 82.

172 "The Doctor Will See You Now." *New Yorker* 1 Apr 1939: 26; *CP* 121-122; *NSP* 72-73.

174 "Readings, Forecasts, Personal Guidance." *New Yorker* 20 May 1939: 23; *CP* 148; *NSP* 90.

176 "Net." *New Yorker* 12 Aug 1939; *CP* 134.

177 "Agent No. 174 Resigns." *New Yorker* 26 Aug 1939: 19, as "Operative No. 174 Resigns"; *CP* 117-119; *NSP* 68-70. Strophe 6, line 3, "Krueger-Musica denouement": Ivar Krueger (1880-1932), a Swedish industrialist known as the "Match King," created a financial empire based on fraud and forgery. Philip Musica (1877?-1938), an Italian immigrant to the U.S., served three years in prison for fraud and later plundered McKesson and Robbins, the pharmaceutical company, which he had bought under an alias. Both men committed suicide.

180 "Jackpot." *New Yorker* 9 Sep 1939: 19; *CP* 128-129.

182 "Pact." *New Yorker* 23 Sep 1939: 25; *CP* 120; *NSP* 71. The publication of this poem followed by one month the signing of the Hitler-Stalin pact, to which it obviously alludes.

183 "Yes, the Agency Can Handle That." *New Yorker* 2 Dec 1939: 30, as "Yes, the Serial Will Continue"; *CP* 133; *NSP* 81.

184 "Homage." *New Yorker* 30 Dec 1939: 19; *CP* 123; *NSP* 74.

185 "Any Man's Advice to His Son." *New Yorker* 13 Jan 1940: 22; *CP* 127; *NSP* 77.

186 "Discussion After the Fifth or Sixth." *Poetry* 56 (May 1940): 82-84. *CP* 144-145; *NSP* 86-87.

189 "Pay-Off." *Poetry* 56 (May 1940): 84; *CP* 146; *NSP* 88.

190 "Five A.M." *Poetry* 56 (May 1940): 85, as "5 A.M."; *CP* 147; *NSP* 89.

191 "Payday in the Morgue." *Direction* 2 (May-Jun 1939): 13; *CP* 139-141.

194 "Class Reunion." *Common Sense* 9 (Jun 1940): 25; *CP* 137-138; *NSP* 83-84.

196 "Portrait of a Cog." *New Yorker* 27 Jul 1940: 20; *CP* 125-126; *NSP* 76.

198 "American Rhapsody (5)." *New Yorker* 14 Sep 1940: 25, as "American Rhapsody"; *CP* 131-132, as "(4)"; *NSP* 79-80, as "(2)." The worksheets for this poem (10 versions in 25 pages), evidently the only surviving complete draft of a published work by Fearing, are in the Poetry/Rare Books Collection, University Libraries, SUNY at Buffalo. These have been described and analyzed in some detail by Charles D. Abbott in "The Poetics of Mr. Fearing," *University of Colorado Studies in Literature and Language*, Ser. B, 2 (Oct 1945): 382-387. According to Abbott (383), the poem was written in 1939.

200 "A la Carte." *New Republic* 7 Oct 1940: 470; *CP* 130; *NSP* 78.

201 "Gentleman Holding Hands with Girl." *CP* 124; *NSP* 75. Strophe 3, line 3: Like Freud, Baron Richard von Kraft-Ebing (1840-1902) and Havelock Ellis (1859-1939) wrote extensively on the psychology of sex.

202 "Love, 20¢ the First Quarter Mile." *CP* 142-143; *NSP* 85.

204 "Statistics." *New Yorker* 15 Nov 1941: 32; *AP* 9.

205 "Suburban Sunset, Pre-War, or What Are We Missing?" *Compass: A Quarterly Anthology of Modern Poetry*, ed. James A. Decker (Prairie City, IL: Decker [1941]), 9-10; *AP* 23-24.

207 "Beware." *New Yorker* 26 Sep 1942: 42; *AP* 27-28; *NSP* 103.

208 "Thirteen O'Clock." *New Yorker* 28 Nov 1942: 26; *AP* 13-14; *NSP* 98.

210 "Cracked Record Blues." *New Yorker* 12 Dec 1942: 32; *AP* 7-8; *NSP* 95.

211 "Continuous Performance." *An American Anthology*, ed. Tom Boggs (Prairie City, IL: James A. Decker, 1942), 38-39; *AP* 3-4; *NSP* 92-93.

213 "Public Life." *An American Anthology*, ed. Tom Boggs (Prairie City, IL: James A. Decker, 1942), 37; *AP* 43-44.

215 "Elegy in a Theatrical Warehouse." *New Yorker* 2 Jan 1943: 40; *AP* 29-30; *NSP* 104.

216 "Certified Life." *New Yorker* 6 Feb 1943: 24; *AP* 15-16.

218 "King Juke." *Poetry* 61 (Mar 1943): 663-664; *AP* 25-26; *NSP* 102.

219 "Confession Overheard in a Subway." *Poetry* 61 (Mar 1943): 664-666; *AP* 19-22; *NSP* 99-101.

222 "Art Review." *New Yorker* 24 Apr 1943: 24; *AP* 5-6; *NSP* 94.

223 "The Joys of Being a Businessman." *New Yorker* 10 Jun 1943: 23; *AP* 41-42.

224 "Travelogue in a Shooting Gallery." *New Yorker* 26 Jun 1943: 24; *AP* 11-12; *NSP* 96-97.

226 "Afternoon of a Pawnbroker." *New Republic* 23 Aug 1943: 250; *AP* 47; *NSP* 111-112.

229 "Monograph on International Peace." *New Yorker* 6 Nov 1943: 28. Strophe 4, line 3, "*Lebensraum*": German for "living space," the alleged need for which was used by Hitler to justify aggressive German expansionism.

231 "Model for a Biography." *AP* 33-34; *NSP* 106.

232 "Piano Tuner." *AP* 31-32; *NSP* 105.

233 "Reception Good." *AP* 17-18.

235 "End of the Seers' Convention." *AP* 35-37; *NSP* 107-108.

237 "Finale." *AP* 39; *NSP* 109.

238 "A Tribute, and a Nightmare." *AP* 45-46; *NSP* 110. In the Wellesley manuscript (see note on the following poem), Fearing made two revisions in ink in the last line of the third strophe, changing "rightfully" to "rightly" and "investigate" to "probe." Martin Dies, Jr. (1900-1972), chairman of the House Committee on Un-American Activities in the late thirties and early forties, advocated that the Communist Party be made illegal, that government employees be required to sign loyalty oaths, and that known Communists be eliminated from government service.

240 "[Somebody's War Bonds]." This untitled poem appears only on the back of the *AP* dustcover, the Treasury Department having asked writers to contribute to the war effort by urging readers to buy bonds. In spite of the apparent cynicism of the poem, Fearing donated the typescript of *AP* to the Treasury Department through the Book and Authors War Bond Committee, which in 1945 used it as an award in a Wellesley College Book and Authors Rally for the purchase of bonds in a Victory Loan Drive. The winner, Washington House, donated the typescript to the Margaret Clapp Library, where it is now in Special Collections.

241 "Sherlock Spends a Day in the Country." *New Yorker* 11 Mar 1944: 32; *SCI* 22; *NSP* 126. A memoir prepared for the editor by Nan Lurie, Fearing's second wife, indicates that this poem, drafted in the winter of 1942-43, was his answer to her complaint that he had not shared her enthusiasm for identifying animal tracks after a snow storm at Yaddo.

242 "4 A.M." *Poetry* 64 (Jun 1944): 188-189; *SCI* 6-7; *NSP* 116-117.

244 "Spotlight." *New Yorker* 4 Nov 1944, as "Possession." *SCI* 5; *NSP* 115.

245 "Museum." *New Yorker* 9 Dec 1944: 38; *SCI* 35-36; *NSP* 132-133.

247 "Once Upon a Time." *New Yorker* 27 Jan 1945: 20; *SCI* 29.

248 "M.D." *New Yorker* 8 Feb 1947: 28; *SCI* 12-13; *NSP* 120.

249 "Bryce & Tomlins." *New Yorker* 29 Mar 1947: 34; *SCI* 20-21; *NSP* 125.

251 "The Face in the Bar Room Mirror." *Poetry* 71 (Oct 1947): 24-25; *SCI* 25-26; *NSP* 128.

252 "The Juke-Box Spoke and the Juke-Box Said:" *Poetry* 71 (Oct 1947): 25-26; *SCI* 14-15; *NSP* 121.

253 "Newspaperman." *Poetry* 71 (Oct 1947): 26-27; *SCI* 18-19; *NSP* 124.

255 "The People v. the People." *New Yorker* 6 Mar 1948: 36; *SCI* 30-31; *NSP* 129-130.

257 "Castaway." *Tomorrow* Apr 1947: 28, as "O Castaway"; *SCI* 8-9; *NSP* 118. Of three poems in the *SCI* acknowledgments said to have been first published in *Tomorrow*, "Castaway" is the only one to have appeared there. Cf. the note on "Long Journey."

259 "Stranger at Coney Island." *SCI* 3-4; *NSP* 113-114.

261 "Higher Mathematics." *SCI* 10-11; *NSP* 119.

262 "Decision." *SCI* 27-28.

264 "Irene Has a Mind of Her Own." *SCI* 32-33.

265 "Lanista." *SCI* 16-17; *NSP* 122-123. The title is Latin for "a trainer of gladiators."

267 "Elegy." *SCI* 34; *NSP* 131. Like the Dakota hunter and the Egyptian king, the Greenpoint child is presumably a representative fiction. Greenpoint, the northernmost section of Brooklyn, was known for its slums and its industrial grime. It does not have a cemetery.

268 "Minutes from the Chamber of Commerce." *SCI* 37; *NSP* 134.

269 "This Day." *SCI* 38-39; *NSP* 135.

270 "Long Journey." *SCI* 40-41; *NSP* 136-7. In the *SCI* acknowledgments, this and the following poem are said to have been first published in *Tomorrow* but cannot be found there.

272 "Mrs. Fanchier at the Movies." *SCI* 24; *NSP* 127.

273 "Family Album (1)." *NSP* 138-139. Line 2, "graver and subtle risks": Thus, *NSP*, the only extant text, though "graver" may be a misprint for "grave."

275 "Family Album (2)." *NSP* 140.

277 "Family Album (3)." *NSP* 141.

278 "Family Album (4)." *NSP* 142-143.

Index of TITLES and First Lines

1-2-3 was the number he played but today the number came
    3-2-1; 109
$2.50 113
4 A.M. 242
1933 94

A butterfly whose wings 15
A cigarette burning— 4
A few of them, sometimes, choose record number 9, 252
A LA CARTE 200
A man is a maze of ants in dark endeavor. 20
Acid for the whorls of the fingertips; for the face, a surgeon's
    knife; oblivion to the name; 107
ACT ONE, Madrid-Barcelona, 152
AD 149
AFTERNOON OF A PAWNBROKER 226
AFTERNOON OF COLONEL BRADY 49
AGENT NO. 174 RESIGNS 177
ALAN STRACHE 39
All right, I may have lied to you, and about you, and made a
    few pronouncements a bit too sweeping, perhaps, and
    possibly forgotten to tag the bases here or there, 202
AMERICAN RHAPSODY (1) 88
AMERICAN RHAPSODY (2) 101
AMERICAN RHAPSODY (3) 122
AMERICAN RHAPSODY (4) 146
AMERICAN RHAPSODY (5) 198
And now you see the artificial sun come up, everywhere
    suffusing a marvelously painted sky; 245
And Steve, the athlete, where is he? 194
ANDY AND JERRY AND JOE 61

ANGEL ARMS 44
ANTON RUBIN, ARTIST 40
ANY MAN'S ADVICE TO HIS SON 185
APHRODITE METROPOLIS I 24
APHRODITE METROPOLIS II 25
APHRODITE METROPOLIS III 26
APHRODITE METROPOLIS IV 27
ART REVIEW 222
AS THE FUSE BURNS DOWN 121
ASHES 4

BAL MASQUE 10
BALLAD OF THE SALVATION ARMY 30
Bankers and priests and clerks and thieves, 62
Before warmth and sight and sound are gone, 122
Behold the afternoon sun, how slowly it withdraws from the
    sand, those darker stains within the shadows, though they
    have been covered and covered again, growing darker still,
    265
BEWARE 207
BLAIR AND BLAIR'S FRIENDS 8
Blood in my veins that seems not mine 38
Bought at the drug store, very cheap; and later pawned. 75
BRACELET 46
BREAKFAST WITH HILDA 57
Broadway was a rash of fire, 27
BRYCE & TOMLINS 249
BULLETIN 133
BULLETIN see also EN ROUTE (note)
BUSINESS AS USUAL 29
Business of forcing a showdown. 170
But it could never be true; 127
But that dashing, dauntless, delphic, diehard, diabolic cracker

likes his fiction turned with a certain elegance and wit; and that anti-anti-slum-congestion clublady prefers romance; 113

BUTTERFLY ARRAS 15

C STANDS FOR CIVILIZATION 145
CABINET OF SIMPLICITY, THE 79
CANNIBAL LOVE 14
CARICATURE OF FELICE RICARRO 54
CARMICHAEL 19
CASTAWAY 257
CERTIFIED LIFE 216
Cherubs of stone, smiling, wait and watch above the grave of the Greenpoint child, 267
CITY TAKES A WOMAN, THE 53
CLASS REUNION 194
Coffee for Hilda, 57
Cold street beneath the winter moon; 10
CONCLUSION 86
CONFESSION OVERHEARD IN A SUBWAY 219
CONTINUOUS PERFORMANCE 211
CRACKED RECORD BLUES 210
CULTURAL NOTES 51

DANCE OF THE MIRRORS 163
DEAR BEATRICE FAIRFAX: 100
DEATH AND TRANSFIGURATION OF FOURTEENTH STREET 34
DEBRIS 158
DECISION 262
Deep city, 164
DENOUEMENT 115
DEVIL'S DREAM 127

DIRGE 109
DISCUSSION AFTER THE FIFTH OR SIXTH 186
DIVAN AND MORRIS CHAIR 6
DIVIDENDS 98
Do you, now, as the news becomes known, 189
DOCTOR WILL SEE YOU NOW, THE 172
DOLLAR'S WORTH OF BLOOD, PLEASE, A 139
Dragons love the world in rain. 55
DRINKERS, THE 59
DRUNKEN FLY, THE 37

ELEGY 267
ELEGY IN A THEATRICAL WAREHOUSE 215
EN ROUTE 135
END OF THE SEERS' CONVENTION 235
ENGAGEMENTS FOR TOMORROW 170
Enter the proprietor of the Riviera Cafe; 223
ESCAPE 107
"Etch me in black and white. 54
Even when your friend, the radio, is still; even when her
     dream, the magazine, is finished; even when his life, the
     ticker, is silent; even when their destiny, the boulevard, is
     bare; 97
EVENING SONG 47
Ever, ever, ever, ever, ever so long ago, 247
Every need analyzed, each personal problem weighed,
     carefully, and solved according to the circumstance of
     each 249
Except for their clothing and the room, 59

FACE IN THE BAR ROOM MIRROR, THE 251
FAMILY ALBUM (1) 273
FAMILY ALBUM (2) 275

FAMILY ALBUM (3) 277
FAMILY ALBUM (4) 278
Fifteen gentlemen in fifteen overcoats and fifteen hats holding
    fifteen glasses in fifteen hands, 251
FINALE 16
FINALE 237
First you bite your fingernails. And then you comb your hair
    again. And then you wait. And wait. 198
FIVE A.M. 190
FLOPHOUSE 157
Flourish your cigarette, 18
Foolproof baby with that memorized smile, 100
Fourteenth street, with a bad cold in its head, 34

GENTLEMAN HOLDING HANDS WITH GIRL 201
GEORGE MARTIN 62
Get this straight, Joe, and don't get me wrong. 168
Go ahead, will you, see who's there, knocking at the door.
    191
Go to sleep, McKade; 47
GREEN LIGHT 75

HAPPY NEW YEAR 154
Harry loves Myrtle—He has strong arms, from the
    warehouse, 26
HAS LITTLE TO SAY 22
Having weighed, as a man must weigh, having measured for
    precision, as a person must, having tested, as one must
    test, for safety, for convenience, and for strength, 180
He, forty-five years old, 49
HELL 17
HIGHER MATHEMATICS 261
HOLD THE WIRE 137

HOMAGE 184

How cold, how very cold is the wind that blows out of
    nowhere into nowhere, 237

HOW DO I FEEL? 168

I have never seen him, this invisible member of the panel, this
    thirteenth juror, but I have certain clues; 255

I know your neckties where they line the rack, orderly from
    day to day, from year to year, 257

I sing of simple people and the hardier virtues, by Associated
    Stuffed Shirts & Company, Incorporated, 358 West 42d
    Street, New York, brochure enclosed; 147

If I am to live, or be in the studios, 64

If I could reply, but once, to these many new and kindly
    companions I have found 272

IF MONEY 162

If the doorbell rings, and we think we were followed here; or
    if the bell should ring but we are not sure— 137

If you have lost the radio beam, then guide yourself by the
    sun or the stars. 185

If you watch it long enough you can see the clock move, 210

Illimitable grief, at night, 28

IN CONCLUSION see CONCLUSION

In me slumber the strong secrets 40

In the small but crowded attic of Irene's mind there is room
    for everything except confusion, hesitancy, and doubt;
    264

Innocent of the mean or stupid, and innocent of crime, 82

INVITATION 77

IRENE HAS A MIND OF HER OWN 264

Is there still any shadow there, on the rainwet window of the
    coffee pot, 153

It comes to this, 133

It does no good 11
[IT HAPPENED IN FAR OFF FROZEN NOME] 90
It is early evening, still, in Honolulu, and in London, now, it
    must be well past dawn, 242
It is not—I swear it by every fiery omen to be seen these
    nights in every quarter of the heavens, I affirm it by all the
    monstrous portents of the earth and of the sea— 174
It is posted in the clubrooms, 148
It is the sound of a cat like no cat ever seen before walking
    back and forth on ivory keys; 232
It is written in the skyline of the city (you have seen it, that
    bold and accurate inscription), where the gray and gold
    and soot-black roofs project against the rising or the
    setting sun, 182
It will be known as Doctor Barky's cabinet, a new magic, 79

JACK KNUCKLES FALTERS 22
JACKPOT 180
JAKE 35
JOHN STANDISH, ARTIST 64
JOYS OF BEING A BUSINESSMAN, THE 223
JUKE-BOX SPOKE AND THE JUKE-BOX SAID:, THE
    252

KING JUKE 218

LANISTA 265
Let us present, 88
Like a window blind that shakes all night; 6
LITERARY 147
LITHOGRAPHING 58
LONG JOURNEY 270
LONGSHOT BLUES 129

LOUIS MENDELE 38
LOVE, 20¢ THE FIRST QUARTER MILE 202
LULLABY 123
LUNCH WITH THE SOLE SURVIVOR 131

M.D. 248
MAN DEAD 9
MANHATTAN 164
Meaning what it seems to when the day's receipts are counted
    and locked inside the store and the keys are taken home;
    131
MEDUSA 20
MEMO 153
MINNIE AND MRS. HOYNE 68
MINUTES FROM THE CHAMBER OF COMMERCE
    268
[MOA MOA MUNE] 132
MODEL FOR A BIOGRAPHY 231
MONOGRAPH ON INTERNATIONAL PEACE 229
MORAL (OP. 1) 11
MORAL (OP. 2) 12
MR. JESSE JAMES WILL SOME DAY DIE see WHAT IF
    MR. JESSE JAMES SHOULD SOME DAY DIE?
MRS. FANCHIER AT THE MOVIES 272
MUSEUM 245
My darling spurns the tea cup's waves, 41
MY MERMAID 41
"Myrtle loves Harry"—It is sometimes hard to remember a
    thing like that, 25

NATHAN SCHAFFRIN see DRUNKEN FLY, THE
NET 176
NEVER, NEVER, NEVER see DEVIL'S DREAM

NEWSPAPERMAN 253

Next door there's happened something strange. 9

NIGHT OF A JEW, THE 28

NO CREDIT 105

No violence, 135

NO WAR see NOW

NOCTURNE 70

Not here, but a little farther, after we have passed through the hall of mirrors, 259

Not the saga of your soul at grips with fate, bleedingheart, for we have troubles of our own, 167

NOW 65

Now, about that other one, the sober one 186

Now, at a particular spot on the radio dial, "—in this corner, wearing purple trunks," 233

Now, in this moment that has no identical twin throughout all time, 269

Now that the others are gone, all of them, forever, 159

Now that we know life: 65

O CASTAWAY see CASTAWAY

OBITUARY 84

Of you, both the known and unknown quantities, but more especially, of those unknown, 201

OLD MEN 56

OLD STORY 21

On Fourteenth street the bugles blow, 30

ONCE UPON A TIME 247

One time across the hills of Rome, 42

OPERATIVE NO. 174 RESIGNS see AGENT NO. 174 RESIGNS

Our scholars say of this latest find, the boat uncovered in the desert sands, 277

Out of the frailest texture, somehow, and by some means
   from the shabbiest odds and ends, 157

PACT 182
PANTOMIME 126
Patient are the winds that blow 2
PATTERN, A 142
PAY-OFF 189
PAYDAY IN THE MORGUE 191
PEOPLE v. THE PEOPLE, THE 255
PIANO TUNER 232
Poem? You call that a poem—that little line 8
Poor old codger! you seem to realize 13
PORTRAIT (1) 71
PORTRAIT (2) 140
PORTRAIT OF A COG 196
POSSESSION see SPOTLIGHT
Professor Burke's symphony, "Colorado Vistas," 51
PROGRAM, THE 152
PUBLIC LIFE 213

Q & A 156

RADIO BLUES 150
RAIN 55
Read, as the dreamer reads, 12
READINGS, FORECASTS, PERSONAL GUIDANCE
   174
Recently displayed at the Times Square Station, a new
   Vandyke on the face-cream girl. 222
RECEPTION GOOD 233
REQUIEM 160
RESURRECTION 92

Return to me now, 46
REVEILLE 36
REVEILLE—7TH AVENUE see REVEILLE
RIALTO EQUATION see X MINUS X

SOS 148
SATURDAY NIGHT 66
SCHEHERAZADE 167
SCOTTWELL 5
Scottwell could project his soul 5
SECRET 7
She could die laughing, 68
She is the little pink mouse, his far away star, 44
She said did you get it, and he said did you get it, 101
She sleeps, lips round, see how at rest, 126
SHERLOCK SPENDS A DAY IN THE COUNTRY 241
Silent . . something white . . went "flick" . . 7
Sixty souls, this day, will arrange for travel to brighter lands
    and bluer skies. 204
Sky, be blue, and more than blue; wind, be flesh and blood;
    flesh and blood, be deathless; 115
So many asteroids speed and flash and spin along the
    heavenly way where Francis L. Regan travels his regular
    rounds 261
Some take to liquor, some turn to prayer, 200
Somebody's War Bonds aren't going to be worth a damn.
    240
Someone, a dissatisfied customer, has thrown a brickbat
    through the plate-glass window of the Riviera Café 229
Someone, somewhere, is always starting trouble, 207
Somewhere beyond the wall of blue 17
SONNET TO A PROMINENT FIGURE ON THE
    CAMPUS 13

Sounds at night 37
Speak as you used to; 154
SPOTLIGHT 244
ST. AGNES' EVE 31
STATISTICS 204
Still they bring me diamonds, diamonds, always diamonds,
    226
STRANGER AT CONEY ISLAND 259
Street by street the lights go out, and the night turns gray,
    bringing respite to this and to all other agencies, 190
SUBURBAN SUNSET, PRE-WAR, OR WHAT ARE WE
    MISSING? 205
SUNDAY TO SUNDAY 103
Surely, surely, whether broken on the wheel, or burned at the
    stake, or nailed to the cross, 176

TAKE A LETTER 143
Take him away, he's as dead as they die, 84
Ten divisions of bacillus Z stand poised at strategic points
    along the last frontier, 268
TESTAMENT 1
That is not blood on the shiny street 66
The alarm that shatters sleep, at least, is real; 142
The clear brown eyes, kindly and alert, with 12-20 vision,
    give confident regard to the passing world through R. K.
    Lampert & Company lenses framed in gold; 140
The crime, if there was a crime, has not been reported as yet;
    241
The drummer lad who marched away, 21
The falcon is a star that broods of plunder 39
The floor of the blue night, 70
The furious giant who rifled him 16
The hour that was bleak, as he worked, does not betray itself

in the gem that the craftsman has polished; 244

The juke-box has a big square face, 218

The neighborhood athlete is in love again, staring about him with sightless eyes, and that, for him, is the same as having a patent on life; 216

The place seems strange, more strange than ever, and the times are still more out of joint; 211

The settings include a fly-specked Monday evening, 31

The subject was put to bed at midnight, and I picked him up again at 8 A.M. 177

The windows, faintly blue and gold in the sun's first light; 158

Then enter again, through a strange door, into a life again all strange, 213

There is a jungle, there is a jungle, there is a vast, vivid, wild, wild, marvelous, marvelous, marvelous jungle, 224

These are the live, 58

These models (they were the very last word) arrived in the morning. 205

These small, cool kisses, love, what good are they? 14

They are able, with science, to measure the millionth of a millionth of an electron-volt, 145

They are the raw, monotonous skies, 56

They have laid the penthouse scenes away, after a truly phenomenal run, 215

THEY LIKED IT 73

They lived with dangers they alone could see, 273

They said to him, "It is a very good thing that you have done, yes, both good and great, proving this other passage to the Indies. Marvelous," they said. "Very. But where, Señor, is the gold?" 184

They tremble in the morning eye 36

They watched the lights go on when night fell. 73

THIRTEEN O'CLOCK 208

This advantage to be seized; and here, an escape prepared
    against an evil day; 98

This charge was laid upon me long ago: Do not forget; 253

THIS DAY 269

This is Grandmother Susan, in one of the few pictures taken
    by the press, 275

This is the poet 29

This patient says he is troubled by insomnia, and that one
    finds it difficult to stay awake. 172

Tip-toeing softly through the sky, 3

TO A DAFFODIL, OR PERHAPS A LITTLE GOSSIP
    ABOUT FLAUBERT see LITERARY

TO A DYING MAN 18

TOMORROW 159

Tomorrow, yes, tomorrow, 146

Too bad for her with the kids and all 35

TRAVELOGUE IN A SHOOTING GALLERY 224

TRIBUTE, AND A NIGHTMARE, A 238

TRIUMPH 42

Try 5 on the dial, try 10, 15; 150

TWENTIETH-CENTURY BLUES 124

"Twilights that are deathless 53

Unknown to Mabel, who works as cook for the rich and
    snobbish Aldergates, 103

Unto the panoramic skies, 1

VILLANELLE OF MARVELOUS WINDS 2

VIOLENCE 3

WANTED: Men; 149

We cough. We shiver. We have seizures of pain, and

weakness. Often there is blood. 248
We were staring at the bottles in the restaurant window, 61
We were walking and talking on the roof of the world, 235
We will make love, when the hospitals are quiet and the blue
    police car stops to unload prisoners, 77
What do you call it, bobsled champion, and you, too,
    Olympic roller-coaster ace, 124
What if all the money is bet on the odd; 129
WHAT IF MR. JESSE JAMES SHOULD SOME DAY
    DIE? 111
What will you do when the phone rings and they say to you:
    What will you do? 121
When the stars speak out above 24
Where analgesia may be found to ease the infinite, minute
    scars of the day; 156
Where will we ever again find food to eat, clothes to wear, a
    roof and a bed, now that the Wall Street plunger has gone
    to his hushed, exclusive, paid-up tomb? 111
Whether dinner was pleasant, with the windows lit by
    gunfire, and no one disagreed; or whether, later, we
    argued in the park, and there was a touch of vomit-gas in
    the air; 105
WHO DO YOU, WHO DO YOU, WHO DO YOU, WHO? 278
Why do they whistle so loud, when they walk past the
    graveyard late at night? 208
Why do you glance above you, for a moment, before you stop
    and go inside, 162
Wide as this night, old as this night is old and young as it is
    young, still as this, strange as this; 123
Will they stop, 160
William Lowell is drunk again. 71
WINNER TAKE ALL 82
With so much at stake, an inhuman risk for a prize until now
    beyond all grasp, 262

With the last memo checked: *They will sign, success*; with the
    phone put down upon the day's last call; then with the
    door locked at last, 139
With us, on this journey that begins in the green and chilly
    suburbs on a late Spring afternoon 270
Would you like to live, yourself, the way that other people do,
    143

X MINUS X 97

Years in sporting goods, rich in experience, were followed by
    years in soda, candy, and cigars. 231
YES, THE AGENCY CAN HANDLE THAT 183
YES, THE SERIAL WILL CONTINUE see YES, THE
    AGENCY CAN HANDLE THAT
You, 163
"You are sure you love me? 19
You have forgotten the monthly conference. Your four
    o'clock appointment waits in the ante-room. The uptown
    bureau is on the wire again. 196
You heard the gentleman, with automatic precision, speak the
    truth. 94
You recommend that the motive, in Chapter 8, should be
    changed from ambition to a desire, on the heroine's part,
    for doing good; yes, that can be done. 183
You will ask how I came to be eavesdropping, in the first
    place. 219
You will give praise to all things, praise without end; 86
You will remember the kisses, real or imagined; 92
You wonder, sometimes, but more often worry, and feel
    dismayed in a world of change, 238
YOUR MOVE see BULLETIN